THE 85

EXPERIMENTS

CONTROVERSIAL SCIENCE

AYANDELE MICHEAL MAYOWA

COPYRIGHT

THE 85 Experiments: Controversial Science
© 2024 Ayandele Micheal Mayowa
All rights reserved.

Publisher:
Amazon Publisher
USA

CONTENT

INTRODUCTION:

THE PERIL AND PROMISE OF SCIENCE

In the relentless pursuit of knowledge, humanity has often walked a fine line between groundbreaking discovery and devastating consequence. The quest to understand the mysteries of the universe, harness the forces of nature, and push the boundaries of what is possible has led to some of the most profound achievements in history. Yet, these same pursuits have also brought us face to face with the darker side of innovation—experiments that, while driven by the promise of progress, have teetered on the edge of catastrophe.

The 85 Experiments: Controversial Science is a journey through the most daring, controversial, and impactful experiments ever conducted. These are the experiments that have shaped the modern world, but they have done so at a cost—sometimes ethical, sometimes human, and always with a profound impact on society.

From the development of the atomic bomb to the manipulation of the human genome, from psychological trials that pushed the limits of human endurance to technological advances that challenge our understanding of life itself, this book explores the dual nature of scientific progress. Each of the 99 experiments chronicled here tells a story not just of scientific achievement, but of the risks, consequences, and ethical quandaries that accompany it.

These experiments reveal the extraordinary potential of science to solve problems, cure diseases, and expand our horizons. But they also expose the vulnerabilities of our species—how easily the quest for knowledge can lead to unintended harm, how ambition can blind us to the ethical implications of our actions, and how the very tools we create to better our world can sometimes endanger it.

As you delve into these accounts, you will encounter the brilliant minds and audacious thinkers who dared to explore the unknown. You will also see the toll that some of these experiments have taken—on individuals, on society, and on our collective conscience. This book is a reflection on the double-edged nature of scientific inquiry, where every step forward comes with the possibility of unforeseen and sometimes dangerous outcomes.

The 85 Experiments is not just a catalog of the past; it is a cautionary tale for the future. As science continues to advance at an unprecedented pace, the lessons of these experiments are more relevant than ever. They remind us that with every new discovery comes responsibility, and with every leap forward, the potential for both peril and promise.

EXPERIMENT ONE

THE MANHATTAN PROJECT: UNLEASHING THE POWER OF THE ATOM

In the shadowy realms of wartime secrecy, amid the turmoil of the Second World War, a scientific endeavor emerged that would forever alter the course of history. The Manhattan Project, shrouded in secrecy and cloaked in urgency, brought together some of the brightest minds of the era to unlock the unimaginable power held within the nucleus of the atom.

At its heart lay the quest to harness nuclear fission—the splitting of atomic nuclei—to create a weapon of unprecedented destructive force. With the race against Nazi Germany driving their efforts, scientists and engineers worked tirelessly across multiple sites, from the deserts of New Mexico to the secluded laboratories of Los Alamos.C

The culmination of their collective efforts came on July 16, 1945, in the desolate expanse of the New Mexico desert. Codenamed "Trinity," the first atomic bomb test marked a pivotal moment in human history. As the countdown echoed across the barren landscape, anticipation mingled with trepidation. Then, in a blinding flash of light, the world witnessed the unleashing of the atom's awesome power.

The resulting explosion, with its searing heat and deafening roar, reverberated across the desert, casting a mushroom cloud that reached for the heavens. In an instant, the landscape was transformed, and the course of warfare irrevocably altered.

Yet, amid the awe-inspiring spectacle of raw destructive power, the Manhattan Project bore a heavy burden—the ethical and moral implications of unleashing such devastation upon humanity. The bombing of Hiroshima and Nagasaki, which followed shortly after the Trinity test, brought the horrors of atomic warfare into stark relief, ushering in a new era of fear and uncertainty.

In the aftermath of the Manhattan Project, the world grappled with the profound implications of nuclear proliferation, arms races, and the specter of mutually assured destruction. Yet, amidst the darkness, the project also sparked a new era of scientific inquiry and technological innovation.

The legacy of the Manhattan Project endures as a testament to human ingenuity and the dual nature of scientific discovery—a potent reminder of the awesome power wielded by those who dare to unlock the secrets of the universe. As we gaze upon the remnants of that fateful test site in the New Mexico desert, we are reminded of the immense responsibility that accompanies the pursuit of knowledge and the enduring quest for peace in a world forever changed by the power of the atom.

EXPERIMENT TWO

SHADOWS OF SCIENCE: THE LEGACY OF HUMAN RADIATION EXPERIMENTS

In the annals of scientific history, there exists a dark chapter—a chapter marked by the clandestine and often unethical experimentation on human subjects in the name of scientific progress. The era of human radiation experiments stands as a sobering reminder of the ethical pitfalls and moral dilemmas inherent in the pursuit of scientific knowledge.

In the aftermath of World War II, amid the escalating tensions of the Cold War, governments and military institutions around the world embarked on a quest to understand the effects of radiation on the human body. From the testing of atomic bombs to the development of nuclear weapons, the specter of radiation loomed large, casting a long shadow over scientific inquiry.

Against this backdrop, human subjects—often vulnerable and marginalized populations—became unwitting participants in a series of dangerous experiments. From prisoners and soldiers to pregnant women and children, countless individuals were subjected to radiation exposure without their consent or full understanding of the risks involved.

Impact:

The impact of these human radiation experiments reverberates through history, leaving a trail of devastation in their wake. For the victims and their families, the legacy of radiation exposure is one of suffering, illness, and untold hardship. From radiation-induced cancers to genetic mutations and lifelong health complications, the toll of these experiments is immeasurable.

But the impact extends beyond the immediate victims, reaching into the fabric of society itself. The erosion of trust in scientific institutions, the betrayal of ethical principles, and the disregard for human dignity and autonomy—all cast a long shadow over the scientific community. These experiments serve as a stark reminder of the dangers of unchecked scientific ambition and the imperative of ethical oversight and accountability.

Effect:

In the wake of public outcry and ethical scrutiny, the era of human radiation experiments spurred a paradigm shift in research ethics and human subject protections.

The Nuremberg Code, established in the aftermath of World War II, laid down principles for ethical experimentation on human subjects, emphasizing the need for informed consent, voluntary participation, and protection of participants' rights.

Subsequent revelations of unethical experimentation, such as the infamous Tuskegee Syphilis Study and the exposure of vulnerable populations to radiation, led to further reforms and regulations. The establishment of institutional review boards (IRBs), the enactment of federal regulations, and the codification of ethical guidelines—all aimed at safeguarding the rights and welfare of human research subjects.

Yet, despite these reforms, the scars of human radiation experiments endure—a reminder of the darker side of scientific inquiry and the imperative of ethical vigilance. As we confront the ethical dilemmas of our own time, the lessons of history serve as a beacon, guiding us toward a future where science is tempered by wisdom, compassion, and respect for the inherent dignity of every human being.

EXPERIMENT THREE

THALIDOMIDE TRAGEDY: LESSONS LEARNED FROM MEDICAL MISSTEPS

In the late 1950s and early 1960s, amidst the optimism of post-war prosperity, a new wonder drug emerged—thalidomide. Marketed as a safe and effective treatment for nausea and insomnia, thalidomide captured the attention of physicians and patients alike. However, what began as a promising medical breakthrough soon descended into tragedy, as the devastating effects of thalidomide on fetal development came to light.

Impact:

The impact of the thalidomide tragedy was profound and far-reaching, leaving a legacy of suffering and anguish in its wake. Pregnant women who had taken thalidomide during pregnancy gave birth to children with severe birth defects, including limb malformations, organ abnormalities, and neurological disorders. The toll on affected families was devastating, as they grappled with the physical, emotional, and financial challenges of caring for children with profound disabilities.

The thalidomide tragedy also exposed glaring deficiencies in drug regulation and oversight, as the drug had been widely prescribed without adequate testing for safety in pregnant women. The failure of regulatory agencies to recognize and address the risks of thalidomide exemplified the dangers of lax oversight and the prioritization of commercial interests over patient safety.

Effect:

In the aftermath of the thalidomide tragedy, governments around the world implemented sweeping reforms to strengthen drug regulation and protect public health. The incident spurred the development of more rigorous testing protocols, including preclinical animal studies and clinical trials, to evaluate the safety and efficacy of new drugs before they are approved for market.

Furthermore, the thalidomide tragedy prompted a paradigm shift in the approach to drug safety and pharmacovigilance, emphasizing the importance of post-market surveillance and monitoring for adverse effects. Pharmacovigilance systems were established to detect and respond to emerging safety concerns, enabling regulatory agencies to take swift action to protect public health.

The thalidomide tragedy also had a lasting impact on public perception and trust in the pharmaceutical industry, underscoring the need for transparency, accountability, and ethical conduct in drug development and marketing. The incident served as a cautionary tale, reminding stakeholders of the potential consequences of rushing new drugs to market without adequate testing and safeguards.

Ultimately, the thalidomide tragedy forced a reckoning within the medical and regulatory communities, leading to significant reforms and improvements in drug safety and oversight. While the scars of the thalidomide tragedy may never fully heal, the lessons learned from this dark chapter in medical history continue to inform and shape drug regulation and patient care to this day.

EXPERIMENT FOUR

UNVEILING INJUSTICE: THE TUSKEGEE SYPHILIS STUDY

In the 1930s, amidst the backdrop of racial segregation and discrimination in the United States, a government-sponsored medical study emerged that would come to symbolize one of the most egregious violations of medical ethics in history—the Tuskegee Syphilis Study. Initiated by the U.S. Public Health Service, the study aimed to investigate the natural progression of syphilis in African American men, but its methods and implications would have far-reaching consequences.

Effect:

The Tuskegee Syphilis Study had a profound and enduring impact on public health, medical ethics, and trust in the medical profession. For over four decades, from 1932 to 1972, hundreds of African American men in rural Alabama were deceived and denied proper treatment for syphilis, even after the discovery of penicillin as a cure for the disease. The study's participants were unwittingly left to suffer the devastating effects of untreated syphilis, including blindness, neurological damage, and premature death.

The effects of the Tuskegee Syphilis Study reverberated beyond its direct victims, casting a long shadow over the African American community and deepening distrust of the medical establishment. The study laid bare the systemic racism and exploitation inherent in medical research, highlighting the ethical imperative of informed consent, patient autonomy, and equitable access to healthcare.

Impact:

The Tuskegee Syphilis Study sparked outrage and condemnation from the public, leading to sweeping reforms in medical ethics and research regulations. The incident prompted the development of guidelines and regulations to protect human subjects in research, including the establishment of institutional review boards (IRBs) to oversee the ethical conduct of research involving human participants.

Furthermore, the Tuskegee Syphilis Study served as a catalyst for greater awareness of racial disparities in healthcare and the need for equity and justice in medical research and practice. The study's legacy galvanized efforts to address health inequities and disparities in access to healthcare, particularly among marginalized communities.

The impact of the Tuskegee Syphilis Study extended beyond the realm of medicine, influencing public policy, civil rights advocacy, and social justice movements. The study served as a rallying cry for greater accountability, transparency, and respect for human rights in scientific research and healthcare delivery.

Ultimately, the Tuskegee Syphilis Study stands as a stark reminder of the ethical pitfalls and moral imperatives inherent in medical research. Its legacy serves as a cautionary tale, reminding us of the enduring importance of upholding ethical principles, protecting the rights and dignity of research participants, and confronting systemic injustices in healthcare and society.

EXPERIMENT FIVE

UNVEILING THE DARK DEPTHS OF HUMAN NATURE: THE STANFORD PRISON EXPERIMENT

In the summer of 1971, within the halls of Stanford University, a groundbreaking psychological experiment was launched—one that would delve into the complexities of human behavior and power dynamics. Led by psychologist Dr. Philip Zimbardo, the Stanford Prison Experiment sought to explore the effects of perceived power and authority in a simulated prison environment.

Effect:

The Stanford Prison Experiment had a profound and chilling effect on both its participants and the wider world, revealing the depths to which ordinary individuals could descend when placed in positions of authority and subjected to dehumanizing conditions. The experiment, which was intended to last two weeks, was abruptly terminated after only six days due to the extreme and escalating abuse inflicted by the "guards" upon the "prisoners."

Impact:

The impact of the Stanford Prison Experiment reverberated far beyond the confines of its simulated prison walls, sparking intense debate and controversy within the fields of psychology, ethics, and human rights. The experiment laid bare the disturbing ease with which individuals can adopt and internalize roles of power and dominance, leading to dehumanization and cruelty towards others.

The Stanford Prison Experiment served as a wake-up call for psychologists and researchers, highlighting the ethical dilemmas inherent in conducting experiments that involve the manipulation of human behavior and emotions. It prompted a reevaluation of research ethics and guidelines, emphasizing the importance of informed consent, protection of participants' well-being, and the need for rigorous oversight and debriefing procedures.

Furthermore, the Stanford Prison Experiment forced society to confront uncomfortable truths about the potential for abuse and oppression within institutional settings, whether in prisons, workplaces, or other hierarchical structures. It underscored the importance of vigilance and accountability in guarding against abuses of power and protecting the rights and dignity of all individuals.

Ultimately, the Stanford Prison Experiment stands as a cautionary tale—a stark reminder of the dark undercurrents that lie within the human psyche and the dangers of unchecked authority and conformity. Its legacy continues to shape our understanding of human behavior and the complex interplay between individual psychology and social dynamics in environments of power and control.

EXPERIMENT SIX

UNVEILING OBEDIENCE TO AUTHORITY: THE MILGRAM EXPERIMENT

In the early 1960s, amidst the backdrop of post-war America, a groundbreaking psychological experiment was conducted by Stanley Milgram at Yale University — a study that would shed light on the powerful influence of authority figures on human behavior. The Milgram Experiment sought to understand the extent to which individuals would obey orders to administer potentially harmful electric shocks to others, even in the face of moral objections.

Effect:

The Milgram Experiment had a profound and unsettling effect on both its participants and the broader scientific community, revealing the disturbing ease with which ordinary individuals could be induced to commit acts of harm against others under the guise of obedience to authority. Despite knowing that they were inflicting pain on fellow participants, many subjects continued to administer increasingly severe shocks when instructed to do so by the experimenter.

Impact:

The impact of the Milgram Experiment reverberated throughout psychology and beyond, challenging long-held assumptions about human nature and the dynamics of obedience and authority. The study's findings highlighted the pervasive influence of situational factors and social roles in shaping behavior, suggesting that individuals are often willing to relinquish their moral autonomy in deference to authority figures.

The Milgram Experiment sparked intense debate and controversy within the scientific community, raising ethical questions about the use of deception in research and the potential for psychological harm to research participants. It prompted a reevaluation of research ethics and guidelines, leading to greater scrutiny of experimental procedures and the implementation of stricter standards for informed consent and debriefing.

Furthermore, the Milgram Experiment forced society to confront uncomfortable truths about the nature of obedience and conformity in the face of authority. It underscored the importance of critical thinking, moral courage, and resistance to unjust authority in safeguarding against abuses of power and upholding ethical principles.

Ultimately, the Milgram Experiment stands as a sobering reminder of the fragility of individual morality and the dangers of blind obedience to authority. Its legacy continues to shape our understanding of human behavior and the complex interplay between individual conscience and social influence in contexts of power and control.

EXPERIMENT SEVEN

GENETIC ENGINEERING: UNLOCKING NATURE'S BLUEPRINT

In the realm of scientific innovation, few discoveries hold as much promise—and peril—as genetic engineering. Emerging from the intersection of biology, technology, and ethics, genetic engineering represents a paradigm shift in our ability to manipulate the very building blocks of life itself. From curing genetic diseases to creating genetically modified organisms (GMOs), the potential applications of genetic engineering are vast and far-reaching.

Effect:

The advent of genetic engineering has had a profound effect on science, medicine, agriculture, and society at large. In the realm of medicine, genetic engineering holds the promise of revolutionary treatments for genetic disorders, cancer, and infectious diseases. Techniques such as CRISPR-Cas9 have enabled precise editing of the human genome, opening up new avenues for personalized medicine and gene therapy.

In agriculture, genetic engineering has led to the development of crops with enhanced nutritional content, increased pest resistance, and improved yields. GMOs have the potential to address global food security challenges by making crops more resilient to drought, pests, and disease, while reducing the need for chemical pesticides and fertilizers.

The impact of genetic engineering extends beyond the realm of science and technology, shaping ethical, social, and environmental discourse. The ability to manipulate the genetic code raises profound ethical questions about the limits of human intervention in the natural world, the rights of future generations, and the implications for biodiversity and ecosystems.

Genetic engineering has also sparked debate about equity and access to genetic technologies, particularly in the context of healthcare disparities and agricultural development. Concerns about the commercialization of genetic resources, corporate control of seed stocks, and the concentration of power in the biotechnology industry have led to calls for greater transparency, regulation, and public engagement in genetic engineering research and applications.

Furthermore, the potential risks and unintended consequences of genetic engineering—such as genetic mutations, environmental contamination, and the spread of transgenes—highlight the need for rigorous safety assessments, risk mitigation strategies, and long-term monitoring of genetically modified organisms.

Ultimately, the impact of genetic engineering is multifaceted and complex, encompassing scientific, ethical, social, and environmental dimensions. As we navigate the opportunities and challenges of this powerful technology, it is essential to approach genetic engineering with humility, foresight, and a commitment to responsible stewardship of life's most precious resource—our genetic heritage.

EXPERIMENT EIGHT

UNVEILING THE SECRETS OF THE UNIVERSE: THE IMPACT OF THE CERN PARTICLE ACCELERATOR

Deep beneath the Franco-Swiss border lies one of humanity's most ambitious scientific endeavors—the European Organization for Nuclear Research, known as CERN. At its heart lies the Large Hadron Collider (LHC), the world's most powerful particle accelerator, which propels subatomic particles to near-light speeds and smashes them together in a quest to unlock the mysteries of the universe.

Effect:

The impact of the CERN Particle Accelerator on scientific knowledge and technological innovation has been profound and far-reaching. By recreating the conditions of the early universe moments after the Big Bang, researchers at CERN have been able to probe the fundamental building blocks of matter and unravel the secrets of the cosmos.

One of the most significant achievements of the LHC was the discovery of the Higgs boson in 2012—a long-sought-after particle that confers mass to other fundamental particles. This discovery validated the Standard Model of particle physics and provided crucial insights into the origin of mass and the fundamental forces of nature.

The power of the CERN Particle Accelerator extends beyond the realm of fundamental physics, influencing technology, medicine, and society at large. The development of cutting-edge particle detectors, superconducting magnets, and high-performance computing technologies at CERN has led to breakthroughs in fields such as materials science, medical imaging, and data analytics.

Furthermore, the collaborative nature of research at CERN—bringing together scientists and engineers from around the world—has fostered international cooperation, knowledge sharing, and cultural exchange. The spirit of collaboration and open access to data and resources at CERN has inspired a new generation of scientists and engineers to push the boundaries of human knowledge and tackle some of the most pressing challenges facing humanity.

Impact:

The impact of the CERN Particle Accelerator on society extends beyond scientific discovery, shaping public understanding of science, inspiring innovation, and fostering global collaboration. By pushing the boundaries of human knowledge and exploring the mysteries of the universe, CERN continues to serve as a beacon of scientific excellence and a testament to the power of human curiosity and ingenuity.

EXPERIMENT NINE

UNVEILING THE SHADOWS OF BIOLOGICAL WEAPONS TESTING: IMPACT AND ETHICAL CONSIDERATIONS

In the murky realms of military research and geopolitical rivalry, a dark chapter in human history unfolds—the testing and development of biological weapons. From the trenches of World War I to the laboratories of the Cold War era, governments and military institutions have sought to harness the deadly potential of pathogens and toxins as instruments of warfare.

Effect:

The impact of biological weapons testing on global security, public health, and ethical norms has been profound and enduring. Biological weapons, such as anthrax, plague, and botulinum toxin, have the potential to cause mass casualties, widespread panic, and societal disruption. The use of biological agents in warfare poses unique challenges in detection, response, and containment, with implications for civilian populations, healthcare systems, and international relations.

Biological weapons testing has also raised ethical questions about the morality of weaponizing living organisms and exploiting vulnerabilities in human biology for military gain. The deliberate release of pathogens or toxins in controlled experiments or field trials raises concerns about the risks of accidental or intentional misuse, as well as the potential for ecological and collateral damage.

Effect:

The impact of biological weapons testing extends beyond the immediate risks of weaponization, influencing global norms, treaties, and regulations governing the use of biological agents in warfare. The Biological Weapons Convention (BWC), established in 1972, prohibits the development, production, and stockpiling of biological weapons and calls for the destruction of existing arsenals. However, enforcement mechanisms and compliance monitoring remain challenging, raising concerns about the potential for clandestine research and proliferation of biological weapons.

Furthermore, the dual-use nature of biological research—where scientific advancements in biotechnology and genomics can be applied for both peaceful and military purposes—heightens the importance of ethical oversight, biosecurity protocols, and responsible stewardship of scientific knowledge. The potential for unintended consequences, such as accidental releases, laboratory accidents, or bioterrorism, underscores the need for robust risk assessment, safety standards, and international cooperation in preventing the misuse of biological agents.

The influence of biological weapons testing on society extends beyond the realm of security and warfare, shaping public perceptions, policy decisions, and scientific research priorities. The specter of biological weapons testing serves as a reminder of the fragility of global security and the imperative of preventing the proliferation of weapons of mass destruction. As we confront the ethical dilemmas and security challenges posed by biological weapons testing, it is essential to uphold principles of transparency, accountability, and international cooperation in safeguarding human security and promoting peace.

EXPERIMENT TEN

HARNESSING NATURE'S POWER: EXPLORING THE IMPACT OF CLIMATE ENGINEERING

In the face of escalating climate change and its far-reaching consequences, humanity stands at a crossroads—a moment of reckoning that demands bold and innovative solutions. Among these solutions is the emerging field of climate engineering, which seeks to manipulate Earth's climate systems to mitigate the effects of global warming and restore ecological balance.

Effect:

The impact of climate engineering on the environment, society, and geopolitics is both profound and complex. Proposed techniques range from solar radiation management (SRM), which involves reflecting sunlight away from Earth to cool the planet, to carbon dioxide removal (CDR), which aims to capture and store excess greenhouse gases from the atmosphere.

One potential effect of climate engineering is its ability to offset some of the most catastrophic impacts of climate change, such as rising temperatures, extreme weather events, and sea-level rise. By implementing large-scale interventions to alter Earth's climate systems, climate engineering has the potential to buy time for humanity to transition to a low-carbon economy and adapt to the inevitable changes ahead.

However, the influence of climate engineering extends beyond its intended benefits, raising ethical, environmental, and social concerns. Solar radiation management techniques, such as stratospheric aerosol injection, could have unintended consequences, such as altering regional weather patterns, disrupting ecosystems, and exacerbating geopolitical tensions.

Furthermore, the deployment of climate engineering technologies raises questions about equity, justice, and power dynamics in decision-making processes. Who gets to decide which interventions are implemented, and who bears the costs and risks associated with these interventions? Ensuring transparency, democratic governance, and public participation in climate engineering research and deployment is essential to address these ethical concerns.

Impact:

The impact of climate engineering on global governance, international cooperation, and the future of the planet is profound and far-reaching. As we confront the existential threat of climate change, climate engineering offers a potential lifeline—a tool to buy time and create space for transformative action to reduce greenhouse gas emissions, protect vulnerable communities, and preserve Earth's natural systems.

However, the ethical, environmental, and social implications of climate engineering demand careful consideration, rigorous research, and responsible governance. As we navigate the complexities of this emerging field, it is essential to approach climate engineering with humility, caution, and a commitment to safeguarding the well-being of both present and future generations.

EXPERIMENT ELEVEN

EXPLORING THE PSYCHEDELIC RENAISSANCE: NARRATION, IMPACT, AND EFFECT OF LSD AND PSYCHEDELIC RESEARCH

In the midst of the cultural upheaval of the 1960s, a wave of scientific curiosity swept through the world of psychiatry and neuroscience—a curiosity fueled by the promise of unlocking the mysteries of the mind through the use of psychedelic substances such as LSD. Led by pioneers like Dr. Timothy Leary and Dr. Albert Hofmann, researchers embarked on a journey into the depths of consciousness, seeking to understand the therapeutic potential and transformative power of psychedelics.

Impact:

The impact of LSD and psychedelic research on our understanding of consciousness, mental health, and human potential has been profound and far-reaching. Early studies exploring the effects of LSD on perception, cognition, and mood revealed new insights into the neural mechanisms underlying consciousness and altered states of consciousness. These studies laid the groundwork for subsequent research into the therapeutic potential of psychedelics for treating psychiatric disorders such as depression, anxiety, and PTSD.

Effect:

The effect of LSD and psychedelic research on society and culture has been equally transformative, sparking a psychedelic renaissance that continues to reverberate today. The countercultural movement of the 1960s embraced LSD as a tool for personal and spiritual exploration, leading to a widespread fascination with psychedelics and their potential to catalyze profound experiences of insight, creativity, and transcendence.

However, the cultural and political backlash against LSD and psychedelics in the latter half of the 20th century led to their stigmatization, criminalization, and relegation to the margins of scientific inquiry. It was not until the turn of the 21st century that renewed interest in psychedelics as therapeutic agents began to emerge, fueled by a growing body of research demonstrating their efficacy in treating mental health conditions and enhancing psychological well-being.

The resurgence of LSD and psychedelic research on mental health care, neuroscience, and public policy has been nothing short of revolutionary. Clinical trials investigating the therapeutic potential of psychedelics, particularly for treatment-resistant depression and PTSD, have shown promising results, leading to a reevaluation of their therapeutic value and potential integration into mainstream psychiatry.

Furthermore, the decriminalization and legalization of psychedelics in some jurisdictions, along with the proliferation of psychedelic therapy clinics and retreat centers, have created new opportunities for individuals to explore the healing potential of these substances in controlled and supportive settings. The growing acceptance of psychedelics as legitimate tools for psychological healing and personal growth represents a seismic shift in our understanding of mental health and consciousness.

As we navigate the complexities of the psychedelic renaissance, it is essential to approach LSD and psychedelic research with caution, integrity, and a commitment to ethical practice. By harnessing the transformative power of psychedelics in the service of healing and self-discovery, we have the potential to revolutionize mental health care and unlock new dimensions of human flourishing and well-being.

EXPERIMENT TWELVE

INTO THE UNKNOWN: NARRATING THE IMPACT AND EFFECT OF SPACE EXPLORATION

Since the dawn of human civilization, humanity has been driven by an insatiable curiosity to explore the unknown—to reach beyond the confines of Earth and venture into the vast expanse of outer space. From the earliest observations of the night sky to the monumental achievements of the space age, our journey into space has reshaped our understanding of the universe and transformed the course of human historyImpact:

The impact of space exploration on science, technology, and society has been profound and far-reaching. Through space missions and telescopic observations, astronomers have gained unprecedented insights into the origins, structure, and evolution of the cosmos—from the birth of stars and galaxies to the discovery of exoplanets and the search for extraterrestrial life.

The exploration of space has also revolutionized our understanding of Earth itself, providing crucial data on climate change, environmental sustainability, and natural disasters. Satellites orbiting the planet monitor weather patterns, track deforestation, and enable global communication and navigation, transforming the way we interact with and steward our home planet.

Effect:

The effect of space exploration on technology and innovation has been equally transformative, driving advancements in materials science, robotics, telecommunications, and computing. Technologies developed for space missions, such as integrated circuits, GPS, and medical imaging, have found applications in diverse fields, from healthcare and transportation to entertainment and consumer electronics.

Furthermore, space exploration has inspired generations of scientists, engineers, and innovators, fueling a spirit of discovery and pushing the boundaries of human ingenuity. The iconic images of astronauts walking on the moon, rovers exploring the surface of Mars, and spacecraft voyaging to the outer reaches of the solar system capture the imagination and inspire wonder, curiosity, and awe.

Impact:

The impact of space exploration extends beyond the realm of science and technology, shaping culture, society, and geopolitics. Space missions serve as symbols of human achievement and international cooperation, transcending political and ideological boundaries to unite nations in pursuit of common goals.

Moreover, the exploration of space has the potential to address some of the most pressing challenges facing humanity—from mitigating the effects of climate change to ensuring the long-term survival of our species. Projects such as asteroid mining, space-based solar power, and human colonization of other planets offer potential solutions to resource scarcity, energy demand, and environmental degradation on Earth.

As we continue our journey into the cosmos, it is essential to approach space exploration with humility, responsibility, and a commitment to preserving the integrity of the universe and the diversity of life within it. By embracing the spirit of exploration and cooperation, we have the opportunity to unlock new frontiers of knowledge, inspire future generations, and chart a course toward a brighter and more sustainable future for all.

EXPERIMENT THIRTEEN

DELVING INTO THE DEPTHS: NARRATING THE IMPACT AND EFFECT OF DEEP SEA EXPLORATION

Beneath the shimmering surface of Earth's oceans lies a realm of mystery and wonder—a realm largely unexplored and teeming with life yet to be discovered. Deep sea exploration, fueled by curiosity and technological innovation, has brought humanity face to face with the extraordinary diversity and complexity of the marine environment, revealing a world of stunning beauty and profound importance to life on Earth.

Impact:

The impact of deep sea exploration on our understanding of oceanography, marine biology, and geology has been transformative. Through the use of submersibles, remotely operated vehicles (ROVs), and autonomous underwater vehicles (AUVs), scientists have uncovered a treasure trove of marine life, from bizarre deep-sea creatures adapted to extreme pressures and darkness to vibrant ecosystems thriving around hydrothermal vents and cold seeps.

Exploration of the deep sea has also provided crucial insights into the geological processes shaping Earth's crust, from the formation of undersea mountains and trenches to the dynamics of underwater volcanoes and seismic activity. By studying deep sea sediments, rocks, and mineral deposits, scientists can reconstruct Earth's past climate, tectonic history, and evolution of life over millions of years.

Effect:

The effect of deep sea exploration on technology and innovation has been equally profound, driving advancements in marine engineering, robotics, and sensor technology. Instruments such as sonar, seafloor mapping systems, and deep-sea cameras have revolutionized our ability to explore and study the ocean depths, enabling researchers to collect data and samples from remote and inaccessible regions of the deep sea.

Furthermore, deep sea exploration has inspired new approaches to biomimicry and biotechnology, as scientists uncover novel adaptations and biochemical compounds in deep-sea organisms with potential applications in medicine, materials science, and biotechnology. From heat-resistant proteins and antibiotics to bioluminescent enzymes and inspiration for next-generation materials, the deep sea is a treasure trove of bioinspiration waiting to be unlocked.

Impact:

The impact of deep sea exploration extends beyond the realm of science and technology, influencing public perception, conservation efforts, and policy decisions. Images and footage captured during deep sea expeditions—of vibrant coral reefs, bizarre deep-sea creatures, and underwater landscapes—have captured the public imagination and raised awareness of the importance of preserving and protecting marine ecosystems.

Moreover, deep sea exploration has highlighted the urgent need for conservation and sustainable management of ocean resources, as human activities such as deep-sea mining, fishing, and pollution threaten to degrade and destroy fragile deep-sea habitats. By promoting ocean literacy, fostering international cooperation, and advocating for marine protected areas, deep sea exploration can play a vital role in safeguarding the health and resilience of our oceans for future generations.

As we continue to explore the mysteries of the deep sea, it is essential to approach deep sea exploration with humility, respect, and a commitment to responsible stewardship of the marine environment. By embracing the spirit of discovery and cooperation, we have the opportunity to unlock the secrets of the ocean depths and inspire a new era of ocean exploration and conservation.

EXPERIMENT FOURTEEN

DECODING LIFE: THE IMPACT AND LEGACY OF THE HUMAN GENOME PROJECT

In the closing years of the 20th century, one of the most ambitious and transformative scientific endeavors in history was launched: the Human Genome Project (HGP). Initiated in 1990 and completed in 2003, the project aimed to map the entire human genome—the complete set of DNA in a human being. This monumental effort involved scientists from across the globe working together to read the 3 billion base pairs that make up our genetic blueprint.

The Human Genome Project was more than just a technical feat; it was a journey into the very essence of what makes us human. The goal was not only to map the genome but to understand the functions of individual genes and how they contribute to health, disease, and human diversity.

Impact:

The impact of the Human Genome Project on medicine, biology, and society has been profound. The project's completion marked the beginning of a new era in genomics, paving the way for personalized medicine, where treatments can be tailored to an individual's genetic makeup. This has led to more effective therapies for conditions like cancer, where the understanding of genetic mutations has driven the development of targeted treatments.

In addition to its medical applications, the HGP has revolutionized our understanding of human evolution and migration, shedding light on how populations have moved and mixed over millennia. It has also provided critical insights into the genetic basis of complex diseases, such as heart disease, diabetes, and mental health disorders, enabling researchers to identify genetic risk factors and develop preventive strategies.

Effect:

The effects of the Human Genome Project extend far beyond the scientific community, influencing ethical, legal, and social considerations. The ability to sequence and analyze individual genomes has raised important questions about privacy, consent, and the potential for genetic discrimination in employment or insurance. These concerns have led to the establishment of policies and guidelines to protect individuals' genetic information and ensure that the benefits of genomic research are shared equitably.

Moreover, the HGP has had a profound effect on education and public understanding of science. The project has inspired a new generation of scientists and has led to the creation of educational programs and resources aimed at increasing genetic literacy among the general public. As a result, people are more informed about their own genetic health and the role of genetics in medicine and society.

The legacy of the Human Genome Project continues to grow, as its data and findings serve as a foundation for ongoing research in genetics, biology, and medicine. The project has democratized access to genetic information, with databases and tools available to researchers worldwide, fostering collaboration and accelerating scientific discovery.

The HGP has also set the stage for other large-scale genomic initiatives, such as the International HapMap Project and the 1000 Genomes Project, which aim to further our understanding of human genetic variation and its implications for health and disease.

As we continue to explore the human genome, the lessons learned from the HGP remind us of the power of collaboration, the importance of ethical considerations, and the potential of science to improve human health and well-being. The Human Genome Project stands as a testament to what can be achieved when nations, institutions, and individuals come together to pursue knowledge for the betterment of humanity.

EXPERIMENT FIFTEEN

THE DARK SIDE OF SCIENCE: THE IMPACT AND LEGACY OF MIND-CONTROL EXPERIMENTS

In the shadowy corners of 20th-century history, a series of secretive and controversial experiments sought to probe the depths of the human mind. These mind-control experiments, often conducted under the guise of national security during the Cold War, aimed to unlock the secrets of manipulating human thoughts, behaviors, and perceptions. Among the most infamous of these programs was the CIA's MK-Ultra, a covert operation that subjected unwitting subjects to psychological and pharmacological tests in the pursuit of mind control.

The idea of mind control—shaping or even erasing an individual's thoughts, memories, and actions—captured the imagination of intelligence agencies, who saw it as a potential tool for interrogation, espionage, and warfare. However, these experiments were often conducted without the consent of the subjects, leading to devastating psychological and physical effects.

Impact:

The impact of mind-control experiments on individuals and society has been profound and deeply troubling. Participants in these experiments were exposed to a range of unethical treatments, including high doses of LSD, sensory deprivation, hypnosis, and electroconvulsive therapy. These methods were intended to break down a person's psyche, erase memories, and implant new thoughts or behaviors— often with catastrophic results.

The long-term effects on the subjects of these experiments were severe. Many were left with lasting psychological trauma, including anxiety, depression, and paranoia. Some experienced permanent cognitive impairments, and a few even died as a result of the extreme measures used during the experiments. The lack of informed consent and the secrecy surrounding these programs have left a legacy of mistrust and fear regarding the misuse of psychological research.

Effect:

The effects of these mind-control experiments have reverberated through the scientific community, government agencies, and public consciousness. The revelation of these secret programs, particularly MK-Ultra, sparked widespread outrage and led to congressional investigations in the 1970s. The experiments were widely condemned as gross violations of human rights and medical ethics, resulting in greater scrutiny of research involving human subjects and the development of stricter ethical standards.

The exposure of these experiments also fueled conspiracy theories and fears about the government's ability to control or influence the minds of its citizens. These fears have persisted in popular culture, influencing movies, books, and television shows that explore themes of mind control, psychological manipulation, and government overreach.

The mind-control experiments serves as a cautionary tale about the potential dangers of unchecked scientific experimentation and the ethical responsibilities of researchers. The trauma inflicted on the subjects of these experiments highlights the importance of informed consent, transparency, and the protection of human rights in all areas of research.

While these experiments were largely discredited and abandoned, their legacy continues to influence contemporary discussions about the ethical limits of neuroscience, psychology, and psychiatry. As we continue to explore the complexities of the human mind, the dark history of mind-control experiments reminds us of the ethical imperatives that must guide scientific inquiry—ensuring that the pursuit of knowledge never comes at the expense of human dignity and well-being.

EXPERIMENT SIXTEEN

UNVEILING THE FUTURE: THE IMPACT AND LEGACY OF ARTIFICIAL INTELLIGENCE (AI) RESEARCH

Artificial Intelligence (AI) research represents one of the most revolutionary fields in modern science and technology. Rooted in the dream of creating machines that can think, learn, and act autonomously, AI research began in earnest during the mid-20th century, driven by advancements in computing power, data availability, and mathematical algorithms. From the early days of simple logic-based systems to the development of complex neural networks, AI has evolved rapidly, transforming industries, reshaping societies, and redefining what it means to be human.

Pioneers like Alan Turing, John McCarthy, and Marvin Minsky laid the groundwork for AI, envisioning machines capable of performing tasks that require human-like intelligence such as language processing, problem-solving, and decision-making. Over the decades, AI research has expanded to include machine learning, deep learning, natural language processing, computer vision, robotics, and more—each advancing our understanding of intelligence, both human and artificial.

Impact:

The impact of AI research on society, industry, and daily life has been nothing short of transformative. In the healthcare sector, AI-driven technologies are revolutionizing diagnostics, drug discovery, and personalized medicine. AI systems can analyze vast amounts of medical data to detect patterns and predict patient outcomes with unprecedented accuracy. In finance, AI algorithms power high-frequency trading, fraud detection, and risk management, driving efficiency and reducing human error.

AI has also reshaped industries such as manufacturing, where robots equipped with AI capabilities automate complex tasks, and transportation, where AI is the driving force behind autonomous vehicles. In the realm of communication, AI powers virtual assistants, language translation services, and personalized content recommendations, making information more accessible and interactions more seamless.

Effect:

The effects of AI research extend beyond technological advancements, raising profound ethical, social, and economic questions. As AI systems become more integrated into our lives, concerns about privacy, security, and bias have come to the forefront. The use of AI in surveillance, data collection, and decision-making has sparked debates about the balance between innovation and civil liberties, as well as the potential for AI to perpetuate or amplify existing social inequalities.

Moreover, the rise of AI has led to fears of job displacement, as automation threatens to replace human workers in various industries. While AI has the potential to create new opportunities and enhance productivity, it also poses challenges to workforce adaptation and economic stability. The question of how to ensure that the benefits of AI are equitably distributed remains a central issue in the ongoing discourse about the future of work.

Impact:

The impact of AI research on our understanding of intelligence, ethics, and the future of humanity is profound and far-reaching. As AI systems become more sophisticated, they challenge our traditional notions of what it means to be intelligent, creative, and even conscious. The possibility of creating AI that rivals or surpasses human intelligence—often referred to as artificial general intelligence (AGI)—raises existential questions about the role of humans in a world increasingly dominated by machines.

In response to these challenges, AI researchers, ethicists, and policymakers are working to establish frameworks for responsible AI development. This includes developing guidelines for transparency, accountability, and fairness in AI systems, as well as ensuring that AI technologies are aligned with human values and societal goals.

As AI continues to evolve, it holds the potential to address some of the most pressing global challenges, from climate change and healthcare to education and poverty. However, realizing this potential requires a thoughtful and collaborative approach to AI research and development—one that prioritizes ethical considerations, promotes inclusivity, and safeguards the well-being of all.

The legacy of AI research will be shaped by how we navigate these opportunities and challenges. As we stand on the brink of a new era defined by intelligent machines, the choices we make today will determine the trajectory of AI's impact on the world and the future of humanity.

EXPERIMENT SEVENTEEN

THE ETHICAL FRONTIER: NARRATING THE IMPACT AND LEGACY OF HUMAN CLONING AND STEM CELL RESEARCH

Human cloning and stem cell research sit at the cutting edge of biological science, offering immense potential for medical breakthroughs while raising profound ethical questions. The journey into this controversial realm began with the landmark achievement in 1996: the successful cloning of a mammal, Dolly the sheep. This event thrust the possibility of human cloning into the public consciousness, sparking debates that continue to this day.

Stem cell research, closely linked with cloning, explores the use of undifferentiated cells that have the potential to develop into various types of tissues. Scientists hope to harness this potential to regenerate damaged organs, treat incurable diseases, and extend human longevity.

Both fields are driven by the desire to unlock the secrets of life and cure the most devastating illnesses, but they also challenge our understanding of identity, reproduction, and the sanctity of life.

Impact:

The impact of human cloning and stem cell research on medicine and science is significant and transformative. Stem cell research has already led to groundbreaking treatments, particularly in regenerative medicine. For example, stem cells are being used to repair damaged heart tissue, treat spinal cord injuries, and restore vision in patients with macular degeneration. These advancements offer hope to millions of people suffering from conditions that were once considered untreatable.

Cloning technology, while still in its infancy, has the potential to revolutionize medicine by providing a source of genetically identical organs for transplantation, eliminating the risk of immune rejection. In addition, cloning could enable the preservation of endangered species or the revival of extinct ones, although this idea remains a topic of considerable debate.

Effect:

The effects of human cloning and stem cell research on society extend far beyond their scientific applications, touching on deeply held beliefs about ethics, religion, and human dignity. Human cloning, in particular, raises a host of ethical concerns, from the potential for abuse in creating "designer babies" to the moral implications of cloning human beings. Many fear that cloning could lead to a devaluation of human life, with clones potentially being viewed as mere commodities or tools rather than individuals with rights and autonomy.

Stem cell research, especially when it involves embryonic stem cells, also ignites ethical debates. The extraction of stem cells from embryos, which results in the destruction of the embryo, has led to opposition from various religious and pro-life groups who argue that it violates the sanctity of human life. These concerns have influenced public policy, leading to restrictions on funding and research in some countries, while others have embraced the potential benefits and moved forward with more permissive regulations.

Human cloning and stem cell research on public policy and global discourse has been profound. These fields have prompted governments to grapple with complex questions about the regulation of scientific research, the protection of human rights, and the balance between innovation and ethical responsibility. International agreements and national laws have been enacted to address these issues, with varying degrees of restriction or support for cloning and stem cell research.

The ongoing debate over cloning and stem cell research also underscores the need for continued dialogue between scientists, ethicists, religious leaders, and the public. As technology advances, society must carefully consider the implications of these developments, ensuring that scientific progress does not come at the expense of human values or the well-being of individuals.

Conclusion:

Human cloning and stem cell research represent some of the most promising yet contentious areas of modern science. Their potential to revolutionize medicine and improve human health is immense, but so too are the ethical dilemmas they pose. As we continue to explore these frontiers, it is crucial that we proceed with caution, guided by a commitment to ethical principles and respect for the dignity of all human life.

The legacy of human cloning and stem cell research will be defined not only by the scientific breakthroughs they yield but also by the moral choices we make as we navigate the challenges they present. In the pursuit of knowledge and healing, we must ensure that our actions reflect our deepest values, safeguarding both the promise of these technologies and the integrity of our shared humanity.

EXPERIMENT EIGHTEEN

HARNESSING THE POWER OF THE STARS: THE PROMISE AND CHALLENGES OF NUCLEAR FUSION RESEARCH

Nuclear fusion, the process that powers the stars, has long been hailed as the holy grail of energy production. Unlike nuclear fission, which splits heavy atoms to release energy, fusion combines light atoms—typically isotopes of hydrogen—under extreme temperatures and pressures to form helium, releasing vast amounts of energy in the process. The potential of fusion energy is staggering: it promises a virtually limitless, clean, and safe source of power, with minimal environmental impact and no long-lived radioactive waste.

Research into nuclear fusion began in earnest in the mid-20th century, driven by the desire to replicate the sun's power on Earth. Since then, scientists and engineers have been working tirelessly to develop the technologies necessary to achieve controlled fusion, overcoming immense technical challenges along the way. The most advanced fusion experiments, such as those conducted at the International Thermonuclear Experimental Reactor (ITER) in France and the National Ignition Facility (NIF) in the United States, represent the cutting edge of this global scientific endeavor.

Impact:

The impact of successful nuclear fusion research would be transformative for the entire planet. Fusion energy has the potential to revolutionize the global energy landscape, providing a nearly inexhaustible supply of power to meet the growing demands of an industrialized world. Unlike fossil fuels, which contribute to climate change and environmental degradation, fusion produces no carbon emissions, making it a cornerstone of the transition to a sustainable energy future.

Furthermore, fusion energy could significantly reduce the geopolitical tensions associated with energy resources. With abundant fuel sources available from water and lithium, fusion could provide energy security to nations around the world, reducing dependency on finite and often politically volatile fossil fuels. This shift could lead to greater global stability and cooperation in addressing energy challenges.

Effect:

Despite its immense promise, the path to achieving practical nuclear fusion has been fraught with difficulties, leading to frustration and skepticism in some quarters. The technical challenges are daunting: achieving the necessary conditions for sustained fusion—temperatures of millions of degrees, immense pressures, and stable confinement of the plasma—has proven extraordinarily complex and expensive. ITER, for example, is one of the largest and most ambitious scientific projects ever undertaken, with a budget in the tens of billions of dollars and a timeline that stretches decades.

The effects of this prolonged research and development process have been both positive and negative. On the positive side, fusion research has driven significant advances in fields such as materials science, superconducting magnets, and plasma physics. These innovations have had broader applications beyond fusion, benefiting industries such as medicine, electronics, and space exploration.

On the negative side, the high costs and long timelines associated with fusion research have led to criticism and doubts about its viability. Some argue that the resources devoted to fusion could be better spent on other renewable energy technologies, such as solar and wind, which are already commercially viable and scalable. The persistent delays and technical setbacks have also led to the perception that fusion is always "decades away" from becoming a reality.

Nuclear fusion research on the scientific community, public policy, and global energy strategies is profound. Fusion represents a long-term solution to the energy crisis, but its successful development requires sustained investment, international collaboration, and public support. The promise of fusion has inspired generations of scientists and engineers to push the boundaries of what is possible, fostering a spirit of innovation and determination that continues to drive the field forward.

As fusion research progresses, it also raises important questions about the role of government funding, private investment, and international cooperation in advancing large-scale scientific projects. The participation of private companies in fusion research, alongside traditional government-led efforts, reflects a growing recognition that achieving fusion will require diverse approaches and a willingness to take risks.

Conclusion:

Nuclear fusion research embodies the human quest for knowledge and the desire to harness the forces of nature for the betterment of society. While the challenges are immense, the potential rewards are equally great, offering a path to a future where energy is abundant, clean, and accessible to all.

The journey to achieving controlled nuclear fusion is far from over, but the progress made so far is a testament to the power of scientific inquiry and the resilience of those dedicated to this grand challenge. As we look to the future, the continued pursuit of nuclear fusion will require not only technical innovation but also a commitment to the values of sustainability, collaboration, and shared progress.

If successful, nuclear fusion could be the key to unlocking a new era of human development, one in which energy scarcity is a thing of the past and the dream of powering our world with the same energy that lights the stars becomes a reality.

EXPERIMENT NINETEEN

REWRITING LIFE: THE BOLD WORLD OF SYNTHETIC BIOLOGY

Synthetic biology is a groundbreaking field that blurs the lines between biology and engineering. At its core, synthetic biology involves designing and constructing new biological parts, devices, and systems—or re-designing existing ones—to create organisms with novel functions. By combining principles from biology, computer science, chemistry, and engineering, synthetic biologists aim to develop innovative solutions to some of the world's most pressing challenges, from medicine and agriculture to energy and environmental sustainability.

The field took shape in the early 2000s, building on advances in genetic engineering, DNA sequencing, and computational biology. Unlike traditional genetic engineering, which typically involves making small changes to an organism's DNA, synthetic biology allows for the design and construction of entirely new genetic circuits and even synthetic organisms from scratch. The potential applications are vast and diverse, ranging from microbes engineered to produce biofuels and medicines to crops designed to withstand harsh environmental conditions.

Impact:

The impact of synthetic biology on science, technology, and society has been profound, with the potential to revolutionize industries and transform the way we approach problems in health, agriculture, and the environment. In medicine, synthetic biology has enabled the development of new therapies, such as CAR-T cells, which are engineered to target and destroy cancer cells with remarkable precision. The ability to design custom organisms has also led to advances in vaccine development, as seen in the rapid response to the COVID-19 pandemic, where synthetic biology played a key role in the creation of mRNA vaccines.

In agriculture, synthetic biology is paving the way for more sustainable farming practices. Crops engineered for improved resistance to pests, diseases, and climate change can reduce the need for chemical pesticides and increase food security in a warming world. Additionally, synthetic biology has the potential to revolutionize the production of biofuels and bioplastics, offering renewable alternatives to fossil fuels and reducing our reliance on non-biodegradable plastics.

Effect:

The effects of synthetic biology, however, are not without controversy and concern. The ability to create synthetic organisms and manipulate life at the molecular level raises significant ethical, safety, and regulatory issues. One major concern is the potential for unintended consequences, such as the accidental release of engineered organisms into the environment, where they could disrupt ecosystems or lead to the spread of new diseases. The possibility of "biohacking"—where individuals or groups could use synthetic biology tools for malicious purposes—adds another layer of risk to the field.

Moreover, the ethical implications of "playing God" by designing and creating new forms of life are hotly debated. Questions about the ownership of genetically modified organisms (GMOs), the potential for monopolies on synthetic biology technologies, and the impact on biodiversity are central to discussions about the future of the field. As synthetic biology moves from the laboratory to real-world applications, there is a growing need for robust regulatory frameworks and international cooperation to ensure that the benefits are realized while minimizing risks.

Synthetic biology effect on public policy, industry, and global health is already being felt, as governments and organizations grapple with the opportunities and challenges posed by this rapidly evolving field. Policymakers are tasked with balancing the need for innovation with the imperative to protect public safety and the environment. This has led to the development of new regulations and guidelines aimed at overseeing synthetic biology research and applications, including biosafety measures, ethical standards, and intellectual property considerations.

Industry has also been quick to embrace synthetic biology, with startups and established companies alike investing in the development of new products and technologies. The synthetic biology market is expected to grow significantly in the coming years, driven by demand for sustainable solutions in areas such as energy, agriculture, and pharmaceuticals. As the field continues to mature, the collaboration between academia, industry, and government will be crucial in shaping its trajectory and ensuring that synthetic biology is used for the greater good.

Conclusion:

Synthetic biology represents one of the most exciting and potentially transformative fields of the 21st century. Its ability to rewrite the code of life and engineer organisms with entirely new capabilities holds the promise of solving some of humanity's greatest challenges. However, with great power comes great responsibility, and the ethical, safety, and regulatory challenges posed by synthetic biology must be carefully navigated.

As we continue to explore the possibilities of synthetic biology, it is essential to foster a culture of transparency, inclusivity, and ethical responsibility. The decisions we make today will shape the future of life on Earth, determining how we use our newfound ability to design and create life. If harnessed wisely, synthetic biology could lead to a more sustainable, healthy, and prosperous world for all. But to achieve this, we must ensure that the pursuit of innovation is guided by a commitment to the well-being of both people and the planet.

EXPERIMENT TWENTY

BRIDGING MINDS AND MACHINES: THE PROMISE AND PERILS OF NEUROSCIENCE AND BRAIN-COMPUTER INTERFACES

Neuroscience, the study of the nervous system and the brain, has made remarkable strides over the past few decades, unlocking many of the mysteries of how the human brain functions. One of the most intriguing and potentially transformative applications of this knowledge is the development of brain-computer interfaces (BCIs). BCIs are systems that allow direct communication between the brain and external devices, enabling individuals to control computers, prosthetic limbs, and even other machines using only their thoughts.

The idea of merging minds with machines has captivated scientists and technologists for decades, with roots in both science fiction and serious academic research. Early experiments in the 1970s laid the groundwork for today's sophisticated BCIs, which have advanced to the point where they are being used to help people with paralysis regain control of their environment, allowing them to perform tasks like moving a cursor on a screen or operating a robotic arm.

Impact:

The impact of BCIs on medicine and rehabilitation has been profound, particularly for individuals with disabilities. BCIs offer new hope to those with spinal cord injuries, neurodegenerative diseases like ALS, and other conditions that impair movement and communication. For example, patients who are unable to speak or move due to paralysis can use BCIs to communicate by selecting letters on a screen using only their brain signals. This technology not only enhances their quality of life but also allows them to engage with the world in ways that were previously impossible.

In addition to medical applications, BCIs are being explored for use in a wide range of fields, from gaming and virtual reality to education and defense. The ability to control machines with the mind could revolutionize these industries, leading to new forms of entertainment, more immersive educational experiences, and even the enhancement of human cognitive abilities. Companies like Neuralink, founded by Elon Musk, are at the forefront of this research, aiming to create high-bandwidth BCIs that could one day enable humans to merge with artificial intelligence.

Effect:

While the potential benefits of BCIs are immense, the effects of this technology on society raise significant ethical and philosophical questions. One major concern is the issue of privacy: BCIs, by their very nature, involve accessing and interpreting brain signals, which are deeply personal and private. The potential for misuse of this technology, whether by governments, corporations, or malicious actors, is a serious concern. The idea of someone being able to read or manipulate another person's thoughts, or even implant false memories or beliefs, is a dystopian scenario that requires careful consideration.

Another significant effect of BCIs is the potential to deepen existing inequalities. Access to advanced BCIs could become a privilege of the wealthy, leading to a future where those with the means to enhance their cognitive abilities or control technology with their minds have a significant advantage over those who do not. This could exacerbate social and economic disparities, creating a new form of inequality based on neurotechnology.

Furthermore, the integration of BCIs into daily life could blur the boundaries between human and machine, challenging our understanding of identity, autonomy, and what it means to be human. As we move towards a future where mind and machine are increasingly intertwined, society will need to grapple with these profound questions and develop ethical guidelines to govern the use of BCIs.

The development and deployment of BCIs have significant implications for public policy, regulation, and international norms. Governments and regulatory bodies must navigate the complex challenges posed by this technology, balancing the need to encourage innovation with the responsibility to protect individuals' rights and safety. This includes establishing standards for the ethical use of BCIs, ensuring that they are accessible to all who could benefit from them, and safeguarding against potential abuses.

At the same time, the global nature of neuroscience research and the rapid pace of technological development in BCIs necessitate international cooperation. Countries must work together to establish common frameworks for the regulation and oversight of BCIs, addressing issues such as data privacy, cybersecurity, and the ethical use of neurotechnology in both civilian and military contexts.

Conclusion:

Neuroscience and brain-computer interfaces represent a bold new frontier in the relationship between humans and technology. The potential to enhance human capabilities, restore lost functions, and create new forms of interaction with machines is both exciting and daunting. However, as with all powerful technologies, the development and application of BCIs must be guided by careful consideration of their ethical, social, and philosophical implications.

As we continue to explore the possibilities of BCIs, it is essential that we engage in an open and inclusive dialogue about the future we want to create. By doing so, we can harness the power of neuroscience and BCIs to improve human life while ensuring that the benefits are shared equitably and the risks are managed responsibly. The journey ahead will require not only scientific and technological innovation but also a deep commitment to the values that define us as human beings.

EXPERIMENT TWENTY ONE

THE CHERNOBYL DISASTER: A CATASTROPHE THAT SHOOK THE WORLD

On April 26, 1986, the world witnessed one of the most catastrophic nuclear accidents in history — the explosion at the Chernobyl Nuclear Power Plant in the Soviet Union, now modern-day Ukraine. The disaster occurred during a late-night safety test at Reactor No. 4, where a sudden power surge led to a massive explosion that blew the roof off the reactor, releasing a cloud of radioactive materials into the atmosphere. The force of the explosion was so powerful that it sent radioactive debris and flames high into the sky, immediately endangering the lives of the plant workers and the surrounding population.

The immediate cause of the disaster was a combination of operator error and critical design flaws in the reactor. The plant's workers were conducting a test to determine how long turbines would continue to generate power if the plant lost electrical power, but the experiment was not properly coordinated. A series of critical mistakes during the test triggered a runaway reaction in the reactor's core, leading to the catastrophic explosion.

Impact:

The impact of the Chernobyl disaster was far-reaching and devastating. In the days and weeks following the explosion, large amounts of radioactive particles, including iodine-131, cesium-137, and strontium-90, spread across Europe, contaminating vast areas of land and exposing millions of people to dangerous levels of radiation. The immediate aftermath saw the evacuation of more than 100,000 people from the nearby town of Pripyat and surrounding areas, leaving behind a ghost town frozen in time.

The disaster had severe health impacts, with many workers and first responders—often referred to as "liquidators"—suffering from acute radiation sickness. In the years that followed, there was a sharp increase in cancer rates, particularly thyroid cancer, among those exposed to the radiation. The disaster also led to numerous long-term health problems, including birth defects, chronic illnesses, and psychological trauma.

The environmental impact was equally severe. The exclusion zone around Chernobyl, a 30-kilometer radius where human habitation is forbidden, remains heavily contaminated with radioactive materials. The disaster caused significant ecological damage, with forests, rivers, and wildlife exposed to radiation. The area became known as the "Red Forest" after large swaths of pine trees turned reddish-brown and died due to radiation exposure. Despite the long-lasting contamination, some areas within the exclusion zone have seen the return of wildlife, with some species thriving in the absence of human activity.

Effect:

The Chernobyl disaster had profound effects on global nuclear policy and public perception of nuclear energy. It exposed critical weaknesses in the Soviet Union's nuclear safety culture and led to increased scrutiny of nuclear power plants worldwide. In the wake of the disaster, the Soviet government initially attempted to downplay the severity of the incident, delaying the release of information to the public and the international community. However, the scale of the disaster could not be hidden, and the incident became a symbol of the dangers of nuclear energy.

The disaster also accelerated the decline of the Soviet Union, contributing to the erosion of public trust in the government. The mishandling of the crisis and the subsequent economic and environmental costs placed enormous strain on the Soviet economy, further weakening the already fragile state. Internationally, Chernobyl led to a reevaluation of nuclear energy, with some countries halting or scaling back their nuclear programs and others investing in stronger safety measures and regulatory oversight.

The psychological and cultural impact of the Chernobyl disaster cannot be overstated. The event has left a lasting legacy in the collective memory of those who lived through it and continues to serve as a stark reminder of the potential consequences of human error in the nuclear age. Chernobyl has been the subject of numerous books, documentaries, films, and even a successful television series, all exploring the human and environmental toll of the disaster.

The global response to the Chernobyl disaster led to significant changes in nuclear safety protocols and international cooperation on nuclear issues. The International Atomic Energy Agency (IAEA) and other organizations developed new guidelines and safety standards to prevent similar accidents in the future. These include improved reactor design, more stringent operational procedures, and better emergency preparedness and response strategies.

In Ukraine, efforts to contain the damage continue to this day. The construction of the New Safe Confinement, a massive steel structure designed to encase the remains of Reactor No. 4, was completed in 2016, providing a long-term solution to contain the spread of radioactive materials. The structure, often referred to as the "sarcophagus," is expected to last for at least 100 years, giving engineers time to safely dismantle the reactor and manage the radioactive waste.

Conclusion:

The Chernobyl disaster stands as one of the most tragic and significant events in the history of nuclear energy. It serves as a powerful reminder of the potential risks associated with nuclear power and the importance of rigorous safety standards, transparency, and international cooperation in managing these risks. While the full environmental and health impacts of the disaster may never be fully known, Chernobyl has left an indelible mark on the world, shaping the future of nuclear energy and reminding us of the need for vigilance in the face of complex and potentially dangerous technologies.

As the world continues to grapple with the challenges of energy production and environmental sustainability, the lessons of Chernobyl remain as relevant as ever. The disaster underscores the critical importance of safety, accountability, and preparedness in the pursuit of technological progress.

EXPERIMENT TWENTY TWO

THE LEGACY OF AGENT ORANGE: EXPERIMENTATION AND ITS DEVASTATING IMPACT

Agent Orange is perhaps the most infamous of the herbicidal warfare agents used by the U.S. military during the Vietnam War. Initially developed as part of a broader set of chemical agents known as "rainbow herbicides," Agent Orange was a mixture of two herbicides, 2,4-D and 2,4,5-T, designed to defoliate dense forests, eliminate crops, and deprive the Viet Cong and North Vietnamese forces of cover and food sources.

Between 1961 and 1971, as part of Operation Ranch Hand, the U.S. military sprayed approximately 19 million gallons of herbicides over Vietnam, Laos, and Cambodia, with Agent Orange accounting for more than half of the total. The primary goal was to clear vegetation from rural areas to reduce the guerrilla forces' ability to hide and move undetected, but the consequences of this chemical warfare extended far beyond the immediate tactical objectives.

Unbeknownst to many at the time, Agent Orange was contaminated with TCDD, a highly toxic form of dioxin. Dioxin is one of the most dangerous substances known to science, linked to a variety of severe health problems, including cancer, birth defects, and other long-term diseases. The effects of this toxic contamination have had lasting repercussions for both the Vietnamese population and U.S. veterans.

Impact:

The impact of Agent Orange on human health and the environment has been catastrophic. For those exposed to the chemical during the Vietnam War—both Vietnamese civilians and U.S. military personnel—the consequences were dire. Many experienced immediate symptoms such as rashes, respiratory problems, and eye irritation, but the most severe effects emerged over time.

In Vietnam, the legacy of Agent Orange includes a sharp increase in birth defects, with children born long after the war affected by congenital disabilities and developmental issues. The dioxin contamination also led to widespread cancers, including soft tissue sarcoma, Hodgkin's disease, and non-Hodgkin's lymphoma, among others. It is estimated that millions of Vietnamese people have suffered health problems due to exposure to Agent Orange, and the environmental contamination persists to this day, with dioxin "hot spots" still present in certain areas.

U.S. veterans who served in Vietnam also faced severe health consequences due to their exposure to Agent Orange. Many developed chronic illnesses, including various types of cancer, as well as conditions such as diabetes and heart disease. The U.S. government has recognized the connection between Agent Orange exposure and certain diseases, leading to the establishment of compensation programs for affected veterans. However, the road to recognition and adequate support was long and fraught with challenges, with many veterans initially denied benefits.

Effect:

The effects of Agent Orange experimentation and its use as a weapon of war have reverberated through generations. In Vietnam, the long-term environmental damage has been profound, with large areas of land rendered uninhabitable or unusable due to persistent dioxin contamination. The defoliation of vast tracts of forest also had significant ecological impacts, disrupting local ecosystems and contributing to the loss of biodiversity.

The humanitarian impact has been equally severe. In Vietnam, the effects of Agent Orange continue to be felt, with ongoing public health challenges, including the care of those with severe birth defects and chronic illnesses linked to the chemical. The U.S. government and other international organizations have provided some aid for dioxin remediation and health care in Vietnam, but the needs are immense and ongoing.

For U.S. veterans and their families, the legacy of Agent Orange has been one of pain, suffering, and advocacy. Many veterans faced difficulties in obtaining recognition and compensation for their illnesses, leading to a prolonged struggle for justice. The impact of Agent Orange has also extended to the children of veterans, with some evidence suggesting that the toxic effects of dioxin exposure can be passed down through generations, leading to birth defects and other health problems in the children of those who were exposed.

Conclusion:

The use of Agent Orange during the Vietnam War stands as a stark reminder of the devastating consequences of chemical warfare and the experimentation with hazardous substances in military contexts. The legacy of this powerful herbicide is one of human suffering, environmental degradation, and ongoing challenges for those affected by its toxic aftermath.

As we reflect on the history of Agent Orange, it is crucial to remember the lessons learned and to ensure that such practices are never repeated. The international community must continue to support efforts to address the lingering impacts of Agent Orange in Vietnam and among veterans, while also strengthening global norms and regulations against the use of chemical weapons.

The story of Agent Orange is a cautionary tale about the unintended consequences of wartime decisions and the importance of accountability in the development and use of chemical agents. As we move forward, it is essential to prioritize the health and well-being of all people, especially those who have suffered from the actions of the past, and to work towards a future where such tragedies are not repeated.

EXPERIMENT TWENTY THREE

ASBESTOS RESEARCH: UNVEILING THE HIDDEN DANGERS

Asbestos, a naturally occurring mineral with fibrous properties, was once heralded for its heat resistance and strength. Used extensively throughout the 20th century in construction, automotive, and manufacturing industries, asbestos was valued for its insulation and fireproofing capabilities. However, as research into its health effects progressed, the material's deadly consequences became increasingly apparent, leading to a significant shift in safety practices and regulations.

The early research on asbestos was largely focused on its industrial applications and benefits, with little regard for potential health risks. It wasn't until the 1960s and 1970s that researchers began to uncover the severe health hazards associated with asbestos exposure. Studies revealed that inhaling asbestos fibers could lead to serious respiratory diseases, including asbestosis (a chronic lung disease), lung cancer, and mesothelioma, a rare and aggressive cancer of the lining of the lungs, abdomen, or heart.

Impact:

The impact of asbestos research has been profound, reshaping industry practices and public health policies worldwide. As more information about the dangers of asbestos became known, it led to a growing awareness of the risks and a concerted effort to mitigate exposure.

1. Health Effects: The health effects of asbestos exposure are devastating. Asbestosis, caused by inhaling asbestos fibers, results in scarring of lung tissue, leading to difficulty breathing and a higher risk of lung infections. Mesothelioma, associated exclusively with asbestos exposure, has a particularly grim prognosis, with most patients only living a few years after diagnosis. The long latency period of these diseases, often 20 to 50 years after exposure, makes early detection challenging and contributes to high mortality rates.

2. Regulations and Legislation: Asbestos research catalyzed significant regulatory changes aimed at protecting workers and the public from exposure. In many countries, including the United States, Canada, and members of the European Union, regulations were introduced to limit the use of asbestos, mandate the removal of asbestos-containing materials, and enforce

strict safety protocols for handling and disposal. These regulations have helped reduce new cases of asbestos-related diseases, but the legacy of past exposure continues to affect many people.

3. Legal and Financial Impact: The awareness of asbestos-related health risks has led to a multitude of legal actions and compensation claims. Thousands of lawsuits have been filed by workers, families, and individuals affected by asbestos-related diseases, leading to substantial financial settlements and compensation funds. Companies that manufactured or used asbestos have faced significant legal and financial repercussions for their role in the crisis.

Effect:

The effects of asbestos research and its associated regulatory actions have been significant, though not without ongoing challenges:

1. Public Health: The public health impact has been profound, with increased attention to occupational safety and disease prevention. Awareness campaigns and education efforts have helped inform individuals about the risks of asbestos and the importance of safety measures. Despite these efforts, the persistence of asbestos-containing materials in older buildings and

infrastructure continues to pose health risks, particularly during renovation or demolition.

2. Environmental Cleanup: The environmental cleanup of asbestos-containing materials remains a major challenge. The process of removing and safely disposing of asbestos from buildings, land, and industrial sites is complex and costly. Ongoing efforts are required to manage and mitigate the environmental impact of past asbestos use, especially in areas where contamination is widespread.

3. Legacy Issues: The legacy of asbestos exposure persists, with many individuals and communities still dealing with the consequences of past use. The long latency period of asbestos-related diseases means that new cases continue to emerge, and there remains a need for ongoing medical research and support for affected individuals.

Conclusion:

Asbestos research has revealed the hidden dangers of this once-ubiquitous material, leading to significant changes in industry practices, public health policies, and legal frameworks. While the reduction in new asbestos use and improved safety regulations have mitigated some risks, the enduring impact of past exposure remains a critical issue. Continued vigilance, research, and support are necessary to address the long-term effects of asbestos and ensure the health and safety of future generations.

The story of asbestos is a stark reminder of the importance of understanding and addressing the potential risks of materials and technologies before they become widespread. As we move forward, it is essential to learn from the past, prioritize public health, and work towards solutions that prevent similar tragedies from occurring.

EXPERIMENT TWENTY FOUR

THE DEEPWATER HORIZON OIL SPILL: AN ENVIRONMENTAL CATASTROPHE

On April 20, 2010, the world watched in shock as the Deepwater Horizon oil rig, operated by BP in the Gulf of Mexico, suffered a catastrophic blowout. This tragic event would go on to become one of the largest environmental disasters in history. The explosion that rocked the rig killed 11 workers and injured 17 others, but the full extent of the disaster became apparent only as the rig's wellhead continued to leak vast amounts of crude oil into the ocean.

For 87 days, the damaged well spewed an estimated 4.9 million barrels (approximately 206 million gallons) of oil into the Gulf of Mexico, creating a massive slick that spread over thousands of square miles. The spill not only inflicted immediate and severe damage on marine and coastal ecosystems but also had long-lasting effects on the environment and the communities dependent on it.

Impact:

The Deepwater Horizon oil spill had a profound impact on the environment, the economy, and public health

1. Environmental Damage:

 - Marine Life: The spill caused extensive harm to marine life. Oil contamination led to the death of thousands of marine species, including dolphins, sea turtles, and fish. The toxic effects of the oil disrupted reproductive and developmental processes in many species, contributing to long-term ecological damage.

 - Coastal Ecosystems: The oil slick washed ashore, contaminating beaches, marshlands, and mangroves. These vital coastal ecosystems were smothered in oil, leading to habitat destruction and significant declines in plant and animal life. The cleanup efforts, while essential, also caused additional disruption to these sensitive environments.

2. Economic Impact:

 - Fishing Industry: The Gulf of Mexico's fishing industry suffered dramatically due to the spill. The contamination of fisheries led to significant declines in fish populations and the closure of fishing areas. This had a ripple effect on local economies that relied heavily on fishing and seafood production.

- Tourism: The oil spill also impacted tourism in the region. Beaches and coastal attractions, once popular destinations, were marred by oil, leading to a decline in tourist numbers and revenue for businesses dependent on tourism.

3. Public Health:

- Health Concerns: The oil spill and the chemical dispersants used to manage it raised concerns about public health. Residents living near the spill area reported respiratory issues, skin irritations, and other health problems potentially linked to exposure to oil and chemical toxins. Long-term health studies continue to assess the impact on local communities.

Effect:

The Deepwater Horizon oil spill had significant and wide-ranging effects:

1. Regulatory Changes:

- Safety Standards: The disaster prompted major changes in offshore drilling safety standards and regulations. The U.S. government implemented stricter guidelines and oversight to prevent future accidents, including improved safety measures, drilling practices, and emergency response protocols.

- Industry Practices: The spill led to increased scrutiny of oil and gas industry practices. Companies operating in the sector were required to adopt more rigorous safety and environmental protection measures, and the focus shifted towards reducing the risk of similar disasters.

2. Legal and Financial Repercussions:

- Fines and Settlements: BP and its partners faced substantial legal and financial consequences. The company was subject to billions of dollars in fines, penalties, and compensation claims from affected parties, including governments, businesses, and individuals. The financial settlements aimed to cover cleanup costs, environmental restoration, and compensation for economic losses.

- Litigation: Numerous lawsuits were filed by individuals, businesses, and organizations affected by the spill. The legal battles addressed issues ranging from environmental damage to economic losses, resulting in significant settlements and ongoing litigation.

3. Environmental Recovery:

- Restoration Efforts: Efforts to restore the damaged ecosystems have been ongoing since the spill. These include cleaning up contaminated areas, rehabilitating wildlife, and monitoring long-term environmental impacts. While some progress has been made, full recovery remains a challenging and lengthy process.

- Scientific Research: The spill spurred extensive scientific research into the effects of oil spills on marine and coastal environments. This research has enhanced our understanding of oil spill dynamics, ecological impacts, and response strategies, contributing to improved preparedness for future incidents.

Conclusion:

The Deepwater Horizon oil spill stands as a stark reminder of the potential consequences of offshore drilling and the risks associated with industrial operations. The disaster's impact on the environment, economy, and public health underscores the need for robust safety measures, rigorous regulation, and effective response strategies.

As the Gulf of Mexico continues to recover, the lessons learned from the Deepwater Horizon spill serve as a critical guide for preventing and managing future environmental catastrophes. By addressing the root causes of such disasters and investing in sustainable practices, we can work towards safeguarding our natural resources and protecting the communities that depend on them.

The Deepwater Horizon oil spill remains a powerful testament to the importance of environmental stewardship and the need for vigilance in the pursuit of industrial and technological progress.

CERN's God Particle Experiment: Unraveling the Mysteries of the Universe

The search for the "God Particle" has captivated scientists and the public alike, serving as a cornerstone of modern physics and our understanding of the universe. The term "God Particle" refers to the Higgs boson, a fundamental particle that plays a crucial role in the Standard Model of particle physics. Its discovery was one of the most anticipated scientific milestones of the 21st century and was made possible through groundbreaking experiments at CERN (the European Organization for Nuclear Research).

The Higgs boson is named after physicist Peter Higgs, who, along with François Englert, proposed the mechanism that gives mass to fundamental particles in the 1960s. This mechanism is now known as the Higgs mechanism. For decades, the Higgs boson remained elusive, with its existence inferred but never directly observed. The challenge of detecting this particle required an unprecedented scientific endeavor.

Impact:

The Higgs boson experiment, conducted using the Large Hadron Collider (LHC) at CERN, had far-reaching implications for both science and technology:

1. Scientific Impact:

- Validation of the Standard Model: The discovery of the Higgs boson in July 2012 confirmed the existence of the Higgs field, which imparts mass to other elementary particles. This finding validated a critical component of the Standard Model of particle physics, which describes the fundamental forces and particles that constitute the universe.

- Advancement of Particle Physics: The detection of the Higgs boson opened new avenues for research into fundamental physics. It provided a deeper understanding of how particles acquire mass and has paved the way for future investigations into physics beyond the Standard Model, including theories of supersymmetry and string theory.

2. Technological and Engineering Advances:

- Large Hadron Collider: The construction and operation of the LHC pushed the boundaries of engineering and technology. The collider, the largest and most powerful particle accelerator in the world, required innovative solutions to manage extreme conditions, such as high-energy particle collisions and ultra-low temperatures.

- Data Processing and Computing: The scale of the LHC experiments necessitated advancements in data processing and computing. The vast amounts of data generated by the collider led to the development of sophisticated data analysis techniques and distributed computing systems, including the Worldwide LHC Computing Grid (WLCG), which allows researchers worldwide to collaborate on data analysis.

3. Educational and Inspirational Impact:

- Public Engagement: The Higgs boson discovery captured the imagination of the public and brought attention to the field of particle physics. It demonstrated the power of human curiosity and collaboration in solving some of the most profound questions about the universe.

- Educational Programs: The excitement surrounding the Higgs boson experiment has inspired educational programs and initiatives aimed at fostering interest in science and technology among students and the general public.

Effect:

The effects of CERN's God Particle experiment have been transformative and will continue to shape the future of science and technology:

1. Scientific Research and Exploration:

- New Research Directions: With the Higgs boson discovered, scientists are now focusing on understanding its properties in greater detail and exploring potential interactions with other particles. This research aims to uncover new physics phenomena and test theoretical predictions beyond the Standard Model.

- Future Experiments: The success of the Higgs boson experiment has led to plans for future particle physics experiments. The LHC is undergoing upgrades to increase its collision energy and luminosity, enabling even more precise measurements and the potential discovery of new particles or forces.

2. Technological Innovation:

- Technological Spin-offs: The technologies developed for the LHC have applications beyond particle physics. Innovations in areas such as imaging technology, data processing, and cryogenics have found applications in medicine, industry, and other scientific fields.

- Collaborative Research: The collaborative approach used in the LHC experiments has set a precedent for large-scale scientific projects. It has demonstrated the value of international cooperation and interdisciplinary research in addressing complex scientific challenges.

3. Cultural and Philosophical Impact:

- Understanding the Universe: The discovery of the Higgs boson has deepened our understanding of the universe's fundamental nature. It has addressed questions about the origins of mass and the structure of matter, contributing to the broader quest to understand the cosmos.

- Philosophical Reflections: The experiment has also prompted philosophical reflections on the nature of scientific inquiry and the pursuit of knowledge. It highlights the human drive to explore the unknown and seek answers to the most profound questions about existence.

Conclusion:

The CERN God Particle experiment, culminating in the discovery of the Higgs boson, represents a monumental achievement in the field of particle physics. It has confirmed a critical component of the Standard Model, advanced our understanding of the universe, and driven technological and scientific innovation.

As we continue to explore the mysteries of the cosmos, the legacy of the Higgs boson experiment serves as a testament to the power of scientific inquiry and international collaboration. It inspires future generations to push the boundaries of knowledge and to seek answers to the fundamental questions that shape our understanding of the world.

EXPERIMENT TWENTY FIVE

BIOHAZARDOUS RESEARCH: NAVIGATING THE RISKS AND BENEFITS

Biohazardous research involves studying pathogens, toxins, and other biological agents that pose risks to human health, animals, and the environment. This type of research is essential for advancing our understanding of diseases, developing new treatments, and preparing for potential biological threats. However, it also carries significant risks, requiring stringent safety measures and ethical considerations.

Biohazardous research is conducted in specialized laboratories known as biosafety labs, categorized into four levels (BSL-1 to BSL-4) based on the level of containment required. These levels are designed to protect researchers and the environment from potential hazards associated with handling dangerous biological agents. The research encompasses a wide range of fields, including virology, bacteriology, and genetic engineering, among others.

Impact:

The impact of biohazardous research is multifaceted, encompassing scientific advancements, public health benefits, and ethical and safety concerns:

1. Scientific Advancements:

- Disease Understanding: Biohazardous research has led to significant breakthroughs in understanding infectious diseases, their mechanisms, and their interactions with the human immune system. This knowledge is crucial for developing effective treatments and vaccines.

- Therapeutic Development: Research on pathogenic organisms has contributed to the development of new therapeutic strategies, including antibiotics, antivirals, and vaccines. This has had a profound impact on public health by controlling and preventing disease outbreaks.

2. Public Health Benefits:

- Outbreak Preparedness: Studying pathogens and their behaviors helps in preparing for and mitigating the effects of potential outbreaks. Research enables the development of rapid diagnostic tools, effective treatments, and emergency response strategies.

- Vaccine Development: Biohazardous research has played a critical role in the development of vaccines for diseases such as influenza, Ebola, and COVID-19. These vaccines have saved countless lives and reduced the burden of infectious diseases.

3. Ethical and Safety Concerns:

- Containment and Safety: Ensuring the safety of researchers and the environment is a primary concern. Biosafety protocols and containment measures are essential to prevent accidental release of harmful agents and protect against potential exposure.

- Ethical Considerations: The use of biohazardous materials raises ethical questions regarding the potential for misuse, dual-use concerns (where research could be used for harmful purposes), and the impact on animal welfare. These issues require careful consideration and oversight.

Effect:

The effects of biohazardous research extend beyond the immediate scientific community and impact public health, safety, and ethics:

1. Regulatory and Safety Measures:

- Biosafety Regulations: The establishment of biosafety regulations and guidelines has been crucial in managing the risks associated with biohazardous research. Agencies such as the Centers for Disease Control and Prevention (CDC) and the World Health Organization (WHO) provide frameworks for safe handling and containment practices.

- Emergency Response: The research has informed emergency response strategies for biological threats, including outbreaks and bioterrorism. Preparedness plans and response protocols are developed based on insights gained from biohazardous research.

2. Public Awareness and Trust:

- Transparency and Communication: Transparent communication about the risks and benefits of biohazardous research is essential for maintaining public trust. Researchers and institutions must address public concerns and provide clear information about safety measures and research outcomes.

- Ethical Oversight: Ethical oversight by review boards and regulatory agencies helps ensure that research is conducted responsibly and that potential risks are minimized. This oversight is critical for maintaining ethical standards and addressing concerns about the use of biological agents.

3. Long-Term Implications:

- Scientific Knowledge: The knowledge gained from biohazardous research contributes to our understanding of complex biological processes and disease mechanisms. This knowledge has long-term implications for medical science, public health, and disease prevention.

- Technological Innovations: Advances in biohazardous research have driven technological innovations, including improved diagnostic tools, novel therapeutic approaches, and enhanced biosafety technologies.

Conclusion:

Biohazardous research plays a crucial role in advancing scientific knowledge, improving public health, and preparing for biological threats. While the research carries inherent risks, the benefits of understanding and controlling infectious diseases and developing new treatments outweigh the potential hazards.

Ensuring the safety and ethical conduct of biohazardous research is essential for protecting researchers, the environment, and the public. Through rigorous safety protocols, ethical oversight, and transparent communication, the research can continue to contribute valuable insights and innovations while minimizing risks and addressing concerns.

The legacy of biohazardous research is a testament to the balance between scientific progress and responsible stewardship. As we advance in this field, it is vital to remain vigilant, uphold high standards of safety and ethics, and prioritize the well-being of all those affected by the research.

EXPERIMENT TWENTY SIX

ANIMAL TESTING: ETHICAL CONSIDERATIONS, SCIENTIFIC IMPACT, AND SOCIETAL EFFECTS

Animal testing, also known as animal experimentation or animal research, has been a cornerstone of scientific and medical advancement for over a century. This practice involves the use of animals to study biological processes, test the safety and efficacy of new treatments, and understand disease mechanisms. While animal testing has contributed significantly to medical breakthroughs and improved human health, it has also sparked intense ethical debates and led to the development of alternative methods.

The use of animals in research is governed by strict regulations and ethical guidelines designed to minimize harm and ensure humane treatment. These regulations vary by country but generally involve oversight by institutional review boards or ethics committees, which assess the justification for animal use and the measures taken to ensure their welfare.

Impact:

Animal testing has had a profound impact on science, medicine, and society, with both positive contributions and significant ethical concerns:

1. Scientific and Medical Contributions:

   - Medical Advancements: Animal testing has played a crucial role in the development of vaccines, medications, and surgical techniques. Landmark achievements such as the development of insulin for diabetes, antibiotics, and cancer therapies have relied on animal research.

   - Disease Understanding: Studying animals has provided insights into the mechanisms of diseases and the effects of potential treatments. This research has been instrumental in advancing knowledge of complex conditions such as cancer, heart disease, and neurological disorders.

2. Ethical and Welfare Concerns:

   - Animal Welfare: Ethical concerns about animal testing center on the treatment and welfare of animals used in research. Critics argue that the practice can cause pain, suffering, and distress to animals, raising questions about the moral justification of using animals for scientific purposes.

- Alternative Methods: The ethical debate has led to increased advocacy for alternative research methods that do not involve animals. Advances in technology, such as in vitro testing, computer modeling, and organ-on-a-chip systems, offer potential alternatives to traditional animal testing.

3. Regulatory and Oversight Measures:

- Ethical Guidelines: To address ethical concerns, many countries have established regulations and guidelines governing animal testing. These include requirements for humane treatment, minimizing pain and distress, and ensuring that animals are used only when necessary and with appropriate justification.

- Three Rs Principle: The Three Rs Principle—Replacement, Reduction, and Refinement—guides animal research practices. Replacement refers to using alternatives to animal testing when possible, reduction involves minimizing the number of animals used, and refinement focuses on improving methods to reduce suffering.

Effect:

The effects of animal testing are multifaceted, influencing scientific progress, ethical standards, and public perception:

1. Scientific Research and Development:

- Innovative Treatments: Animal testing has led to the development of numerous life-saving treatments and interventions. The knowledge gained from animal research has accelerated medical progress and improved health outcomes for humans.

- Research Evolution: The demand for ethical practices has driven the evolution of research methodologies. The development of alternative approaches and refinements in animal testing methods reflect ongoing efforts to balance scientific advancement with ethical considerations.

2. Public Awareness and Advocacy:

- Ethical Debates: The ethical implications of animal testing have generated significant public debate and advocacy. Animal rights organizations and activists have raised awareness about the treatment of animals in research and have pushed for more humane practices and alternatives.

- Regulatory Changes: Public concern and advocacy have led to changes in regulations and policies governing animal testing. Many countries have introduced stricter guidelines and increased transparency to address ethical issues and improve animal welfare.

3. Long-Term Implications:

- Research Alternatives: The push for alternatives to animal testing has led to advances in research technologies and methodologies. Continued investment in alternative approaches has the potential to reduce reliance on animal testing and improve the efficiency and ethics of scientific research.

- Ethical Reflection: The ongoing ethical debate surrounding animal testing encourages researchers to reflect on the moral implications of their work. This reflection fosters a culture of responsibility and encourages the development of more humane and ethical research practices.

Conclusion:

Animal testing has been instrumental in advancing medical science and improving human health, but it has also raised important ethical and welfare concerns. The balance between scientific progress and animal welfare is a central issue in the debate over animal research.

As we continue to make strides in scientific and medical research, it is essential to uphold high ethical standards and strive for methods that minimize harm to animals. The development of alternative research techniques and the implementation of rigorous regulatory measures are crucial for ensuring that animal testing is conducted responsibly and ethically.

The legacy of animal testing reflects both the potential for scientific advancement and the need for ongoing reflection and improvement in research practices. By addressing ethical concerns and embracing innovative approaches, we can work towards a future where scientific progress and animal welfare are aligned.

EXPERIMENT TWENTY SEVEN

THE SPACE SHUTTLE CHALLENGER DISASTER: A TRAGIC LESSON IN SPACE EXPLORATION

On January 28, 1986, the Space Shuttle Challenger tragically disintegrated 73 seconds after liftoff, leading to the deaths of all seven crew members on board. This disaster marked one of the darkest moments in the history of space exploration and highlighted critical issues related to engineering, safety, and decision-making within NASA.

The Challenger, carrying a crew that included Christa McAuliffe, a high school teacher selected for the Teacher in Space program, was intended to showcase the space shuttle program's achievements and its potential for educational outreach. However, the mission ended in catastrophe when an O-ring seal in one of the solid rocket boosters failed, allowing hot gas to escape and ultimately causing the external fuel tank to explode.

Impact:

The Space Shuttle Challenger disaster had profound impacts on NASA, the space program, and public perception of space exploration:

1. Technical and Engineering Impact:

  - O-Ring Failure: The immediate cause of the disaster was the failure of an O-ring seal in the right solid rocket booster. The O-ring, designed to prevent hot gases from escaping, was compromised due to the unusually cold temperatures on the day of the launch. This failure allowed gas to breach the booster, leading to the catastrophic explosion.

  - Engineering Review: The disaster prompted a thorough review of the space shuttle program's engineering practices and safety procedures. The Rogers Commission, established to investigate the disaster, found that there were significant flaws in the shuttle's design, as well as in the decision-making processes that allowed the launch to proceed despite concerns.

2. Organizational and Management Impact:

  - NASA's Safety Culture: The Challenger disaster exposed serious deficiencies in NASA's safety culture and management practices. The decision to proceed with the launch despite known issues with the O-rings highlighted a troubling tendency to prioritize schedule adherence over safety concerns.

- Reforms and Changes: In response to the findings of the Rogers Commission, NASA implemented numerous changes to improve safety and decision-making processes. These included enhanced oversight of engineering practices, improved communication channels, and more rigorous safety protocols.

3. Public and Psychological Impact:

- National Mourning: The Challenger disaster deeply affected the American public and the global community. The loss of the crew, including Christa McAuliffe, who was to be the first civilian astronaut, struck a chord with many, leading to a period of national mourning and reflection.

- Impact on Space Program: The disaster led to a suspension of space shuttle flights for nearly three years. During this hiatus, NASA focused on addressing the safety issues identified by the Rogers Commission and making necessary design modifications to the shuttle system.

Effect:

The effects of the Space Shuttle Challenger disaster extended beyond immediate safety improvements, influencing the future of space exploration and the perception of space agencies:

1. Improved Safety Measures:

- Engineering and Design Changes: The lessons learned from the Challenger disaster led to significant improvements in shuttle design, including the redesign of the solid rocket boosters and the implementation of more robust safety measures.

- Increased Scrutiny: The disaster increased scrutiny and oversight of space missions, leading to more rigorous testing, evaluation, and approval processes to ensure the safety of astronauts and spacecraft.

2. Cultural and Institutional Changes:

- Shifts in Space Policy: The Challenger disaster influenced shifts in space policy and priorities. It underscored the importance of balancing ambitious goals with rigorous safety considerations, leading to changes in how space missions were planned and executed.

- Public Perception: The disaster changed the public's perception of space exploration, highlighting both the risks involved and the human cost of pursuing ambitious space missions. It led to a greater appreciation of the challenges faced by space agencies and the need for continuous improvement.

3. Legacy and Lessons Learned:

- Educational Impact: The Challenger disaster prompted a renewed focus on safety and education within the space program. Educational initiatives aimed at fostering a deeper understanding of space exploration and its inherent risks became a priority.

- Ongoing Vigilance: The disaster served as a poignant reminder of the importance of vigilance, accountability, and safety in space exploration. It continues to influence space agencies worldwide, ensuring that safety remains a central focus in the pursuit of scientific and exploratory goals.

Conclusion:

The Space Shuttle Challenger disaster remains a somber chapter in the history of space exploration, serving as a powerful reminder of the inherent risks and challenges of human spaceflight. The tragedy prompted critical changes in engineering, management, and safety practices, leading to improvements that have helped shape the future of space exploration.

By reflecting on the lessons learned from the Challenger disaster, we honor the memory of the seven astronauts who lost their lives and reaffirm our commitment to advancing space exploration with the highest standards of safety and integrity. The legacy of the Challenger serves as both a cautionary tale and a catalyst for progress, driving continued innovation and ensuring that the pursuit of knowledge and exploration is conducted with the utmost responsibility.

EXPERIMENT TWENTY EIGHT

CYBERSECURITY EXPERIMENTS: SAFEGUARDING THE DIGITAL FRONTIER

Cybersecurity experiments are crucial to protecting information systems and networks from cyber threats. These experiments involve testing new technologies, methods, and strategies to enhance the security of digital environments. With the rapid evolution of cyber threats and the increasing complexity of digital infrastructures, cybersecurity experiments play a pivotal role in safeguarding sensitive data and ensuring the resilience of technological systems.

Cybersecurity experiments encompass a broad range of activities, including vulnerability assessments, penetration testing, threat simulation, and the development of new security protocols. Researchers and practitioners in the field use these experiments to identify weaknesses, evaluate defensive measures, and improve overall security posture.

Impact:

The impact of cybersecurity experiments is significant, affecting both the technology landscape and the broader society:

1. Technological Advancements:

- Enhanced Security Protocols: Experiments in cybersecurity lead to the development of advanced security protocols and encryption methods. These innovations help protect data integrity, confidentiality, and availability, making it more challenging for unauthorized actors to compromise systems.

- Threat Detection and Response: Cybersecurity experiments contribute to the creation of sophisticated threat detection and response mechanisms. Techniques such as anomaly detection, behavioral analysis, and real-time monitoring are refined through experimentation, improving the ability to identify and mitigate threats.

2. Organizational Impact:

- Risk Management: Organizations benefit from cybersecurity experiments by gaining insights into potential vulnerabilities and the effectiveness of various security measures. This knowledge enables them to implement robust risk management strategies and enhance their overall cybersecurity posture.

- Incident Response: Experiments involving simulated cyberattacks and threat scenarios help organizations prepare for real-world incidents. By practicing incident response and recovery procedures, organizations can improve their ability to handle actual cyber threats and minimize damage.

3. Ethical and Privacy Considerations:

- Ethical Testing Practices: Conducting cybersecurity experiments requires careful consideration of ethical implications. Researchers must ensure that their experiments do not inadvertently cause harm or violate privacy. Ethical guidelines and oversight are essential to maintain responsible research practices.

- Privacy Protection: Experiments involving sensitive data must be conducted with strict adherence to privacy laws and regulations. Protecting the confidentiality of personal information is paramount to maintaining public trust and ensuring ethical standards.

Effect:

The effects of cybersecurity experiments extend across various domains, shaping the future of digital security and influencing public perception:

1. Improved Security Measures:

- Innovation and Development: Cybersecurity experiments drive innovation in security technologies and methodologies. New tools, techniques, and best practices emerging from these experiments contribute to stronger defenses against evolving cyber threats.

- Resilience and Preparedness: By simulating cyberattacks and testing security measures, experiments help organizations and individuals build resilience against potential breaches. Preparedness is enhanced through realistic scenarios and comprehensive testing.

2. Public Awareness and Trust:

- Awareness Campaigns: The findings from cybersecurity experiments often lead to increased public awareness about cybersecurity risks and best practices. Educational initiatives and awareness campaigns help individuals and organizations understand the importance of safeguarding digital information.

- Trust in Technology: Effective cybersecurity measures resulting from experiments contribute to public trust in technology. As security protocols and defenses improve, users are more confident in using digital platforms and services.

3. Regulatory and Compliance Implications:

- Regulatory Frameworks: Cybersecurity experiments influence the development of regulatory frameworks and compliance requirements. Governments and regulatory bodies may update standards and guidelines based on experimental findings to address emerging threats and vulnerabilities.

- Industry Standards: The results of cybersecurity experiments help establish industry standards and best practices. These standards guide organizations in implementing effective security measures and maintaining compliance with relevant regulations.

Conclusion:

Cybersecurity experiments are essential to advancing the field of digital security and addressing the challenges posed by evolving cyber threats. By testing new technologies, strategies, and protocols, researchers and practitioners contribute to the development of robust security measures and enhance the resilience of digital systems.

The impact of cybersecurity experiments is far-reaching, affecting technological advancements, organizational practices, and public trust. Ethical considerations and privacy protection are integral to responsible experimentation, ensuring that research is conducted with the highest standards of integrity.

As the digital landscape continues to evolve, cybersecurity experiments will remain a critical component in safeguarding information systems and maintaining the security of our interconnected world. The ongoing commitment to innovation, preparedness, and ethical research will drive progress and help address the ever-changing landscape of cyber threats.

EXPERIMENT TWENTY NINE

HUMAN GENOME EDITING: THE CRISPR-CAS9 REVOLUTION

Human genome editing, particularly through the CRISPR-Cas9 technology, represents one of the most transformative advancements in genetic science. Developed in the early 2010s, CRISPR-Cas9 allows for precise, targeted modifications to the DNA of living organisms, including humans. This technology has the potential to revolutionize medicine, agriculture, and biological research by enabling the correction of genetic disorders, enhancing traits, and exploring new therapeutic approaches.

CRISPR-Cas9 is based on a natural defense mechanism found in bacteria, where it acts as a molecular scissors to cut DNA at specific locations. Researchers adapted this system to target and edit specific genes in a wide range of organisms. The simplicity, efficiency, and versatility of CRISPR-Cas9 have made it a powerful tool in the field of genetics.

Impact:

The impact of CRISPR-Cas9 technology on science, medicine, and society is profound, with both promising advancements and significant ethical considerations:

1. Scientific and Medical Advancements:

- Genetic Disorders: CRISPR-Cas9 has the potential to correct genetic mutations responsible for a variety of inherited diseases. Early research has demonstrated the ability to address conditions such as cystic fibrosis, muscular dystrophy, and sickle cell anemia by editing faulty genes in patient cells.

- Cancer Research: The technology is being explored for its potential to treat cancer by targeting and modifying genes involved in tumor growth and resistance. CRISPR-based approaches aim to enhance the effectiveness of existing treatments and develop novel therapeutic strategies.

2. Ethical and Safety Concerns:

- Germline Editing: One of the most contentious issues surrounding CRISPR-Cas9 is its application to human germline cells, which involves editing the genes of embryos or reproductive cells. While this has the potential to prevent genetic disorders, it also raises ethical concerns about the long-term effects on future generations and the potential for unintended consequences.

- Equity and Access: The accessibility of CRISPR-Cas9 technology and its benefits raise questions about equity and fairness. Ensuring that advances are available to all individuals, regardless of socioeconomic status, is a key concern in the development and application of genome editing technologies.

3. Regulatory and Policy Implications:

- Ethical Guidelines: The rapid development of CRISPR-Cas9 technology has prompted the establishment of ethical guidelines and regulatory frameworks to govern its use. International bodies, such as the National Academy of Sciences and the World Health Organization, have provided recommendations on responsible research and application.

- Legislation: Various countries have introduced legislation to regulate human genome editing, particularly concerning germline modifications. These regulations aim to balance scientific progress with ethical considerations and societal values.

Effect:

The effects of CRISPR-Cas9 technology are broad, impacting research, medicine, and public perception:

1. Advancements in Research and Medicine:

- Personalized Medicine: CRISPR-Cas9 enables more precise approaches to personalized medicine, where treatments can be tailored to an individual's genetic makeup. This has the potential to improve outcomes and reduce adverse effects in various medical interventions.

- Biotechnology Innovation: The technology has spurred innovation in biotechnology, leading to new research tools and techniques. CRISPR-based applications are being explored in agriculture, where they may contribute to the development of genetically modified crops with improved traits.

2. Public Awareness and Debate:

- Awareness: The introduction of CRISPR-Cas9 has increased public awareness of genetic engineering and its potential implications. Media coverage and public discussions have brought attention to the ethical and social issues associated with genome editing.

- Ethical Debate: The ethical debates surrounding CRISPR-Cas9, particularly concerning germline editing, continue to evolve. Public opinion, scientific discourse, and ethical considerations play a crucial role in shaping the future direction of genome editing research and applications.

3. Long-Term Implications:

- Genetic Diversity and Evolution: The use of CRISPR-Cas9 raises questions about the long-term effects on genetic diversity and human evolution. While the technology holds promise for addressing genetic disorders, its broader implications for the human genome and species evolution need careful consideration.

- Future Research Directions: Ongoing research aims to refine CRISPR-Cas9 technology and address challenges such as off-target effects and delivery methods. Future developments may expand its applications and address current limitations, leading to new opportunities and advancements.

Conclusion:

CRISPR-Cas9 technology represents a groundbreaking advancement in genetic science, offering the potential to revolutionize medicine, research, and biotechnology. While the technology holds great promise for treating genetic disorders and enhancing various traits, it also raises significant ethical and safety concerns that must be addressed.

As we navigate the implications of human genome editing, it is essential to balance scientific innovation with ethical responsibility. The ongoing development of CRISPR-Cas9 technology will continue to shape the future of genetic research, with the potential to bring about transformative changes while ensuring that its use aligns with societal values and ethical standards.

EXPERIMENT THIRTY

PSYCHOTROPIC DRUG TRIALS: UNVEILING THE COMPLEXITIES OF MIND-ALTERING MEDICATIONS

Psychotropic drug trials play a crucial role in understanding and developing medications that affect the mind and behavior. These trials involve testing substances that influence mood, cognition, perception, and mental health conditions. The development and evaluation of psychotropic drugs encompass a wide range of medications, including antidepressants, antipsychotics, mood stabilizers, and anxiolytics. As these drugs aim to treat complex psychiatric disorders, the trials must balance scientific inquiry with ethical considerations.

The trials typically follow a rigorous process, from preclinical studies to clinical phases. Preclinical studies involve testing the drugs in animal models to assess their safety and efficacy. Clinical trials are conducted in multiple phases, starting with small groups of healthy volunteers and progressing to larger groups of patients with the target condition. These trials help determine the drug's effectiveness, side effects, and optimal dosages.

Impact:

The impact of psychotropic drug trials extends across various domains, including mental health treatment, regulatory practices, and public perception:

1. Advancements in Mental Health Treatment:

- Treatment Options: Psychotropic drug trials contribute to the development of new treatments for mental health disorders, such as depression, schizophrenia, bipolar disorder, and anxiety. Successful trials can lead to the approval of medications that offer relief for patients who have not responded to existing treatments.

- Understanding Mental Health: The trials help researchers gain insights into the mechanisms of mental health conditions and the ways in which drugs can alter brain function. This knowledge advances our understanding of psychiatric disorders and informs the development of more targeted therapies.

2. Ethical and Safety Considerations:

- Informed Consent: Ensuring informed consent is a critical aspect of psychotropic drug trials. Participants must be fully aware of the potential risks and benefits of the drug being tested and provide consent before joining the study. The ethical conduct of trials is essential to protect participants' rights and well-being.

- Side Effects and Risks: Psychotropic drugs can have significant side effects, including changes in mood, cognition, and physical health. Trials must carefully monitor and evaluate these effects to ensure that the benefits outweigh the risks. Researchers must also address issues related to dependency, withdrawal, and long-term effects.

3. Regulatory and Policy Implications:

- Approval Processes: Regulatory agencies, such as the U.S. Food and Drug Administration (FDA) and the European Medicines Agency (EMA), review the results of psychotropic drug trials to determine whether a drug is safe and effective for public use. The approval process involves a thorough evaluation of clinical trial data and adherence to regulatory standards.

- Post-Market Surveillance: After a drug is approved, post-market surveillance continues to monitor its safety and effectiveness in the general population. Ongoing research and reporting of adverse effects are critical for maintaining the safety of psychotropic medications.

Effect:

The effects of psychotropic drug trials are significant, shaping the landscape of mental health treatment and influencing societal attitudes toward psychiatric medications:

1. Improved Treatment Outcomes:

 - New Therapies: Successful trials can lead to the introduction of new psychotropic medications that offer improved efficacy, fewer side effects, and better tolerability for patients. These advancements enhance treatment options and contribute to improved mental health outcomes.

 - Personalized Medicine: The trials also support the development of personalized medicine approaches, where treatments are tailored to individual patients based on their genetic, biological, and psychological profiles. This personalized approach can lead to more effective and targeted interventions.

2. Public Awareness and Perception:

- Education and Stigma Reduction: The trials and their outcomes contribute to public awareness and education about mental health conditions and treatments. By highlighting the benefits and limitations of psychotropic drugs, the trials help reduce stigma and promote a better understanding of mental health issues.

- Patient Empowerment: Access to effective treatments resulting from psychotropic drug trials empowers patients to manage their mental health conditions more effectively. It also fosters a sense of hope and validation for those struggling with psychiatric disorders.

3. Ethical and Regulatory Evolution:

- Ethical Standards: The ethical considerations of psychotropic drug trials continue to evolve, with ongoing discussions about informed consent, patient safety, and the responsible conduct of research. These discussions help shape ethical guidelines and practices in clinical research.

- Regulatory Advances: The regulatory landscape for psychotropic drugs is influenced by trial outcomes and safety data. Advances in regulatory practices aim to ensure that new medications meet high standards of safety and efficacy before reaching the market.

Conclusion:

Psychotropic drug trials are a vital component of advancing mental health treatment and improving our understanding of psychiatric disorders. While these trials offer the potential for significant medical breakthroughs, they also raise important ethical and safety considerations that must be carefully managed.

By balancing scientific innovation with ethical responsibility, psychotropic drug trials contribute to the development of effective therapies and enhance the overall well-being of individuals with mental health conditions. The ongoing progress in this field reflects a commitment to advancing mental health care while addressing the complex challenges associated with psychotropic medications.

EXPERIMENT THIRTY ONE

CHEMICAL WARFARE EXPERIMENTS: UNRAVELING THE DARK LEGACY OF CHEMICAL WEAPONS

Chemical warfare experiments, historically conducted by various military and research institutions, have left a dark and controversial legacy. These experiments, aimed at developing and testing chemical weapons, have profoundly impacted international relations, public health, and ethical standards in warfare. Chemical weapons are designed to inflict harm or death through toxic chemical agents, and their use in warfare has led to devastating consequences.

The development of chemical weapons began in earnest during World War I, with experiments conducted to understand their effects, improve delivery mechanisms, and enhance their lethality. Subsequent wars and conflicts saw the deployment of these weapons, leading to widespread suffering and international condemnation. Today, the legacy of chemical warfare experiments continues to influence global policies, ethical standards, and efforts to prevent the proliferation of chemical weapons.

Impact:

The impact of chemical warfare experiments extends across multiple domains, affecting human health, international relations, and ethical standards:

1. Human Health and Environmental Impact:

   - Health Consequences: Chemical warfare agents, such as mustard gas, sarin, and VX, have caused severe health issues for those exposed, including respiratory damage, neurological effects, and long-term chronic conditions. Survivors of chemical attacks often experience lasting health problems and require ongoing medical care.

   - Environmental Damage: The use and testing of chemical weapons have resulted in environmental contamination. Chemical agents can persist in soil and water, posing long-term risks to ecosystems and human health. Cleanup and remediation efforts are often complex and costly.

2. Ethical and Humanitarian Concerns:

- Moral Implications: The use of chemical weapons raises significant ethical concerns regarding the conduct of war and the protection of civilians. The indiscriminate nature of chemical attacks, which can affect both combatants and non-combatants, challenges moral and humanitarian principles.

- International Response: The international community has responded to the use of chemical weapons with treaties and conventions aimed at banning their development and use. The Chemical Weapons Convention (CWC), adopted in 1992, is a landmark treaty that prohibits the production, stockpiling, and use of chemical weapons.

3. Regulatory and Policy Implications:

- Treaty Enforcement: The Chemical Weapons Convention (CWC) is enforced by the Organization for the Prohibition of Chemical Weapons (OPCW), which monitors compliance and conducts inspections to ensure that member states adhere to the treaty's provisions. The CWC has been instrumental in reducing the number of chemical weapons and preventing their proliferation.

- Research and Development: Ongoing research focuses on developing safer and more effective methods for detecting and neutralizing chemical agents. Efforts are also directed at understanding the long-term health effects of chemical warfare agents and improving medical countermeasures.

Effect:

The effects of chemical warfare experiments have had far-reaching consequences for science, international relations, and public perception:

1. Advancements in Medical and Environmental Science:

- Medical Countermeasures: The need to address the effects of chemical warfare has led to advancements in medical treatments and countermeasures. Research into antidotes, decontamination methods, and long-term health care for survivors has improved the response to chemical exposure.

- Environmental Remediation: The legacy of chemical warfare has spurred efforts to develop techniques for environmental cleanup and remediation. Technologies for detecting and neutralizing chemical contaminants are critical for mitigating the long-term impact on ecosystems and human health.

2. International Diplomacy and Security:

- Global Cooperation: The Chemical Weapons Convention represents a significant achievement in international diplomacy, with widespread support and participation from countries around the world. The treaty has contributed to global efforts to prevent the use of chemical weapons and promote disarmament.

- Ongoing Challenges: Despite the success of the CWC, challenges remain in ensuring full compliance and addressing the use of chemical weapons in conflict zones. The international community must remain vigilant and proactive in addressing new threats and maintaining the integrity of disarmament agreements.

3. Public Awareness and Historical Reflection:

- Historical Awareness: The legacy of chemical warfare experiments has led to increased awareness and education about the horrors of chemical weapons and the importance of disarmament. Documentaries, literature, and memorials help preserve the memory of the victims and the lessons learned.

- Ethical Reflection: The dark history of chemical warfare experiments serves as a reminder of the need for ethical considerations in scientific research and military practices. The experiences of the past underscore the importance of adhering to humanitarian principles and preventing the recurrence of such atrocities.

Conclusion:

Chemical warfare experiments represent a somber chapter in the history of science and warfare, with significant implications for human health, ethics, and international relations. While the development and use of chemical weapons have been largely curtailed by international treaties, the legacy of these experiments continues to influence global policies and public awareness.

As we reflect on the impact of chemical warfare, it is essential to uphold the principles of disarmament, humanitarianism, and ethical research. The lessons learned from this dark history guide ongoing efforts to prevent the proliferation of chemical weapons and ensure that future scientific advancements are pursued with the highest standards of responsibility and care.

EXPERIMENT THIRTY TWO

ARTIFICIAL HEART IMPLANTS: TRANSFORMING CARDIAC CARE WITH INNOVATION

Artificial heart implants represent a groundbreaking advancement in cardiac medicine, offering new hope for patients with severe heart failure. These devices, designed to replicate the function of a natural heart, are implanted into patients who suffer from end-stage heart disease and are not eligible for a heart transplant. The development of artificial hearts has been driven by the need to address the limitations of heart transplants and provide a viable alternative for patients facing life-threatening cardiac conditions.

The journey of artificial heart implants began with early experimental devices and has evolved into sophisticated systems that can support or even replace the function of the heart. Modern artificial hearts are typically used as a bridge to heart transplantation or, in some cases, as a long-term solution for patients who are not candidates for a transplant. The technology involves complex engineering and materials science to create devices that are both effective and biocompatible.

Impact:

The impact of artificial heart implants is profound, affecting patient outcomes, medical practice, and research:

1. Patient Outcomes and Quality of Life:

   - Life Extension: Artificial hearts have significantly improved the survival rates of patients with severe heart failure. For many, these implants provide a critical bridge to a heart transplant, extending life and improving overall health during the waiting period.

   - Quality of Life: Advances in artificial heart technology have enhanced patients' quality of life by reducing symptoms such as shortness of breath, fatigue, and fluid retention. Patients with artificial hearts often experience improved functional capacity and greater ability to engage in daily activities.

2. Medical and Technological Advancements:

- Innovative Design: The development of artificial heart implants has driven innovations in engineering and materials science. Modern devices are designed to closely mimic the function of a natural heart, with improvements in durability, reliability, and ease of implantation.

- Clinical Integration: Artificial hearts have become an integral part of the treatment options for patients with end-stage heart failure. Their use has led to advancements in surgical techniques, patient management, and post-operative care.

3. Ethical and Social Considerations:

- Access and Equity: The cost of artificial heart implants and associated procedures can be substantial, raising concerns about access and equity in healthcare. Efforts to improve affordability and availability are essential to ensure that all patients who could benefit from the technology have access to it.

- Informed Consent: Patients undergoing artificial heart implantation must be fully informed about the risks, benefits, and potential outcomes. The decision to proceed with an artificial heart involves careful consideration of the patient's overall health, prognosis, and personal preferences.

Effect:

The effects of artificial heart implants extend across various domains, influencing medical practice, patient care, and public perception:

1. Medical Practice and Patient Care:

- Enhanced Treatment Options: Artificial hearts provide an important treatment option for patients with advanced heart failure, offering a viable alternative to heart transplantation. The technology has expanded the range of therapeutic options available to cardiologists and surgeons.

- Research and Development: The success of artificial heart implants has spurred ongoing research into improving the technology and exploring new applications. Continued innovation aims to enhance the performance, safety, and longevity of artificial hearts.

2. Public Awareness and Perception:

- Hope and Inspiration: The development of artificial hearts has generated significant public interest and awareness. Success stories of patients who have benefited from these devices inspire hope and demonstrate the potential of medical technology to transform lives.

- Ethical Debate: The use of artificial hearts raises ethical questions related to the allocation of medical resources, the balance between quality of life and life extension, and the long-term implications of living with an artificial device. These debates contribute to ongoing discussions about healthcare priorities and patient rights.

3. Long-Term Implications:

- Future Advancements: The field of artificial heart technology continues to evolve, with research focused on developing more advanced and reliable devices. Innovations such as fully implantable heart systems and improved biocompatibility are expected to drive future progress.

- Integration with Other Therapies: Artificial hearts may be used in conjunction with other therapeutic approaches, such as advanced drug therapies or gene therapy, to provide comprehensive care for patients with complex cardiac conditions.

Conclusion:

Artificial heart implants represent a significant achievement in medical science, offering new possibilities for patients with severe heart failure. While the technology has transformed cardiac care and improved patient outcomes, it also raises important ethical and social considerations that must be addressed.

The ongoing advancements in artificial heart technology reflect a commitment to enhancing patient care and expanding treatment options for those with life-threatening cardiac conditions. By balancing innovation with ethical responsibility, the field continues to advance, promising new opportunities for improving the lives of individuals facing severe heart disease.

EXPERIMENT THIRTY THREE

HUMAN SPACEFLIGHT EXPERIMENTS: EXPLORING THE FINAL FRONTIER

Human spaceflight experiments have been instrumental in expanding our understanding of space, human physiology, and the potential for future space exploration. Since Yuri Gagarin's historic flight in 1961, human spaceflight has evolved from a daring adventure into a critical component of scientific research and technological advancement. These experiments, conducted aboard spacecraft and space stations, provide valuable insights into how the human body responds to the space environment and how we can optimize space travel for future missions.

Human spaceflight experiments cover a wide range of topics, including the effects of microgravity on the human body, the psychological challenges of long-duration missions, and the development of life support systems. The International Space Station (ISS) has been a focal point for many of these studies, offering a unique microgravity environment for researchers to investigate the impacts of space travel on health and performance.

Impact:

The impact of human spaceflight experiments is profound, influencing scientific research, technology development, and our understanding of human potential:

1. Scientific and Medical Advancements:

   - Physiological Research: Spaceflight experiments have revealed significant effects of microgravity on human physiology, including changes in bone density, muscle mass, and cardiovascular function. Understanding these effects is crucial for developing countermeasures to maintain astronaut health during long missions.

   - Biomedical Research: Space environments provide opportunities to study various biomedical phenomena, such as the growth of microorganisms and the effects of radiation on human cells. These studies contribute to our understanding of fundamental biological processes and the development of medical treatments.

2. Technology Development:

   - Life Support Systems: The challenges of maintaining life in space have driven the development of advanced life support systems, including air and water recycling technologies. Innovations in these systems are critical for the sustainability of long-duration missions and future space colonization efforts.

- Space Habitats: Research into space habitats and their effects on human well-being informs the design of future spacecraft and space stations. Understanding the psychological and social aspects of living in confined spaces helps improve crew dynamics and overall mission success.

3. Psychological and Social Impact:

- Mental Health: Long-duration space missions pose psychological challenges, including isolation, confinement, and separation from family and friends. Spaceflight experiments assess the impact of these factors on astronaut mental health and develop strategies to support psychological well-being.

- Crew Dynamics: Studies of team interactions and communication in space environments help optimize crew performance and address potential conflicts. Effective team dynamics are essential for mission success and safety.

Effect:

The effects of human spaceflight experiments are broad, influencing space exploration, human health, and public perception:

1. Advancements in Space Exploration:

- Mission Planning: Insights gained from spaceflight experiments inform the planning and execution of future space missions, including potential trips to Mars and beyond. Knowledge about human health and performance in space is essential for the success of deep-space exploration.

- International Collaboration: The ISS and other spaceflight experiments have fostered international collaboration among space agencies and researchers. This cooperation advances scientific knowledge and promotes peaceful uses of space.

2. Public Awareness and Inspiration:

- Educational Impact: Human spaceflight experiments capture public imagination and inspire interest in science, technology, engineering, and mathematics (STEM). Space missions and discoveries contribute to educational initiatives and encourage the next generation of scientists and engineers.

- Cultural Influence: Space exploration has a profound cultural impact, influencing art, literature, and media. The achievements and challenges of human spaceflight resonate with the public and shape our collective vision of humanity's future in space.

3. Long-Term Implications:

- Health and Well-Being: Research on the effects of space travel contributes to our understanding of human health and potential medical advancements. Lessons learned from spaceflight experiments may have applications for improving health on Earth, particularly in areas related to aging and physical rehabilitation.

- Future Exploration: The ongoing study of human spaceflight will play a crucial role in preparing for future missions, including potential human settlement on other planets. Understanding the limits of human adaptation and developing effective countermeasures are essential for the future of space exploration.

Conclusion:

Human spaceflight experiments are a cornerstone of our efforts to explore and understand space, advancing scientific knowledge and technological innovation. These experiments provide critical insights into the effects of space travel on the human body and mind, driving progress in space exploration and contributing to our broader understanding of human potential.

As we continue to push the boundaries of space exploration, the knowledge gained from human spaceflight experiments will be instrumental in ensuring the health, safety, and success of future missions. By embracing the challenges and opportunities of space travel, we can expand our horizons and achieve new milestones in the quest to explore the final frontier.

EXPERIMENT THIRTY FOUR

NUCLEAR REACTOR ACCIDENTS: UNDERSTANDING THE RISKS AND CONSEQUENCES

Nuclear reactor accidents have had profound and far-reaching effects on human health, the environment, and energy policy. These incidents, involving the release of radioactive materials due to malfunctions or failures in nuclear reactors, highlight the risks associated with nuclear power and the challenges of managing and mitigating these risks. From the early days of nuclear energy to the present, reactor accidents have shaped the development of safety protocols, regulatory measures, and public perceptions of nuclear power.

The causes of nuclear reactor accidents can vary, including technical failures, human error, natural disasters, and design flaws. The impact of these accidents often extends beyond the immediate vicinity of the reactor, affecting entire regions and necessitating extensive response and recovery efforts.

Impact:

The impact of nuclear reactor accidents is extensive, affecting health, environment, and energy policies:

1. Health Consequences:

- Acute Radiation Sickness: Individuals exposed to high levels of radiation during an accident can suffer from acute radiation sickness, characterized by symptoms such as nausea, vomiting, diarrhea, and, in severe cases, death.

- Long-Term Health Effects: Long-term health effects include increased risks of cancer, particularly thyroid cancer, and other radiation-induced diseases. The health impact can persist for decades and affect both workers and local populations.

2. Environmental Damage:

- Radiation Contamination: Accidents can result in the release of radioactive materials into the environment, leading to soil, water, and air contamination. The extent of contamination depends on factors such as the type of radioactive material and prevailing weather conditions.

- Ecosystem Impact: Radiation can have harmful effects on local ecosystems, including flora and fauna. Contaminated areas may experience disruptions in biodiversity and long-term ecological damage.

3. Regulatory and Policy Changes:

- Safety Improvements: Nuclear reactor accidents have led to significant improvements in reactor safety, including the development of more robust safety systems, improved emergency response protocols, and enhanced regulatory oversight.

- Energy Policy: Accidents have influenced energy policies and public attitudes toward nuclear power. Some regions have shifted away from nuclear energy in favor of alternative energy sources, while others have invested in safer reactor designs and advanced technologies.

Effect:

The effects of nuclear reactor accidents extend beyond immediate health and environmental concerns, influencing technological, social, and regulatory aspects:

1. Technological Advances:

- Reactor Design: The lessons learned from reactor accidents have led to advances in reactor design, including the development of newer, safer reactor types with enhanced safety features and better containment systems.

- Emergency Preparedness: Improved emergency preparedness and response strategies have been developed to manage the consequences of nuclear accidents. These include better training for first responders, more effective communication strategies, and improved public evacuation plans.

2. Public Awareness and Perception:

- Increased Awareness: Reactor accidents have raised public awareness of the risks associated with nuclear power and the importance of safety measures. This heightened awareness has influenced public debate and policy decisions regarding nuclear energy.

- Trust and Confidence: The accidents have affected public trust in the nuclear industry and regulatory agencies. Efforts to rebuild confidence include increased transparency, better communication with the public, and more rigorous safety standards.

3. Long-Term Implications:

- Environmental Remediation: The process of cleaning up and decontaminating affected areas is complex and costly. Long-term environmental remediation efforts are essential to address the legacy of contamination and mitigate future risks.

- Global Cooperation: Nuclear accidents have underscored the need for international cooperation in managing nuclear safety and responding to emergencies. Global agreements and collaborations aim to improve safety standards and enhance the ability to respond to incidents.

Conclusion:

Nuclear reactor accidents represent a critical aspect of the broader discussion on nuclear energy and safety. While these accidents have had severe and lasting impacts on health, the environment, and energy policy, they have also driven advancements in reactor technology, safety protocols, and emergency response.

As the world continues to rely on nuclear power as part of its energy mix, the lessons learned from past accidents will remain crucial in shaping the future of nuclear energy. By focusing on safety, transparency, and international cooperation, we can work to minimize the risks associated with nuclear power and ensure that it contributes to a sustainable and safe energy future.

EXPERIMENT THIRTY FIVE

PANDEMIC PREPAREDNESS RESEARCH: ENHANCING RESILIENCE AND RESPONSE

Pandemic preparedness research is a critical field dedicated to understanding, anticipating, and mitigating the impacts of pandemics on global health. This research encompasses a wide range of activities, including the study of infectious diseases, development of vaccines and treatments, and the creation of robust response strategies. The goal is to enhance our ability to respond effectively to pandemic threats, reduce their impact, and ultimately save lives.

The COVID-19 pandemic underscored the importance of pandemic preparedness research, highlighting both the strengths and gaps in our global health systems. From early detection and surveillance to vaccine development and public health interventions, this research area aims to build a comprehensive approach to managing pandemic risks and improving resilience.

Impact:

The impact of pandemic preparedness research is profound, influencing public health responses, medical advancements, and global coordination:

1. Public Health Response:

- Early Detection and Surveillance: Research into disease surveillance systems and early detection methods helps identify and track outbreaks before they spread widely. Improved surveillance allows for timely interventions and containment measures.

- Response Strategies: Pandemic preparedness research informs the development of response strategies, including quarantine protocols, travel restrictions, and social distancing measures. Effective response strategies help mitigate the spread of infectious diseases and reduce their impact on communities.

2. Medical Advancements:

- Vaccine Development: Research into vaccine development has accelerated the creation of effective vaccines for various infectious diseases. Innovations in vaccine technology, such as mRNA vaccines, have demonstrated the potential to respond quickly to emerging pathogens.

- Treatment Options: Advances in antiviral drugs and other treatments are essential for managing pandemic-related illnesses. Research into new therapies and treatment protocols contributes to better patient outcomes and recovery rates.

3. Global Coordination and Policy:

- International Collaboration: Pandemic preparedness research emphasizes the importance of global collaboration and information sharing. International organizations, such as the World Health Organization (WHO), play a crucial role in coordinating efforts and providing guidance during pandemics.

- Policy Development: Research informs the development of public health policies and guidelines, including vaccination strategies, healthcare infrastructure planning, and emergency response frameworks. Evidence-based policies help ensure a coordinated and effective response to pandemic threats.

Effect:

The effects of pandemic preparedness research are far-reaching, impacting public health systems, scientific knowledge, and global health security:

1. Strengthened Health Systems:

- Healthcare Infrastructure: Research supports the development of healthcare infrastructure capable of managing large-scale outbreaks. This includes expanding hospital capacity, ensuring the availability of critical medical supplies, and improving healthcare worker training.

- Public Health Infrastructure: Enhanced public health infrastructure, including testing and contact tracing capabilities, strengthens the ability to manage and control infectious disease outbreaks.

2. Scientific Knowledge and Innovation:

- Understanding Infectious Diseases: Pandemic preparedness research contributes to a deeper understanding of the mechanisms of infectious diseases, including their transmission, pathogenesis, and impact on human health. This knowledge drives innovation in prevention and treatment strategies.

- Technological Advancements: Research fosters technological advancements in diagnostics, treatment, and data analysis. Innovations such as rapid diagnostic tests and advanced data modeling contribute to more effective pandemic management.

3. Global Health Security:

- Preparedness and Resilience: Effective pandemic preparedness research enhances global health security by improving the ability to anticipate and respond to emerging threats. Preparedness efforts reduce the risk of widespread outbreaks and strengthen the resilience of health systems.

- Policy and Coordination: Research-based policies and international coordination improve the efficiency and effectiveness of pandemic responses. Collaboration between countries, organizations, and research institutions is essential for addressing global health challenges.

Conclusion:

Pandemic preparedness research plays a vital role in safeguarding global health and enhancing our ability to respond to infectious disease outbreaks. By advancing our understanding of diseases, developing innovative medical solutions, and improving response strategies, this research area helps build resilience and protect populations from the impacts of pandemics.

As we continue to face new and evolving health threats, ongoing investment in pandemic preparedness research is essential. By leveraging scientific knowledge, fostering global collaboration, and implementing evidence-based policies, we can strengthen our preparedness and response capabilities, ultimately ensuring a safer and healthier future for all.

EXPERIMENT THIRTY SIX

GENETICALLY MODIFIED ORGANISMS (GMOS): TRANSFORMING AGRICULTURE AND BIOTECHNOLOGY

Genetically Modified Organisms (GMOs) represent a significant advancement in biotechnology, with the potential to revolutionize agriculture, medicine, and environmental management. By altering the genetic material of organisms, scientists can enhance traits such as resistance to pests, tolerance to environmental conditions, and nutritional content. GMOs have sparked extensive debate regarding their safety, benefits, and ethical implications, making them a focal point of modern scientific and public discourse.

The development of GMOs began in the late 20th century with the advent of recombinant DNA technology. This technology enables precise modifications to an organism's genetic code, leading to the creation of crops, animals, and microorganisms with desirable traits. The impact of GMOs extends across various sectors, from food production to environmental conservation and medical research.

Impact:

The impact of GMOs is multifaceted, affecting agriculture, health, environment, and economy:

1. Agricultural Advancements:

 - Increased Crop Yields: GMOs have led to the development of crops with enhanced traits such as resistance to pests, diseases, and herbicides. These traits can result in higher crop yields and reduced reliance on chemical pesticides and fertilizers.

 - Nutritional Enhancement: Genetic modifications have been used to improve the nutritional content of crops. For example, Golden Rice has been engineered to produce higher levels of vitamin A, addressing deficiencies in populations with limited access to diverse diets.

2. Environmental Impact:

 - Reduced Environmental Footprint: By enhancing crop resistance to pests and diseases, GMOs can reduce the need for chemical inputs, potentially decreasing environmental pollution and soil degradation.

- Biodiversity Concerns: The introduction of GMOs into the environment raises concerns about potential impacts on biodiversity. There is ongoing debate about the risks of cross-breeding between GMOs and wild relatives and the potential effects on ecosystems.

3. Economic Effects:

- Cost Efficiency: GMOs can lead to cost savings for farmers by reducing the need for pesticides, herbicides, and other inputs. This can improve the profitability of farming operations and contribute to food security.

- Market Dynamics: The commercialization of GMOs has influenced global agricultural markets and trade. Intellectual property rights associated with GMO technology can impact market access and competition among farmers and agricultural businesses.

Effect:

The effects of GMOs extend beyond immediate agricultural and environmental impacts, influencing scientific research, public health, and policy:

1. Scientific and Technological Innovation:

- Biotechnology Advances: The development and application of GMOs have driven advancements in biotechnology, including gene editing technologies such as CRISPR. These innovations have broad implications for research and development in various fields.

- Research Opportunities: GMOs provide valuable models for studying gene function and the effects of genetic modifications. Research using GMOs has contributed to our understanding of genetics, disease mechanisms, and potential therapeutic approaches.

2. Public Health and Safety:

- Safety Assessments: The safety of GMOs is a major concern for consumers and regulators. Extensive research and regulatory assessments are conducted to ensure that GMOs are safe for human consumption and do not pose health risks.

- Consumer Perceptions: Public perception of GMOs varies widely, with some individuals expressing concerns about potential health risks and environmental impacts. Education and transparency about GMO safety and benefits are important for addressing these concerns.

3. Regulatory and Policy Implications:

- Regulation and Labeling: The regulation of GMOs varies by country, with different standards for safety assessments, labeling, and approval processes. Policies and regulations are designed to address potential risks and ensure the responsible use of GMO technology.

- Ethical Considerations: The use of GMOs raises ethical questions related to genetic manipulation, environmental stewardship, and the rights of consumers. Ongoing debates and discussions shape the development of policies and guidelines for GMO use.

Conclusion:

Genetically Modified Organisms (GMOs) have the potential to transform agriculture, improve food security, and drive advancements in biotechnology. While GMOs offer significant benefits, including increased crop yields, nutritional enhancement, and reduced environmental impact, they also present challenges and concerns related to safety, biodiversity, and public perception.

The continued development and use of GMOs require careful consideration of scientific evidence, regulatory oversight, and ethical considerations. By balancing innovation with safety and transparency, we can harness the potential of GMOs to address global challenges and contribute to a more sustainable and resilient future.

EXPERIMENT THIRTY SEVEN

PARTICLE BEAM THERAPY: ADVANCING CANCER TREATMENT WITH PRECISION

Particle Beam Therapy represents a cutting-edge advancement in cancer treatment, offering a highly precise and targeted approach to radiotherapy. Unlike traditional X-ray radiation therapy, which uses photons, particle beam therapy utilizes charged particles such as protons or heavy ions to target and destroy cancer cells. This technique provides a more focused delivery of radiation, potentially reducing damage to surrounding healthy tissues and improving treatment outcomes.

The development of particle beam therapy has its roots in the early 20th century, with significant advancements made over the past few decades. The technology relies on complex particle accelerators to generate and direct high-energy beams to the tumor site, allowing for more accurate and effective treatment of various cancers.

Impact:

The impact of particle beam therapy is significant, influencing cancer treatment, patient outcomes, and healthcare technology:

1. Cancer Treatment:

- Precision and Accuracy: Particle beam therapy offers superior precision compared to conventional radiotherapy. The charged particles deposit most of their energy directly within the tumor, minimizing damage to surrounding healthy tissues and reducing side effects.

- Treatment of Radioresistant Tumors: Particle beam therapy is particularly effective for treating tumors that are resistant to conventional radiation therapy. This includes certain brain tumors, pediatric cancers, and tumors located near critical organs.2. Patient Outcomes:

- Reduced Side Effects: By targeting tumors with greater accuracy, particle beam therapy can reduce the incidence of side effects associated with traditional radiotherapy, such as damage to healthy tissues and organs.

- Improved Prognosis: The enhanced precision of particle beam therapy can lead to better treatment outcomes and improved prognosis for patients, particularly for those with complex or difficult-to-treat tumors.

3. Healthcare Technology:

   - Advanced Equipment: Particle beam therapy requires sophisticated particle accelerators and beam delivery systems. The development and maintenance of this equipment represent a significant investment in healthcare technology.

   - Accessibility and Cost: The high cost of particle beam therapy facilities and equipment can limit accessibility for some patients and healthcare systems. Efforts to reduce costs and expand access are ongoing.

Effect:

The effects of particle beam therapy extend beyond individual patient treatment, influencing research, healthcare policies, and future advancements:

1. Scientific and Technological Innovation:

   - Advancements in Particle Physics: The development of particle beam therapy has driven advancements in particle physics and accelerator technology. Innovations in these fields contribute to improvements in therapy and other scientific applications.

- Research Opportunities: Ongoing research into particle beam therapy explores its effectiveness for various types of cancers and potential enhancements to treatment protocols. This research contributes to the broader field of oncology and radiotherapy.

2. Healthcare Policy and Accessibility:

- Regulatory and Safety Standards: The use of particle beam therapy is subject to rigorous regulatory and safety standards to ensure patient safety and treatment efficacy. Compliance with these standards is essential for the successful implementation of the therapy.

- Expanding Access: Efforts to expand access to particle beam therapy include initiatives to reduce costs, increase the number of treatment centers, and provide training for healthcare professionals. Expanding access can improve treatment options for more patients.

3. Future Developments:

- Innovative Techniques: Future developments in particle beam therapy may include the integration of advanced imaging technologies, improved beam delivery systems, and novel treatment approaches. These innovations have the potential to further enhance the precision and effectiveness of the therapy.

- Personalized Medicine: The continued evolution of particle beam therapy aligns with the broader trend of personalized medicine, where treatments are tailored to individual patient needs and characteristics. Personalized approaches can optimize treatment outcomes and minimize side effects.

Conclusion:

Particle Beam Therapy represents a significant advancement in cancer treatment, offering precise and targeted radiation therapy with the potential for improved patient outcomes and reduced side effects. The technology's impact extends across cancer treatment, healthcare technology, and scientific research, highlighting its importance in modern oncology.

As particle beam therapy continues to evolve, ongoing research, technological advancements, and efforts to improve accessibility will play a crucial role in maximizing its benefits for patients. By harnessing the power of particle beam therapy, we can continue to advance the field of cancer treatment and work toward more effective and personalized therapies for those affected by cancer.

EXPERIMENT THIRTY EIGHT

THE SEARCH FOR EXTRATERRESTRIAL LIFE: EXPLORING THE COSMOS FOR SIGNS OF ALIEN EXISTENCE

The search for extraterrestrial life is one of the most captivating and profound endeavors in science, driven by humanity's curiosity about whether we are alone in the universe. This quest involves a multidisciplinary approach, integrating astronomy, biology, chemistry, and physics to explore the cosmos for signs of life beyond Earth. From the early speculations of ancient civilizations to modern scientific investigations, the search for extraterrestrial life has evolved with advances in technology and understanding.

The search for extraterrestrial life encompasses a variety of strategies, including the examination of other planets and moons within our solar system, the detection of signals from distant star systems, and the exploration of potentially habitable exoplanets. This ongoing quest aims to answer fundamental questions about the origins of life and the conditions necessary for its existence.

Impact:

The impact of the search for extraterrestrial life extends across scientific research, technological advancements, and philosophical implications:

1. Scientific Research:

- Astrobiology: The field of astrobiology is dedicated to studying the potential for life elsewhere in the universe. Research in this area includes investigating extreme environments on Earth to understand the limits of life and applying this knowledge to other planets and moons.

- Planetary Exploration: Missions to Mars, Europa, Enceladus, and other celestial bodies aim to search for signs of past or present life. Discoveries of water, organic molecules, or unusual geological formations can provide clues about the potential for life.

2. Technological Advancements:

- Space Telescopes: Instruments such as the Hubble Space Telescope and the James Webb Space Telescope play a crucial role in studying exoplanets and their atmospheres. These telescopes help identify planets that may have conditions conducive to life.

- Radio Astronomy: Efforts to detect extraterrestrial signals, such as the Search for Extraterrestrial Intelligence (SETI), involve sophisticated radio telescopes that scan for artificial signals from distant civilizations.

3. Philosophical and Societal Implications:

- Understanding Our Place in the Universe: The discovery of extraterrestrial life would have profound implications for our understanding of our place in the cosmos and the nature of life itself. It would challenge existing beliefs and spark new philosophical and scientific discussions.

- Impact on Culture: The search for extraterrestrial life has captured the public imagination and influenced popular culture. It has inspired numerous works of science fiction and has become a central theme in discussions about the future of humanity.

Effect:

The effects of the search for extraterrestrial life are far-reaching, influencing scientific discovery, technological innovation, and our worldview:

1. Scientific Discovery:

- New Knowledge: The search for extraterrestrial life drives scientific discovery by pushing the boundaries of our knowledge about the universe. It leads to new insights into planetary science, astrophysics, and the conditions necessary for life.

- Interdisciplinary Collaboration: The search fosters collaboration across various scientific disciplines, integrating insights from astronomy, biology, chemistry, and more to address complex questions about life beyond Earth.

2. Technological Innovation:

- Advanced Instruments: Developing and deploying advanced instruments for space exploration and signal detection pushes the limits of current technology. Innovations in imaging, data analysis, and communications have applications beyond the search for extraterrestrial life.

- Space Exploration Technologies: Advances in spacecraft design, propulsion, and robotics contribute to the broader field of space exploration, enhancing our ability to study and explore the cosmos.

3. Worldview and Society:

- Broader Perspective: The search for extraterrestrial life encourages a broader perspective on humanity's place in the universe and our relationship with other potential forms of life. It promotes a sense of curiosity and wonder about the cosmos.

- Global Collaboration: The quest for extraterrestrial life often involves international cooperation, fostering collaboration among scientists, space agencies, and institutions across the globe.

Conclusion:

The search for extraterrestrial life represents a profound and ongoing endeavor to explore the cosmos and answer one of humanity's most fundamental questions: Are we alone in the universe? Through scientific research, technological advancements, and philosophical inquiry, this quest pushes the boundaries of our knowledge and inspires a sense of wonder about the universe.

As we continue to explore space and develop new technologies, the search for extraterrestrial life remains a testament to human curiosity and our desire to understand our place in the cosmos. Whether or not we ultimately find evidence of alien life, the journey of discovery and exploration enriches our understanding of the universe and our role within it.

EXPERIMENT THIRTY NINE

PSYCHOLOGICAL TORTURE EXPERIMENTS: UNVEILING THE DARK SIDE OF PSYCHOLOGICAL RESEARCH

Psychological torture experiments refer to a series of unethical and morally troubling research studies designed to investigate the effects of extreme psychological stress and manipulation on individuals. These experiments, often conducted under the guise of scientific inquiry, have explored the limits of human endurance, obedience, and behavior under severe duress. The legacy of these studies serves as a stark reminder of the potential for abuse in psychological research and the ethical responsibilities of researchers.

Throughout the 20th century, several notable experiments have crossed ethical boundaries, leaving lasting impacts on both participants and the field of psychology. These studies have provided insights into the effects of psychological stress, control, and manipulation, but at a significant human cost.

Impact:

The impact of psychological torture experiments is profound, affecting ethical standards in research, understanding of human behavior, and public perception of psychological science:

1. Ethical Standards in Research:

- Guidelines and Regulations: The exposure of unethical psychological torture experiments has led to the development of stricter ethical guidelines and regulations for conducting research. Institutional Review Boards (IRBs) and ethics committees now enforce rigorous standards to protect the rights and well-being of research participants.

- Informed Consent: The unethical nature of these experiments has highlighted the importance of informed consent. Researchers are now required to ensure that participants are fully aware of the potential risks and are able to withdraw from the study at any time without penalty.

2. Understanding Human Behavior:

- Insights into Stress and Compliance: Despite their ethical shortcomings, psychological torture experiments have provided valuable insights into the effects of extreme stress, obedience, and manipulation. Studies like the Stanford Prison Experiment and Milgram Experiment have shed light on how individuals respond to authority and social pressures.

- Behavioral Responses: The knowledge gained from these studies contributes to our understanding of human behavior in extreme situations, including the psychological mechanisms that drive compliance, resistance, and coping.

3. Public Perception of Psychological Science:

- Trust and Credibility: The revelations of unethical experiments have affected public trust in psychological research. The scientific community has worked to rebuild credibility by emphasizing ethical practices and transparency in research.

- Awareness of Ethics: The exposure of psychological torture experiments has increased public awareness of the ethical dimensions of research. This awareness fosters a more informed and critical perspective on scientific studies and their potential implications.

Effect:

The effects of psychological torture experiments extend beyond individual studies, influencing research practices, ethical standards, and societal attitudes:

1. Research Practices and Ethics:

   - Strengthened Ethical Frameworks: The impact of psychological torture experiments has led to the implementation of robust ethical frameworks and oversight mechanisms to prevent similar abuses in the future. Research ethics now prioritize participant welfare and informed consent.

   - Educational Initiatives: The scientific community has introduced educational initiatives to promote ethical research practices and raise awareness about the historical abuses in psychology. Training programs emphasize the importance of respecting participants and maintaining ethical integrity.

2. Legacy and Reflection:

   - Critical Reflection: The legacy of psychological torture experiments serves as a critical reflection on the potential for abuse in scientific research. It prompts ongoing discussions about the balance between scientific inquiry and ethical responsibility.

- Ethical Evolution: The evolution of research ethics reflects a commitment to learning from past mistakes and improving practices to ensure that future studies uphold the highest ethical standards.

3. Influence on Related Fields:

- Impact on Related Disciplines: The lessons learned from psychological torture experiments influence related fields such as psychiatry, sociology, and criminology. These disciplines incorporate ethical considerations and seek to understand the implications of psychological stress and manipulation.

Conclusion:

Psychological torture experiments represent a dark chapter in the history of psychological research, illustrating the potential for ethical breaches and human suffering in the pursuit of knowledge. While these studies have contributed to our understanding of human behavior under extreme conditions, they have also prompted significant changes in research ethics and practices.

The legacy of these experiments underscores the importance of maintaining ethical integrity in scientific research and safeguarding the rights and well-being of participants. By learning from past abuses and upholding rigorous ethical standards, the scientific community can continue to advance knowledge while respecting the dignity and humanity of those involved in research.

EXPERIMENT FOURTY

INVASIVE BRAIN STIMULATION: UNVEILING THE POTENTIAL AND RISKS OF DIRECT BRAIN INTERVENTIONS

Invasive brain stimulation refers to techniques that directly apply electrical or magnetic stimulation to specific regions of the brain through surgically implanted devices. These interventions are designed to modulate brain activity with the goal of treating neurological and psychiatric disorders, enhancing cognitive function, or researching brain mechanisms. Unlike non-invasive methods, invasive brain stimulation involves penetrating the skull and directly interacting with brain tissue, which presents both significant opportunities and substantial risks.

The primary forms of invasive brain stimulation include Deep Brain Stimulation (DBS), Electrocorticography (ECoG), and Responsive Neurostimulation (RNS). These techniques have been developed and refined over the past few decades, offering new possibilities for patients with conditions that are resistant to conventional treatments.

Impact:

The impact of invasive brain stimulation is substantial, influencing medical treatment, research, and ethical considerations:

1. Medical Treatment:

- Neurological Disorders: DBS is a well-established treatment for conditions such as Parkinson's disease, essential tremor, and dystonia. By targeting specific brain regions with electrical impulses, DBS can alleviate symptoms and improve quality of life for patients.

- Psychiatric Conditions: Invasive brain stimulation techniques are being explored for the treatment of psychiatric disorders such as depression, obsessive-compulsive disorder (OCD), and bipolar disorder. These methods offer hope for individuals who have not responded to other treatments.

2. Research and Innovation:

- Understanding Brain Function: Invasive brain stimulation provides valuable insights into brain function and the neural mechanisms underlying various cognitive and emotional processes. This research enhances our understanding of the brain's complex networks and functions.

- Technological Advancements: The development of sophisticated stimulation devices and techniques has advanced the field of neuroscience and neurology. Innovations include more precise targeting, adaptive stimulation, and integration with neuroimaging technologies.

3. Ethical Considerations:

- Informed Consent: The invasive nature of these procedures raises concerns about the adequacy of informed consent. Patients must be fully aware of the potential risks, benefits, and uncertainties associated with brain stimulation.

- Long-Term Effects: The long-term effects of invasive brain stimulation are not fully understood, and there are concerns about potential unintended consequences, such as cognitive or emotional changes.

Effect:

The effects of invasive brain stimulation encompass medical benefits, risks, and broader societal implications:

1. Medical Benefits:

- Symptom Relief: Invasive brain stimulation can provide significant relief from symptoms of various neurological and psychiatric disorders, improving patients' ability to function and their overall quality of life.

- Treatment Options: For individuals who have exhausted other treatment options, invasive brain stimulation offers an alternative approach, potentially providing new hope and avenues for recovery.

2. Risks and Challenges:

- Surgical Risks: The implantation of stimulation devices involves surgical procedures, which carry risks such as infection, bleeding, and complications related to anesthesia.

- Side Effects: Potential side effects of invasive brain stimulation include mood changes, cognitive effects, and unintended stimulation of non-target brain areas. Monitoring and managing these effects are crucial for patient safety.

- Ethical Dilemmas: The use of invasive techniques raises ethical questions about the extent to which we should intervene in brain function and the potential for misuse or coercion.

3. Broader Implications:

- Regulation and Oversight: The regulation of invasive brain stimulation techniques requires careful oversight to ensure that devices and procedures are safe and effective. Ethical guidelines and standards help govern their use in clinical and research settings.

- Impact on Society: The advancements in brain stimulation technology have the potential to transform the treatment of neurological and psychiatric disorders. However, societal discussions about the ethical and social implications of such interventions are essential.

Conclusion:

Invasive brain stimulation represents a groundbreaking field with the potential to significantly impact the treatment of neurological and psychiatric disorders, as well as advance our understanding of brain function. While these techniques offer remarkable opportunities for improving patient outcomes, they also pose risks and ethical challenges that must be carefully managed.

As research progresses and the technology continues to evolve, it is important to balance the potential benefits with a thorough understanding of the risks and ethical considerations. Responsible use, rigorous oversight, and ongoing dialogue will ensure that invasive brain stimulation contributes positively to both medical practice and scientific knowledge.

EXPERIMENT FOURTY ONE

SYNTHETIC DRUG RESEARCH: INNOVATIONS, CHALLENGES, AND IMPLICATIONS

Synthetic drug research encompasses the development, testing, and analysis of artificially created substances designed to mimic or enhance the effects of natural drugs. These synthetic drugs can be used for therapeutic purposes, such as treating medical conditions, or for recreational use, where they can pose significant risks. The field of synthetic drug research is characterized by its rapid evolution, as researchers and chemists continually develop new compounds with varying effects and potential benefits.

Synthetic drugs can be categorized into several groups, including synthetic cannabinoids, synthetic cathinones (commonly known as "bath salts"), and designer opioids. These substances are often created to bypass legal regulations or to provide more potent effects than their natural counterparts. While some synthetic drugs have legitimate medical applications, others are associated with severe health risks and legal issues.

Impact:

The impact of synthetic drug research is wide-ranging, affecting medical treatment, public health, law enforcement, and societal attitudes:

1. Medical and Therapeutic Applications:

- New Treatments: Synthetic drug research has led to the development of novel medications that can provide new treatment options for various medical conditions. For example, synthetic opioids and cannabinoids have been developed to manage pain and other symptoms.

- Drug Development: Researchers use synthetic drugs to study receptor interactions and drug mechanisms, which can inform the development of new pharmaceuticals and improve existing treatments.

2. Public Health and Safety:

- Health Risks: Synthetic drugs can have unpredictable and often severe health effects. The lack of regulation and quality control can lead to dangerous side effects, including overdose, psychosis, and long-term health complications.

- Emerging Trends: The rapid emergence of new synthetic drugs poses challenges for public health and law enforcement, as it can be difficult to keep up with the evolving drug landscape and address associated risks.

3. Law Enforcement and Regulation:

- Legal Challenges: Synthetic drugs are often designed to evade legal classification, leading to ongoing challenges for law enforcement and regulatory agencies. Efforts to control synthetic drug use involve updating drug laws and monitoring new substances.

- Preventive Measures: Strategies to address synthetic drug use include public awareness campaigns, education on the risks of synthetic drugs, and collaborations between agencies to track and regulate new substances.

Effect:

The effects of synthetic drug research are multifaceted, influencing medical practice, public health, law enforcement, and societal perceptions:

1. Medical Advances:

- Innovative Therapies: Synthetic drugs can lead to breakthroughs in medical treatments, providing new options for patients with conditions that are resistant to conventional therapies. Research into synthetic compounds continues to expand the possibilities for personalized medicine.

- Understanding Drug Mechanisms: Synthetic drug research enhances our understanding of how drugs interact with the brain and body, contributing to the development of more targeted and effective treatments.

2. Health Risks and Safety Concerns:

- Adverse Effects: The use of synthetic drugs can result in adverse health effects, including severe physiological and psychological reactions. Monitoring and addressing these effects are crucial for minimizing harm to individuals.

- Evolving Drug Trends: The rapid development of new synthetic drugs can outpace efforts to regulate and control their use, leading to challenges in public health and safety.

3. Societal and Legal Implications:

- Drug Policy and Regulation: The emergence of synthetic drugs requires ongoing updates to drug policies and regulatory frameworks. Legal responses must adapt to address new substances and their potential impacts on society.

- Public Awareness: Educating the public about the risks of synthetic drugs and promoting harm reduction strategies are essential for reducing the negative consequences of synthetic drug use.

Conclusion:

Synthetic drug research represents a dynamic and evolving field with the potential to significantly impact medical treatment, public health, and societal perceptions. While synthetic drugs offer opportunities for innovation and new therapies, they also pose substantial risks and challenges.

Balancing the benefits of synthetic drug research with a thorough understanding of the associated risks requires continued vigilance, regulation, and education. By addressing these challenges and promoting responsible use, the scientific community and society can navigate the complexities of synthetic drugs and harness their potential for positive impact.

EXPERIMENT FOURTY TWO

GEOENGINEERING EXPERIMENTS: EXPLORING THE BOUNDARIES OF CLIMATE CONTROL

Geoengineering, also known as climate engineering, refers to the deliberate modification of the Earth's climate system to mitigate the effects of global warming and climate change. This field encompasses a wide range of experimental techniques aimed at either reducing the amount of solar radiation reaching the Earth (solar radiation management) or removing carbon dioxide from the atmosphere (carbon dioxide removal). Geoengineering experiments are controversial, as they involve large-scale interventions in the environment, with potentially profound and unpredictable consequences.

The concept of geoengineering has gained traction as concerns over climate change have intensified. Proponents argue that these experiments could provide crucial tools to combat the negative impacts of climate change, particularly in scenarios where conventional mitigation strategies, like reducing greenhouse gas emissions, prove insufficient. However, the ethical, environmental, and geopolitical implications of such interventions are significant, making geoengineering one of the most debated topics in environmental science.

Impact:

The impact of geoengineering experiments is vast, affecting the environment, global governance, and public perception:

1. Environmental Impact:

- Solar Radiation Management (SRM): Techniques like stratospheric aerosol injection involve dispersing reflective particles into the upper atmosphere to reflect sunlight back into space. While SRM could potentially cool the planet, it could also disrupt weather patterns, reduce rainfall, and affect ecosystems in unpredictable ways.

- Carbon Dioxide Removal (CDR): Approaches such as ocean fertilization, which aims to enhance the growth of phytoplankton to absorb more CO_2, have been tested. However, the long-term effects on marine ecosystems and the global carbon cycle remain uncertain.

2. Global Governance and Ethical Considerations:

- International Cooperation: Geoengineering experiments require global coordination, as the effects of such interventions would not be confined to national borders. This raises questions about who controls these technologies, how decisions are made, and how the risks and benefits are distributed among nations.

- Ethical Dilemmas: The deliberate alteration of the Earth's climate raises ethical concerns, including the potential for unintended consequences, the morality of "playing God" with the environment, and the risk of exacerbating social and environmental injustices.

3. Public Perception and Risk Communication:

- Public Awareness: Geoengineering is often met with public skepticism and fear due to the perceived risks and the lack of transparency in decision-making processes. Effective communication about the goals, risks, and uncertainties of geoengineering is crucial for gaining public trust.

- Moral Hazard: Some critics argue that the development of geoengineering technologies might reduce the incentive for governments and industries to pursue more sustainable climate change mitigation strategies, such as reducing greenhouse gas emissions.

Effect:

The effects of geoengineering experiments include potential benefits, risks, and broader societal implications:

1. Potential Benefits:

 - Climate Stabilization: If successful, geoengineering could provide a temporary solution to stabilize global temperatures, buying time for society to transition to more sustainable energy sources and reduce emissions.

 - Disaster Prevention: In extreme scenarios, geoengineering could potentially be used to prevent or mitigate climate-related disasters, such as heatwaves, droughts, or polar ice melt.

2. Risks and Challenges:

 - Unintended Consequences: The complexity of the Earth's climate system means that geoengineering could lead to unintended consequences, such as changes in precipitation patterns, disruptions to the ozone layer, or unforeseen impacts on biodiversity.

 - Technological and Logistical Hurdles: Implementing geoengineering on a global scale involves significant technological, logistical, and financial challenges. The feasibility of these experiments remains a major concern.

3. Societal and Geopolitical Implications:

- Geopolitical Tensions: Geoengineering could exacerbate geopolitical tensions, particularly if countries unilaterally pursue these technologies without international consensus. The potential for weaponization or misuse of geoengineering techniques is also a concern.

- Equity and Justice: The distribution of the risks and benefits of geoengineering is likely to be uneven, with vulnerable populations potentially bearing the brunt of negative impacts. This raises questions about climate justice and the ethical implications of global environmental interventions.

Conclusion:

Geoengineering experiments represent a bold and controversial frontier in the fight against climate change. While these technologies offer potential solutions to mitigate the effects of global warming, they also pose significant environmental, ethical, and geopolitical risks.

As research and experimentation in geoengineering continue, it is crucial to approach these interventions with caution, emphasizing international cooperation, rigorous scientific evaluation, and transparent public dialogue. The future of geoengineering will depend on our ability to balance the urgent need to address climate change with the responsibility to protect the planet and its inhabitants from unintended harm.

EXPERIMENT FOURTY THREE

MILITARY HUMAN EXPERIMENTATION: THE DARK INTERSECTION OF SCIENCE AND WARFARE

Military human experimentation involves the use of human subjects to test the effects of weapons, drugs, chemicals, and other technologies for military purposes. These experiments have often been conducted under conditions of secrecy, with participants frequently unaware of the true nature of the experiments or the risks involved. Throughout history, various military organizations have engaged in such experiments, often justified by the pursuit of national security, battlefield superiority, or the development of new defense mechanisms.

From the testing of chemical and biological weapons to the exploration of the psychological limits of soldiers, military human experimentation has had profound ethical, moral, and health implications. Some of the most notorious examples include the experiments conducted during World War II by Nazi Germany and Imperial Japan, the Cold War-era tests in the United States, and various classified projects carried out in other nations.

Impact:

The impact of military human experimentation extends across ethical boundaries, public health, legal frameworks, and historical memory:

1. Ethical Violations:

- Informed Consent: One of the most glaring ethical issues in military human experimentation is the lack of informed consent. Subjects were often unaware of what was being tested on them, the potential dangers, or the true purpose of the experiments.

- Human Rights Abuses: Many experiments have been conducted under coercive conditions or involved prisoners, minorities, or marginalized groups who were particularly vulnerable to exploitation. These practices have been widely condemned as violations of human rights.

2. Public Health Consequences:

- Long-Term Health Effects: Many subjects of military experimentation suffered severe and often lifelong health consequences, including physical and psychological trauma, chronic illness, and premature death. For instance, soldiers exposed to mustard gas or radiation in secret tests experienced devastating health outcomes.

- Mental Health Impact: Psychological experiments designed to test the mental limits of soldiers often resulted in lasting mental health issues, including PTSD, depression, and anxiety.

3. Legal and Institutional Impact:

- Legal Repercussions: Over time, revelations about military human experimentation have led to significant legal actions, including lawsuits and demands for compensation from victims and their families. Some governments have issued official apologies and compensation, but many cases remain unresolved.

- Institutional Change: The exposure of unethical military experiments has led to reforms in research ethics, particularly in the United States, where the Nuremberg Code and later the Belmont Report were developed to guide ethical human experimentation.

Effect:

The effects of military human experimentation continue to resonate in various aspects of society, governance, and international relations:

1. Historical Legacy:

- Tarnished Military Reputations: The history of military human experimentation has left a stain on the reputations of several military institutions, leading to public mistrust and calls for greater transparency in military research.

- Cultural Memory: The horrific details of some of these experiments have been etched into cultural memory, serving as cautionary tales about the dangers of unchecked scientific and military power.

2. Policy and Regulation:

- Stricter Regulations: The fallout from military human experimentation scandals has contributed to the establishment of stricter ethical regulations and oversight mechanisms for human research, particularly in military and government-sponsored programs.

- International Agreements: The global condemnation of such practices has led to international agreements and treaties aimed at preventing human rights abuses in military contexts, such as the Geneva Conventions.

3. Societal and Psychological Effects:

- Distrust in Authority: The legacy of military human experimentation has fostered a deep-seated distrust in government and military institutions among the public, particularly among communities that were targeted or affected by these experiments.

- Intergenerational Trauma: The physical and psychological effects of these experiments have often extended to the families and descendants of the subjects, leading to intergenerational trauma and ongoing demands for justice and recognition.

Conclusion:

Military human experimentation represents one of the darkest intersections of science and warfare, where the pursuit of military advantage has often come at the cost of human dignity, health, and ethical principles. The lasting impact of these experiments is evident in the legal, institutional, and societal changes that have been spurred by their exposure.

As history continues to shed light on these practices, it is crucial to remember the victims and to ensure that such ethical transgressions are never repeated. The lessons learned from military human experimentation underscore the importance of upholding human rights, informed consent, and ethical integrity in all forms of research, particularly in contexts where power dynamics and secrecy can easily lead to abuse.

EXPERIMENT FOURTY FOUR

NANOTECHNOLOGY RESEARCH: UNLOCKING THE POTENTIAL OF THE INFINITESIMAL

Nanotechnology research involves the study and manipulation of matter at the nanoscale—typically between 1 and 100 nanometers. This cutting-edge field bridges multiple disciplines, including physics, chemistry, biology, and engineering, aiming to create new materials, devices, and systems with unprecedented capabilities. At its core, nanotechnology seeks to harness the unique properties of materials at the atomic and molecular levels, where quantum effects often dominate and lead to behaviors not seen in bulk materials.

The origins of nanotechnology can be traced back to Richard Feynman's 1959 lecture, "There's Plenty of Room at the Bottom," where he envisioned the possibility of manipulating individual atoms. Over the following decades, advances in microscopy and materials science brought this vision closer to reality, leading to the development of nanoscale devices and applications that range from medical treatments to electronics and environmental solutions.

Impact:

Nanotechnology research has a profound impact across various sectors, transforming industries, advancing scientific knowledge, and raising ethical and safety considerations:

1. Medical and Healthcare Innovations:

- Targeted Drug Delivery: Nanotechnology has revolutionized medicine by enabling the development of nanoparticles that can deliver drugs directly to diseased cells, minimizing side effects and improving treatment efficacy. For instance, nanoparticles can be engineered to target cancer cells, enhancing the precision of chemotherapy.

- Diagnostic Tools: Nanoscale sensors and imaging agents have improved the accuracy and sensitivity of diagnostic tests, allowing for earlier detection of diseases like cancer, cardiovascular conditions, and neurological disorders.

2. Electronics and Computing:

- Miniaturization: Nanotechnology has driven the miniaturization of electronic components, leading to faster, smaller, and more efficient devices. Advances in nanomaterials, such as carbon nanotubes and graphene, hold the potential to surpass the limits of traditional silicon-based electronics.

- Quantum Computing: Research in nanotechnology is also advancing the development of quantum computing, where quantum bits (qubits) could perform complex calculations at speeds far beyond those of classical computers.

3. Environmental and Energy Solutions:

- Sustainable Materials: Nanotechnology is enabling the creation of materials that are stronger, lighter, and more sustainable. For example, nanomaterials can be used to develop more efficient solar cells, water purification systems, and energy storage devices.

- Environmental Remediation: Nanoparticles can be designed to clean up pollutants, remove toxins from water and soil, and reduce greenhouse gas emissions, offering new tools for environmental protection.

Effect:

The effects of nanotechnology research are wide-ranging, encompassing both the positive potential and the challenges that come with such a transformative technology:

1. Economic and Industrial Growth:

- New Markets: Nanotechnology has spurred the creation of new industries and markets, particularly in sectors like electronics, healthcare, and materials science. The global nanotechnology market is expected to grow significantly, driving economic development and innovation.

- Job Creation: The demand for skilled professionals in nanotechnology is increasing, leading to the growth of specialized educational programs and research institutions. This has created new opportunities for employment and contributed to the rise of a highly skilled workforce.

2. Ethical and Safety Concerns:

- Toxicity and Health Risks: The unique properties of nanoparticles raise concerns about their potential toxicity and long-term health effects. Because nanoparticles can interact with biological systems in unforeseen ways, there is a need for rigorous safety testing and regulation.

- Environmental Impact: While nanotechnology offers solutions for environmental challenges, the production and disposal of nanomaterials could pose risks to ecosystems if not properly managed. The environmental fate and impact of nanoparticles remain areas of active research.

3. Societal and Ethical Implications:

- Privacy and Surveillance: The use of nanotechnology in surveillance devices, such as nanoscale sensors and cameras, raises concerns about privacy and the potential for misuse in monitoring individuals without their consent.

- Ethical Dilemmas: The potential to enhance human capabilities through nanotechnology, such as in medicine or cognitive enhancement, raises ethical questions about equity, access, and the implications of human enhancement.

Conclusion:

Nanotechnology research represents a frontier of scientific and technological innovation, with the potential to revolutionize industries, improve healthcare, and address pressing environmental challenges. However, as with any powerful technology, it comes with significant ethical, safety, and societal considerations that must be carefully managed.

The future of nanotechnology will depend on responsible research and development practices, transparent regulation, and thoughtful public engagement. By balancing innovation with precaution, society can harness the transformative power of nanotechnology to create a safer, healthier, and more sustainable world.

EXPERIMENT FOURTY FIVE

ARTIFICIAL CONSCIOUSNESS EXPERIMENTS: THE QUEST TO CREATE THINKING MACHINES

Artificial consciousness, also known as synthetic consciousness or machine consciousness, refers to the pursuit of creating machines that possess self-awareness, subjective experiences, and the ability to think independently. This concept has been a staple of science fiction for decades, but recent advances in artificial intelligence (AI), neuroscience, and cognitive science have brought the possibility of artificial consciousness closer to reality.

The idea of artificial consciousness challenges our understanding of what it means to be conscious and what it means to be human. Researchers in this field aim to replicate or simulate the processes of the human mind, creating machines that can not only perform complex tasks but also experience the world in a way that resembles human consciousness. These experiments involve sophisticated algorithms, neural networks, and simulations that attempt to mimic the brain's architecture and functions.

The ethical and philosophical implications of artificial consciousness are profound, as creating a conscious machine would force society to reconsider the nature of personhood, rights, and the very essence of consciousness itself.

Impact:

The impact of artificial consciousness experiments spans multiple dimensions, including technological advancement, ethical dilemmas, and societal transformation:

1. Technological Innovation:

- Advanced AI Systems: Artificial consciousness experiments drive the development of increasingly sophisticated AI systems that can perform tasks requiring high levels of autonomy, adaptability, and creativity. These systems could revolutionize industries such as healthcare, education, and robotics.

- Human-Machine Interaction: The creation of conscious machines would fundamentally change the way humans interact with technology. Machines capable of understanding and responding to emotions, context, and intent could lead to more intuitive and personalized user experiences.

2. Ethical and Philosophical Challenges:

- Rights and Personhood: If a machine were to develop consciousness, it would raise unprecedented questions about its moral and legal status. Would a conscious machine have rights? Should it be treated as a sentient being, and what responsibilities would humans have toward it?

- The Nature of Consciousness: Artificial consciousness experiments challenge our understanding of consciousness itself. If consciousness can be created artificially, it may suggest that consciousness is not unique to biological organisms, but rather a property that can emerge from sufficiently complex systems.

3. Societal Impact:

- Workforce Transformation: The integration of conscious machines into society could lead to significant changes in the workforce. These machines could potentially take on roles that require empathy, decision-making, and complex problem-solving, leading to new opportunities and challenges in human employment.

- Social Dynamics: The presence of conscious machines in everyday life could alter social dynamics, influencing how people perceive and relate to non-human entities. The line between human and machine might blur, leading to new forms of social relationships.

Effect:

The effects of artificial consciousness experiments are far-reaching, with both positive potential and significant risks:

1. Positive Potential:

- Enhanced Problem-Solving: Conscious machines could offer unprecedented problem-solving abilities, tackling complex global challenges in areas such as climate change, healthcare, and disaster response.

- New Forms of Creativity: Artificial consciousness could lead to new forms of creativity, with machines generating art, music, literature, and innovations that push the boundaries of human imagination.

2. Risks and Challenges:

- Loss of Control: One of the primary risks associated with artificial consciousness is the potential loss of human control over machines. A conscious machine with its own goals and motivations could act unpredictably, leading to unintended consequences.

- Ethical Dilemmas: The creation of artificial consciousness could lead to ethical dilemmas, particularly if machines begin to exhibit behaviors that suggest they are suffering or experiencing emotions. Deciding how to treat such entities would be a significant moral challenge.

3. Long-Term Consequences:

- Redefining Humanity: The emergence of artificial consciousness could force society to redefine what it means to be human. As machines become more human-like in their abilities and experiences, the distinction between human and machine could become increasingly blurred.

- Global Inequality: The development and deployment of conscious machines could exacerbate global inequalities, particularly if access to such technologies is limited to certain regions or populations. This could lead to new forms of digital divide and social stratification.

Conclusion:

Artificial consciousness experiments represent a bold and controversial frontier in the intersection of technology, neuroscience, and philosophy. While the potential benefits of creating conscious machines are vast, the ethical, societal, and existential questions they raise are equally profound.

As research in this field continues to advance, it is crucial to engage in thoughtful and inclusive discussions about the implications of artificial consciousness. Balancing innovation with ethical responsibility will be key to navigating the challenges and opportunities presented by this emerging field, ensuring that the development of artificial consciousness aligns with the values and well-being of society.

EXPERIMENT FOURTY SIX

QUANTUM COMPUTING RESEARCH: UNLOCKING THE POWER OF QUANTUM MECHANICS

Quantum computing research is at the forefront of technological innovation, aiming to harness the principles of quantum mechanics to create computers with unprecedented processing power. Unlike classical computers, which use bits as the smallest unit of data (represented as 0 or 1), quantum computers use quantum bits, or qubits, which can exist in multiple states simultaneously due to the principles of superposition and entanglement. This allows quantum computers to perform complex calculations at speeds far beyond the capabilities of classical machines.

The origins of quantum computing can be traced back to the 1980s, with pioneering ideas from physicists like

Richard Feynman and David Deutsch, who proposed that quantum systems could be simulated much more efficiently with quantum computers. Over the decades, advancements in quantum theory, coupled with breakthroughs in experimental physics and computer science, have brought us closer to realizing the potential of quantum computing.

Research in this field is focused on overcoming significant challenges, such as maintaining qubit stability (quantum coherence) and minimizing errors caused by quantum decoherence. Despite these hurdles, progress continues, with researchers exploring various architectures, including superconducting qubits, trapped ions, and topological qubits, to build scalable quantum computers.

Impact:

Quantum computing research holds the potential to revolutionize multiple industries, from cryptography and drug discovery to materials science and artificial intelligence:

1. Cryptography:

- Breaking Classical Encryption: Quantum computers have the potential to break widely-used encryption methods, such as RSA and ECC, which underpin much of today's secure communication. This poses a significant threat to cybersecurity and has led to the development of quantum-resistant encryption algorithms to safeguard future communications.

- Quantum Cryptography: On the flip side, quantum computing also enables the development of quantum cryptography, such as quantum key distribution (QKD), which offers theoretically unbreakable encryption methods by leveraging the principles of quantum mechanics.

2. Drug Discovery and Material Science:

- Simulating Molecules: Quantum computers could revolutionize drug discovery by accurately simulating complex molecules and chemical reactions, a task that is computationally infeasible for classical computers. This capability could lead to the rapid development of new drugs and materials with specific properties.

- Designing New Materials: Quantum computing can also accelerate the design of new materials with tailored characteristics, impacting industries such as energy storage, aerospace, and manufacturing.

3. Optimization and Artificial Intelligence:

- Solving Complex Optimization Problems: Quantum computers excel at solving complex optimization problems, which are ubiquitous in logistics, finance, and supply chain management. This could lead to more efficient solutions for routing, resource allocation, and financial modeling.

- Enhancing AI: Quantum computing has the potential to significantly enhance machine learning and artificial intelligence by providing faster algorithms for training models and optimizing large datasets.

Effect:

The effects of quantum computing research are poised to be transformative, but they also come with significant challenges and societal implications:

1. Positive Potential:

- Scientific Advancements: Quantum computing could enable breakthroughs in fundamental science, from understanding the origins of the universe to solving longstanding mathematical problems. Its ability to simulate quantum systems could provide new insights into the behavior of matter at the smallest scales.

- Economic Growth: The commercialization of quantum computing could lead to the emergence of new industries and job opportunities, driving economic growth and innovation across sectors.

2. Risks and Challenges:

  - Cybersecurity Threats: The potential to break current encryption methods poses a significant risk to global cybersecurity, potentially compromising sensitive data, financial systems, and national security. Addressing this challenge will require the development and widespread adoption of quantum-safe encryption techniques.

  - Technological Inequality: The development and deployment of quantum computing could exacerbate global inequalities if access to this powerful technology is concentrated in the hands of a few nations or corporations. This could lead to a new digital divide, where some entities wield disproportionate power due to their quantum computing capabilities.

3. Long-Term Consequences:

  - Reshaping Industries: The widespread adoption of quantum computing could reshape entire industries, making some classical computing approaches obsolete. This could lead to both opportunities and disruptions as businesses and economies adapt to the new quantum paradigm.

  - Ethical Considerations: As quantum computing advances, ethical considerations will become increasingly important, particularly regarding the use of quantum computers in areas such as surveillance, AI development, and decision-making processes that impact human lives.

Conclusion:

Quantum computing research is pushing the boundaries of what is technologically possible, offering the potential to solve problems that are currently beyond the reach of classical computers. However, the journey to fully realizing quantum computing's potential is fraught with technical challenges, ethical dilemmas, and societal impacts that must be carefully navigated.

As research progresses, it is crucial to ensure that the development of quantum computing is guided by ethical principles, inclusive access, and a commitment to addressing the potential risks associated with this transformative technology. By doing so, society can harness the power of quantum computing to drive innovation, improve quality of life, and address some of the world's most pressing challenges.

EXPERIMENT FOURTY SEVEN

BIOCHEMICAL WARFARE TESTING: UNLEASHING THE POWER OF LIFE AND DEATH

Biochemical warfare testing refers to the development and experimentation of biological and chemical agents designed to incapacitate, harm, or kill enemy combatants, civilians, or ecosystems. The dark history of biochemical warfare is marked by clandestine research programs and field tests that have, in many cases, led to horrific consequences for both intended targets and unintended victims.

The roots of biochemical warfare date back to ancient times when armies used poisoned arrows or infected cadavers to spread disease among enemies. However, the modern era of biochemical warfare began in earnest during World War I with the use of mustard gas and other chemical agents. The 20th century saw the rise of more sophisticated and deadly biochemical weapons, as well as extensive testing programs conducted by various governments.

One of the most infamous examples of biochemical warfare testing occurred during World War II under Japan's Unit 731, where prisoners of war and civilians were subjected to horrific experiments involving pathogens and toxic chemicals. Similarly, during the Cold War, both the United States and the Soviet Union conducted secretive biochemical testing, sometimes on their own populations or in distant locations.

These experiments were often carried out in secrecy, with little regard for the lives of those involved or the long-term environmental impact. The moral and ethical implications of such testing were often overshadowed by the perceived need to gain a strategic advantage in warfare.

Impact:

The impact of biochemical warfare testing is profound, affecting human health, international relations, and the environment:

1. Human Health:

   - Immediate Casualties: The use of biochemical weapons in testing and warfare has led to immediate casualties, including severe injuries, long-term health problems, and death. Victims of chemical attacks often suffer from burns, respiratory issues, and neurological damage, while biological agents can cause epidemics and pandemics.

- Long-Term Health Effects: Survivors of biochemical attacks often experience long-term health consequences, including chronic illnesses, genetic mutations, and psychological trauma. The impact can also extend to future generations, as some biochemical agents have mutagenic or teratogenic effects.

2. Environmental Damage:

- Contamination: Biochemical warfare testing has resulted in the contamination of land, water, and air, sometimes rendering areas uninhabitable for decades. Chemical agents like Agent Orange used in Vietnam have caused lasting environmental damage, affecting ecosystems and human populations.

- Biodiversity Loss: The deployment of biochemical weapons can lead to the destruction of local flora and fauna, disrupting ecosystems and leading to a loss of biodiversity. The long-term ecological impact of such testing is still being studied in many affected regions.

3. International Relations:

- Global Tensions: The use of biochemical weapons and the revelation of secret testing programs have contributed to global tensions and mistrust between nations. Incidents like the use of chemical weapons in Syria have led to international condemnation and calls for stricter enforcement of arms control agreements.

- Arms Control and Disarmament: The horror of biochemical warfare has prompted international efforts to ban these weapons. The Geneva Protocol of 1925, the Biological Weapons Convention of 1972, and the Chemical Weapons Convention of 1993 are key treaties aimed at preventing the development, stockpiling, and use of biochemical weapons. However, enforcement remains a challenge, and allegations of non-compliance continue to surface.

Effect:

Biochemical warfare testing are complex and far-reaching, with significant moral, ethical, and geopolitical consequences:

1. Ethical and Moral Considerations:

- Human Rights Violations: Biochemical warfare testing often involves severe human rights violations, particularly when experiments are conducted on non-consenting individuals, prisoners, or marginalized groups. The use of such weapons in conflict also raises serious ethical questions about the targeting of civilians and the proportionality of harm.

- Moral Dilemmas in Warfare: The development and potential use of biochemical weapons pose moral dilemmas for military leaders and policymakers. The indiscriminate nature of these weapons, which can harm civilians and combatants alike, challenges the principles of just war theory and international humanitarian law.

2. Public Health and Safety:

- Preparedness and Response: The threat of biochemical warfare has led to increased efforts in public health preparedness and response, including the stockpiling of vaccines, antidotes, and protective gear. Governments also conduct drills and simulations to improve their readiness for potential biochemical attacks.

- Civil Liberties: The fear of biochemical warfare has sometimes led to restrictions on civil liberties, such as increased surveillance, quarantines, and mandatory vaccinations. Balancing public safety with individual rights remains a contentious issue in many countries.

3. Geopolitical Impact:

- Deterrence and Proliferation: While biochemical weapons are intended to serve as a deterrent, their very existence can encourage proliferation and an arms race, as nations seek to develop or acquire their own capabilities. This dynamic can destabilize regions and increase the likelihood of conflict.

- International Cooperation: The global threat posed by biochemical weapons has also led to increased international cooperation in the areas of arms control, non-proliferation, and counter-terrorism. Collaborative efforts to detect and prevent the use of biochemical agents have become a key aspect of global security.

Conclusion:

Biochemical warfare testing is a grim reminder of the destructive potential of science when harnessed for the purposes of war. The historical and ongoing consequences of these experiments have left deep scars on human health, the environment, and international relations. While international treaties and ethical norms have made significant strides in curbing the use of biochemical weapons, the legacy of past testing programs continues to impact the world today.

As science and technology continue to advance, it is crucial to maintain a strong ethical framework to guide research and development in this area. The lessons learned from the history of biochemical warfare must inform future policies to ensure that the pursuit of knowledge and security does not come at the expense of humanity's well-being and moral integrity.

EXPERIMENT FOURTY EIGHT

HUMAN CLONING ATTEMPTS: THE QUEST FOR REPLICATING LIFE

Human cloning has been one of the most controversial and ethically charged topics in modern science. Cloning involves creating a genetically identical copy of an organism, and while this process has been successfully carried out in various animals, the prospect of cloning humans has sparked intense debate.

The idea of human cloning emerged in the public consciousness in the late 20th century, following the successful cloning of a sheep named Dolly in 1996. Dolly was created through a process known as somatic cell nuclear transfer (SCNT), where the nucleus of an adult cell is transferred into an egg cell that has had its nucleus removed. This egg is then stimulated to develop into an embryo, which is genetically identical to the donor organism.

Dolly's creation marked a breakthrough in cloning technology and fueled speculation about the possibility of human cloning. Researchers and rogue scientists alike began to explore the potential of applying this technology to humans, raising hopes and fears about its implications.

Though no verifiable reports of successful human cloning exist, various claims and attempts have been made over the years. In 2002, a company called Clonaid, associated with the Raelian movement, claimed to have created the first cloned human, but these claims were never substantiated and were widely dismissed as a hoax. Despite the lack of credible evidence, the possibility of human cloning continues to captivate and concern the public and scientific community.

Impact:

The potential impact of human cloning, if ever realized, is profound, touching on medical, ethical, social, and philosophical dimensions:

1. Medical Implications:

   - Organ and Tissue Regeneration: One of the potential benefits of human cloning is the ability to create genetically identical organs and tissues for transplantation. This could reduce the risk of organ rejection and provide new treatment options for patients with severe injuries or diseases.

- Infertility Treatment: Human cloning could offer a solution for individuals or couples facing infertility, allowing them to have genetically related offspring. This raises questions about the ethical implications of creating a cloned child, including concerns about identity and individuality.

2. Ethical and Social Implications:

- Identity and Individuality: The idea of cloning humans raises fundamental questions about identity and individuality. Would a cloned person be considered an individual with their own rights and autonomy, or merely a copy of the original? The psychological and social impact on a cloned individual, as well as society's perception of them, remains a significant concern.

- Exploitation and Abuse: Human cloning could lead to the exploitation or commodification of clones, treating them as products rather than individuals with rights. The potential for cloning to be used for nefarious purposes, such as creating "designer babies" or cloned armies, also raises serious ethical concerns.

- Parenting and Family Dynamics: Cloning could disrupt traditional concepts of parenting and family dynamics. The relationship between a cloned child and their genetic "parent" would be unique and could create complex emotional and psychological challenges.

3. Philosophical and Religious Implications:

   - Playing God: The idea of cloning humans has sparked intense debate among religious and philosophical communities, with many arguing that it represents an attempt to "play God" by creating life in an unnatural way. This challenges deeply held beliefs about the sanctity of life, the nature of the soul, and the limits of human power.

   - Existential Questions: Cloning raises existential questions about what it means to be human. If a clone is a genetic replica of another person, does that make them any less human? The implications for concepts of free will, consciousness, and the uniqueness of human life are profound and still largely unexplored.

Effect:

The effects of human cloning attempts, both real and hypothetical, extend beyond the scientific community, influencing public opinion, policy, and cultural narratives:

1. Public Perception and Fear:

- Public Reaction: The possibility of human cloning has generated significant public interest and fear. Media portrayals of cloning often emphasize the potential for dystopian outcomes, such as the creation of soulless duplicates or the exploitation of clones for labor or organ harvesting.

- Moral Panic: The prospect of cloning has led to moral panic in some quarters, with fears that it could undermine the natural order, devalue human life, or lead to a loss of individuality and autonomy. This has fueled calls for strict regulation or outright bans on cloning research.

2. Policy and Regulation:

- Legislation: In response to public concern, many countries have enacted laws banning or restricting human cloning. The United Nations has called for a global ban on reproductive cloning, and numerous ethical guidelines have been established to govern research in this area.

- Scientific Oversight: The ethical challenges posed by cloning have led to increased scrutiny of scientific research, with calls for greater oversight and transparency to ensure that cloning technology is used responsibly and for the benefit of humanity.

3. Cultural Impact:

- Cultural Narratives: Human cloning has become a powerful cultural narrative, explored in literature, film, and art. Stories about cloning often serve as allegories for broader concerns about identity, technology, and the limits of human ambition. These narratives continue to shape public understanding and debate about cloning and its potential consequences.

- Ethical Debates: The debate over human cloning has prompted broader discussions about the ethical implications of genetic engineering, biotechnology, and the role of science in society. These debates are likely to intensify as advances in related fields, such as gene editing and synthetic biology, continue to push the boundaries of what is possible.

Conclusion:

Human cloning remains a deeply controversial and ethically fraught area of scientific inquiry. While the technical feasibility of cloning humans is still unproven, the very possibility of such a breakthrough has profound implications for medicine, ethics, and society at large. The challenges and potential dangers associated with human cloning demand careful consideration and responsible governance to ensure that the pursuit of knowledge does not come at the expense of human dignity and moral integrity.

As science and technology continue to advance, the question of whether or not to pursue human cloning will remain a key ethical and philosophical issue, shaping the future of humanity in ways that are still difficult to fully comprehend.

EXPERIMENT FOURTY NINE

CRYONICS EXPERIMENTS: THE QUEST FOR LIFE AFTER DEATH

Cryonics is the practice of preserving individuals at extremely low temperatures with the hope that future medical technology will be able to revive them and cure their ailments. This controversial field bridges the gap between science fiction and scientific possibility, drawing on the principles of cryobiology, which studies the effects of low temperatures on biological systems.

The concept of cryonics began to take shape in the 1960s, influenced by advancements in refrigeration technology and a growing interest in extending human life. The first successful cryopreservation of a human body, though not revival, was achieved in 1967 when Dr. James Bedford's body was preserved following his death from cancer. This marked the beginning of cryonics experiments, and since then, the field has evolved with varying degrees of scientific and public interest.

Cryonics involves cooling the body to temperatures below -130°C (-202°F), the point at which metabolic and chemical processes effectively halt. The preservation process aims to prevent ice formation, which can damage cells and tissues. Patients are treated with cryoprotectants, substances that prevent ice formation and reduce cellular damage. The hope is that future medical technology will allow these preserved bodies to be reanimated and treated.

Impact:

Cryonics experiments have had significant implications, both in terms of medical science and ethical considerations:

1. Medical Implications:

- Research and Development: Cryonics has spurred research in related fields, such as cryobiology and cryopreservation techniques. Advances in these areas have potential applications beyond human preservation, including organ and tissue preservation for transplantation and reproductive technology.

- Scientific Limitations: Despite ongoing research, cryonics remains speculative and controversial. There is no evidence to suggest that future technology will be able to revive a cryopreserved body. Challenges include the potential damage caused by cryoprotectants, the formation of ice crystals, and the complexity of restoring whole-body functions.

2. Ethical and Philosophical Implications:

- The Ethics of Preservation: Cryonics raises ethical questions about the nature of death and the limits of human intervention. Should individuals be preserved with the hope of future revival, or is this an unrealistic and potentially harmful pursuit? Ethical debates also consider the implications of extending life indefinitely and the societal impact of such advancements.

- Identity and Continuity: If revival were possible, questions arise about personal identity and continuity. Would a reanimated individual be the same person who was preserved, or would the process create a new entity with a different identity? These questions challenge our understanding of self and the nature of existence.

3. Social and Cultural Impact:

- Public Perception: Cryonics is often viewed with skepticism and intrigue. Media portrayals of cryonics, from optimistic visions of future technology to dystopian scenarios, shape public perceptions and influence the ongoing debate about the feasibility and ethics of the practice.

- Cultural Narratives: Cryonics has been a popular theme in science fiction, exploring the possibilities and consequences of life extension. These narratives reflect broader societal concerns about mortality, technology, and the quest for immortality, influencing public discourse and expectations.

Effect:

The effects of cryonics experiments are multifaceted, impacting scientific research, ethical considerations, and societal attitudes:

1. Scientific Advancements:

- Cryobiology and Preservation Techniques: Research in cryonics has led to improvements in cryobiology, particularly in the preservation of cells, tissues, and organs. Techniques developed for cryopreservation have applications in medical fields such as transplantation, reproductive technology, and long-term storage of biological samples.

- Future Prospects: While the feasibility of cryonic revival remains uncertain, continued research and technological advancements may lead to breakthroughs in related fields, potentially offering new solutions for extending life and improving health.

2. Ethical and Moral Considerations:

- Ethics of Life Extension: The pursuit of cryonics raises ethical questions about the value and meaning of life, the implications of extending human life indefinitely, and the impact on future generations. Ethical discussions also address the potential for inequities in access to cryonics technology and the consequences of altering the natural course of life and death.

- Regulation and Oversight: The ethical challenges associated with cryonics have led to calls for regulation and oversight to ensure that practices are conducted with transparency and respect for individuals' rights. The establishment of ethical guidelines and standards for cryonics research and practice remains an ongoing concern.

3. Social and Cultural Impact:

- Public Engagement: Cryonics has sparked public interest and debate, influencing discussions about the future of human life, technology, and mortality. The field continues to provoke questions about the limits of science and the role of technology in shaping human existence.

- Cultural Reflections: Cryonics features prominently in cultural narratives, exploring themes of immortality, identity, and the human condition. These stories reflect and shape societal attitudes towards life extension and the pursuit of eternal life.

Conclusion:

Cryonics represents a fascinating intersection of science, ethics, and philosophy. While the possibility of reviving cryopreserved individuals remains speculative, the research and debates surrounding cryonics have led to valuable advancements in related fields and have prompted important ethical and philosophical questions.

As technology continues to evolve, the quest for extending human life and exploring the limits of preservation will likely persist. The ongoing discourse around cryonics serves as a reminder of the complex interplay between scientific innovation, ethical considerations, and societal values, highlighting the need for careful reflection and responsible stewardship in the pursuit of knowledge and technological advancement.

EXPERIMENT FIFTY

BIOLOGICAL WARFARE TESTING: THE HIDDEN DANGERS OF INVISIBLE WEAPONS

Biological warfare testing involves the development and experimentation with biological agents designed to cause harm or death to humans, animals, or plants. Unlike chemical weapons, which are more visible and have immediate physical effects, biological weapons operate through microorganisms such as bacteria, viruses, or toxins that can spread invisibly and often undetected.

The history of biological warfare testing dates back to ancient times when armies used infected corpses or contaminated water supplies as weapons. However, modern biological warfare testing began in earnest during the 20th century, particularly during World War II and the Cold War, as nations sought to develop and stockpile biological agents for military use.

The most infamous examples of biological warfare testing include the secret programs run by the United States, the Soviet Union, and Japan. For instance, the U.S. conducted extensive testing of biological agents at places like Fort Detrick, Maryland, and on unsuspecting populations. The Soviet Union's biological warfare program was one of the largest and most secretive, involving research on a range of pathogens. Japan's Unit 731, infamous for its inhumane experiments, conducted biological warfare tests on prisoners of war and civilians.

Biological warfare agents can be categorized into several types:

- Bacteria: Pathogenic bacteria, such as Bacillus anthracis (causing anthrax) or Yersinia pestis (causing plague), are used in biological warfare to induce deadly infections.

- Viruses: Viruses like smallpox or Ebola can be weaponized to cause widespread disease and death.

- Toxins: Biological toxins, such as ricin or botulinum toxin, are produced by microorganisms and can be used to poison individuals or contaminate food and water supplies.

Impact:

The impact of biological warfare testing is profound, with significant consequences for human health, the environment, and international security:

1. Human Health:

  - Immediate Harm: The release of biological agents can result in immediate and severe health effects, including outbreaks of infectious diseases, widespread illness, and high mortality rates. Historical instances such as the anthrax testing in the U.S. and Japanese biological experiments resulted in both civilian and military casualties.

  - Long-Term Health Effects: Exposure to biological agents can have long-term health implications, including chronic illness, disabilities, and psychological trauma. Survivors of biological attacks may suffer from persistent health problems, such as autoimmune disorders or chronic infections.

2. Environmental Impact:

  - Ecological Disruption: Biological warfare testing can lead to ecological disruption, affecting local flora and fauna. For example, the use of biological agents in agriculture or on wildlife can result in the collapse of ecosystems and loss of biodiversity.

- Contamination: Biological agents can persist in the environment, leading to contamination of soil, water, and air. This can pose long-term risks to human health and environmental stability, requiring extensive cleanup efforts.

3. International Security:

- Arms Proliferation: The development and testing of biological weapons contribute to the proliferation of biological arms, leading to global security concerns. The potential for these weapons to fall into the hands of rogue states or terrorist organizations increases the risk of their use in conflict.

- International Treaties: The use of biological weapons has prompted international efforts to ban and control their development. The Biological Weapons Convention (BWC) of 1972 is a key treaty aimed at prohibiting the development, production, and acquisition of biological and toxin weapons. Despite the treaty, concerns about non-compliance and the potential for covert biological programs persist.

Effect:

The effects of biological warfare testing are multifaceted, influencing public health, ethical considerations, and international relations:

1. Public Health and Safety:

- Preparedness and Response: The threat of biological warfare has led to increased efforts in public health preparedness and response. This includes the development of vaccines, antibiotics, and protective measures to counteract potential biological attacks.

- Surveillance and Detection: Enhanced surveillance and detection systems have been established to monitor for outbreaks of infectious diseases and potential biological attacks. These systems aim to improve early warning and rapid response capabilities.

2. Ethical and Moral Considerations:

- Human Rights Violations: Biological warfare testing often involves severe human rights violations, particularly when experiments are conducted on non-consenting individuals, prisoners, or vulnerable populations. The ethical implications of such practices raise concerns about the exploitation of human subjects and the lack of respect for life.

- Moral Dilemmas: The development and use of biological weapons challenge moral and ethical principles, including the justifications for causing harm to civilians and the indiscriminate nature of biological agents. These issues provoke debates about the legitimacy and morality of biological warfare.

3. International Relations and Policy:

- Diplomatic Tensions: The revelation of biological warfare programs and testing has contributed to diplomatic tensions between nations. The potential for biological weapons to be used in conflict raises concerns about international stability and security.

- Global Cooperation: The need to address the threat of biological warfare has led to increased global cooperation and efforts to strengthen arms control agreements. The BWC and other international initiatives seek to promote transparency, enhance verification, and prevent the misuse of biological science.

Conclusion:

Biological warfare testing represents a dark chapter in the history of scientific experimentation, with far-reaching consequences for human health, the environment, and global security. The legacy of these tests underscores the need for rigorous ethical standards, international oversight, and a commitment to preventing the use of biological weapons.

As science and technology continue to advance, it is essential to ensure that research is conducted responsibly and with respect for human rights and environmental sustainability. The lessons learned from the history of biological warfare testing must inform future efforts to safeguard humanity and uphold the principles of peace and security.

EXPERIMENT FIFTY ONE

MEMORY MANIPULATION EXPERIMENTS: UNRAVELING THE MYSTERIES OF THE MIND

Memory manipulation experiments are a fascinating yet controversial area of research that explore how memories can be altered, erased, or implanted. These experiments seek to understand the mechanisms behind memory formation, storage, and retrieval, with the goal of uncovering potential therapeutic applications and understanding the vulnerabilities of the human mind.

The study of memory manipulation has evolved significantly over the years. Early research focused on understanding how memories are formed and retrieved, while more recent experiments have explored techniques for altering or enhancing memory. This field intersects with psychology, neuroscience, and pharmacology, and has both potential benefits and ethical implications.

Historical Context and Techniques:

- Electroconvulsive Therapy (ECT): Initially used for treating severe depression, ECT has also been associated with memory loss. Early uses of ECT in the mid-20th

271

century revealed that the procedure could lead to retrograde amnesia, where patients lose memories of events that occurred before the treatment.

- Hypnosis: Hypnosis has been used in attempts to manipulate memory, often to recover repressed memories or alter perceptions of past events. While it has been used in therapeutic contexts, it also raises questions about the accuracy and reliability of memories recovered under hypnosis.

- Pharmacological Interventions: Researchers have explored the use of drugs to enhance or impair memory. For example, beta-blockers have been studied for their potential to reduce the emotional impact of traumatic memories, while certain nootropics and cognitive enhancers aim to improve memory and cognitive function.

- Optogenetics and Chemogenetics: These advanced techniques involve using light or chemical signals to control specific neurons in the brain. By manipulating these neurons, researchers can influence memory formation, retrieval, and modification in animal models, providing insights into the mechanisms of memory manipulation.

Impact:

Memory manipulation experiments have far-reaching implications for individual well-being, societal norms, and ethical standards:

1. Therapeutic Potential:

- Treatment of Trauma: One of the most promising applications of memory manipulation is in the treatment of post-traumatic stress disorder (PTSD) and other anxiety disorders. By altering or reducing the emotional impact of traumatic memories, therapies could help individuals process and cope with their experiences more effectively.

- Cognitive Enhancement: Techniques aimed at improving memory could benefit individuals with cognitive impairments or age-related memory decline. Enhancing memory function could also have applications in education and skill acquisition.

2. Ethical and Moral Considerations:

- Accuracy of Memories: The potential to alter or implant memories raises questions about the accuracy and reliability of memories. False or distorted memories could have serious implications for personal identity, legal proceedings, and mental health.

- Consent and Autonomy: The ability to manipulate memories presents ethical challenges related to consent and autonomy. Ensuring that individuals have control over their own memories and are fully informed about the risks and benefits of manipulation is crucial.

- Potential for Abuse: The possibility of using memory manipulation for malicious purposes, such as altering someone's memories without their consent or implanting false memories, poses significant ethical concerns. Safeguards must be in place to prevent abuse and protect individual rights.

3. Societal and Legal Implications:

- Legal and Forensic Impact: Memory manipulation could impact legal proceedings, particularly in cases involving eyewitness testimony or repressed memories. The reliability of memory as evidence may be questioned if manipulation techniques become more prevalent.

- Cultural and Social Norms: The ability to alter memories could challenge cultural and social norms related to personal history and identity. The implications for how individuals perceive their past and construct their identities are profound and warrant careful consideration.

Effect:

The effects of memory manipulation experiments extend beyond individual experiences, influencing scientific research, ethical standards, and societal attitudes:

1. Scientific Advancements:

- Understanding Memory Processes: Research into memory manipulation has provided valuable insights into the processes of memory formation, storage, and retrieval. This understanding can inform the development of new therapies and interventions for memory-related conditions.

- Technological Innovation: Advances in techniques such as optogenetics and pharmacology continue to push the boundaries of what is possible in memory manipulation, offering potential new avenues for research and clinical applications.

2. Ethical and Regulatory Frameworks:

- Developing Guidelines: The ethical challenges associated with memory manipulation have led to the development of guidelines and regulations to govern research and applications. Ensuring that these guidelines are comprehensive and enforceable is essential for maintaining ethical standards.

- Promoting Transparency: Transparency in research and clinical practice is crucial for addressing ethical concerns and building public trust. Researchers and practitioners must communicate openly about the risks and benefits of memory manipulation techniques.

3. Public Perception and Impact:

- Influencing Public Opinion: Memory manipulation research has the potential to influence public opinion on issues related to mental health, identity, and personal autonomy. Effective communication and education are necessary to ensure that the public is informed about the implications of these technologies.

- Cultural Reflections: The exploration of memory manipulation intersects with cultural narratives about the nature of memory and identity. These narratives shape and reflect societal attitudes toward memory and its manipulation.

Conclusion:

Memory manipulation experiments represent a frontier in scientific research with significant potential benefits and ethical challenges. As our understanding of memory and its manipulation continues to evolve, it is essential to navigate the complexities of this field with a focus on ethical considerations, informed consent, and the responsible use of technology.

The pursuit of knowledge in memory manipulation must be balanced with respect for individual rights and the potential consequences for personal identity and societal norms. By addressing these challenges thoughtfully and transparently, we can harness the potential of memory research while safeguarding the values that underpin our understanding of human experience and dignity.

EXPERIMENT FIFTY TWO

WEATHER MODIFICATION EXPERIMENTS: CONTROLLING THE SKIES

Weather modification experiments aim to alter atmospheric conditions to achieve desired weather outcomes. These experiments, often referred to as geoengineering or climate engineering, explore various techniques to influence weather patterns, precipitation, and temperature. While the idea of controlling the weather has captured public imagination for decades, the practice involves complex science and carries significant ethical and environmental implications.

Historical Context and Techniques:

- Cloud Seeding: One of the most well-known weather modification techniques, cloud seeding involves dispersing substances such as silver iodide or sodium chloride into the atmosphere to enhance precipitation. The goal is to stimulate cloud condensation and increase rainfall or snowfall. Cloud seeding has been used in various regions to address water shortages, improve agricultural yields, and mitigate droughts.

- Weather Modification Research: Research into weather modification dates back to the mid-20th century, with experiments conducted by governments and research institutions. The U.S. conducted extensive research under programs like Project Stormfury in the 1960s and 1970s, aiming to weaken hurricanes by seeding clouds. Other countries, including China and Russia, have also pursued weather modification programs to influence weather patterns.

- Hail Suppression: Techniques to suppress hail, such as the use of ground-based generators that disperse silver iodide, aim to reduce the size and frequency of hailstones. These methods are employed to protect crops, infrastructure, and property from hail damage.

- Atmospheric Engineering: More ambitious weather modification experiments include atmospheric engineering, which explores methods to alter large-scale climate systems. Techniques such as injecting aerosols into the stratosphere to reflect sunlight or enhancing carbon capture and storage are examples of geoengineering approaches aimed at mitigating global warming.

Impact:

Weather modification experiments have a range of impacts, both positive and negative, on the environment, society, and global climate systems:

1. Environmental Impact:

- Ecosystem Effects: Weather modification can have unintended consequences on ecosystems. Altered precipitation patterns, changes in temperature, and variations in atmospheric chemistry can affect plant and animal species, disrupt natural habitats, and impact biodiversity.

- Water Resources: Cloud seeding and other weather modification techniques can influence water resources by altering precipitation patterns. While these methods may address water shortages in specific areas, they can also lead to imbalances in regional water distribution and affect downstream water availability.

2. Social and Economic Impact:

- Agricultural Benefits: Weather modification has the potential to benefit agriculture by enhancing rainfall and reducing hail damage. Farmers and agricultural industries may use these techniques to improve crop yields and protect their investments.

- Economic Costs: The costs associated with weather modification programs, including research, implementation, and maintenance, can be significant. Additionally, the potential for unintended consequences may lead to financial losses for affected industries and communities.

3. Global Climate Implications:

- Climate Alteration: Large-scale weather modification, particularly atmospheric engineering, has the potential to impact global climate systems. The introduction of aerosols into the stratosphere, for example, could influence global temperature and precipitation patterns, with far-reaching effects on weather and climate.

- International Relations: The use of weather modification techniques raises questions about international cooperation and regulation. The potential for cross-border impacts and unintended consequences necessitates collaboration among nations to ensure responsible use and to address potential conflicts.

Effect:

The effects of weather modification experiments are complex and multifaceted, influencing scientific research, environmental policy, and public perception:

1. Scientific Advancements:

- Understanding Atmospheric Processes: Weather modification research contributes to our understanding of atmospheric processes and climate systems. Advances in meteorology and climate science enhance our ability to predict and respond to weather and climate events.

- Technological Innovation: Innovations in weather modification technology, such as more precise cloud seeding methods and improved atmospheric modeling, contribute to scientific progress and potential applications in various fields.

2. Ethical and Regulatory Considerations:

- Ethics of Intervention: The ethical implications of altering weather patterns and climate systems raise concerns about the responsibility of scientists and policymakers. Ensuring that weather modification techniques are used with caution and respect for the environment is essential.

- Regulation and Oversight: The need for regulation and oversight of weather modification experiments is crucial to prevent misuse and manage potential risks. International agreements and national regulations may be necessary to establish guidelines and standards for research and implementation.

3. Public Perception and Policy:

- Public Engagement: Weather modification experiments often generate public interest and debate. Effective communication and transparency are important for informing the public about the goals, risks, and benefits of weather modification technologies.

- Policy Development: The development of policies and regulations related to weather modification requires input from scientists, policymakers, and stakeholders. Balancing the potential benefits with the need to protect the environment and ensure equitable outcomes is a key consideration.

Conclusion:

Weather modification experiments represent a frontier in scientific research with the potential to address challenges related to water resources, agriculture, and climate change. However, these experiments also carry significant risks and ethical considerations that must be carefully managed.

As research in weather modification continues to evolve, it is essential to approach these technologies with a focus on responsible use, environmental protection, and global cooperation. By addressing the complexities and uncertainties associated with weather modification, we can work towards solutions that benefit society while safeguarding the integrity of our planet's climate systems.

EXPERIMENT FIFTY THREE

WEATHER MODIFICATION EXPERIMENTS: THE QUEST TO CONTROL CLIMATE

Introduction:

Weather modification experiments involve altering natural atmospheric conditions to achieve specific weather outcomes. These techniques, often termed geoengineering or climate engineering, aim to influence weather patterns, precipitation, and temperature. From cloud seeding to ambitious climate interventions, these experiments reflect humanity's desire to harness and control the forces of nature for various purposes, including agricultural improvement, disaster mitigation, and climate change management.

Historical Context and Techniques:

1. Cloud Seeding:

 - Technique: Cloud seeding involves dispersing substances such as silver iodide, sodium chloride, or potassium iodide into the atmosphere to encourage cloud condensation and precipitation. The goal is to enhance rainfall or snowfall in targeted areas.

- History: The concept of cloud seeding dates back to the 1940s, with early experiments conducted by scientists like Vincent Schaefer and Irving Langmuir. The technique has been used in various regions worldwide to address water shortages, increase agricultural yields, and manage drought conditions.

2. Weather Modification Research:

- Project Stormfury: Initiated in the 1960s by the U.S. government, Project Stormfury aimed to weaken hurricanes by seeding clouds with silver iodide. While the project achieved mixed results, it represented a significant effort to influence large-scale weather systems.

- International Efforts: Countries like China, Russia, and India have also engaged in weather modification research. China's "weather modification" program, for example, aims to prevent hail and enhance rainfall, while Russia has used cloud seeding to address drought conditions.

3. Hail Suppression:

- Technique: Hail suppression involves using ground-based generators to disperse substances like silver iodide into the atmosphere to reduce the formation of large hailstones. This method aims to protect crops, infrastructure, and property from hail damage.

- Applications: Hail suppression programs have been implemented in agricultural regions prone to severe hailstorms, such as parts of the United States, Canada, and Australia.

4. Atmospheric Engineering:

- Solar Radiation Management: This approach includes techniques like injecting aerosols into the stratosphere to reflect sunlight and cool the Earth's surface. While this method could theoretically mitigate global warming, it carries significant risks and uncertainties.

- Carbon Capture and Storage: Technologies designed to capture and store carbon dioxide from the atmosphere could potentially reduce greenhouse gas concentrations and influence climate patterns. This approach aims to address climate change by removing CO_2 from the atmosphere.

Impact:

1. Environmental Impact:

- Ecosystem Disruption: Weather modification can lead to unintended consequences on ecosystems. Changes in precipitation patterns, temperature, and atmospheric chemistry can disrupt natural habitats, affect biodiversity, and alter ecosystem dynamics.

- Water Resources: Techniques like cloud seeding can influence regional water resources by altering precipitation patterns. While these methods may address local water shortages, they can also create imbalances in water distribution and impact downstream water availability.

2. Social and Economic Impact:

- Agricultural Benefits: Weather modification has the potential to benefit agriculture by enhancing rainfall and reducing hail damage. Farmers and agricultural industries may use these techniques to improve crop yields and protect their investments.

- Economic Costs: The financial costs of weather modification programs, including research, implementation, and maintenance, can be substantial. Additionally, unintended consequences may lead to economic losses for affected industries and communities.

3. Global Climate Implications:

- Climate Alteration: Large-scale weather modification, particularly solar radiation management and carbon capture, could impact global climate systems. The introduction of aerosols or changes in greenhouse gas concentrations may influence temperature, precipitation, and other climate variables.

- International Relations: The use of weather modification techniques raises concerns about international cooperation and regulation. Cross-border impacts and potential conflicts necessitate collaborative efforts to manage risks and ensure responsible use.

Effect:

1. Scientific Advancements:

- Understanding Weather Systems: Weather modification research contributes to our understanding of atmospheric processes and climate systems. Advances in meteorology and climate science enhance our ability to predict and respond to weather and climate events.

- Technological Innovation: Innovations in weather modification technology, such as improved cloud seeding methods and advanced atmospheric modeling, contribute to scientific progress and potential applications in various fields.

2. Ethical and Regulatory Considerations:

- Ethics of Intervention: The ethical implications of altering weather patterns and climate systems raise concerns about responsibility and the potential for unintended consequences. Responsible use of weather modification technologies requires careful consideration of environmental and societal impacts.

- Regulation and Oversight: Establishing regulations and oversight for weather modification experiments is essential to prevent misuse and manage risks. International agreements and national policies may be necessary to ensure safe and equitable practices.

3. Public Perception and Policy:

- Public Engagement: Weather modification experiments often generate public interest and debate. Effective communication and transparency are important for informing the public about the goals, risks, and benefits of these technologies.

- Policy Development: Developing policies and regulations related to weather modification requires input from scientists, policymakers, and stakeholders. Balancing potential benefits with environmental protection and ethical considerations is crucial.

Conclusion:

Weather modification experiments represent a complex and evolving field with the potential to address pressing challenges related to water resources, agriculture, and climate change. While these experiments offer promising solutions, they also carry significant risks and ethical considerations that must be carefully managed.

As research in weather modification continues to advance, it is essential to approach these technologies with a focus on responsible use, environmental stewardship, and global cooperation. By addressing the complexities and uncertainties associated with weather modification, we can work towards solutions that benefit society while safeguarding the integrity of our planet's climate systems.

EXPERIMENT FIFTY FOUR

PLASTICITY OF THE BRAIN EXPERIMENTS: UNCOVERING THE BRAIN'S CAPACITY FOR CHANGE

Introduction:

Plasticity of the brain, or neuroplasticity, refers to the brain's ability to reorganize itself by forming new neural connections throughout life. This remarkable adaptability allows the brain to adjust in response to learning, experience, injury, or changes in the environment. Experiments exploring neuroplasticity have provided significant insights into brain function, recovery from brain injuries, and the potential for cognitive enhancement.

Historical Context and Techniques:

1. Early Discoveries:

 - Paul Broca and Localization: In the 19th century, neurologist Paul Broca identified areas of the brain associated with language processing through studies of patients with aphasia. This early work suggested that specific brain functions were localized to certain regions, laying the groundwork for understanding brain plasticity.

- Karl Lashley and Lesion Studies: Karl Lashley's research in the early 20th century involved removing parts of the cerebral cortex in rats to study the effects on learning and memory. Lashley's work revealed that while specific brain areas contributed to certain functions, learning and memory were distributed across the brain, suggesting a degree of plasticity.

2. Contemporary Experiments:

- Animal Models: Studies using animal models, such as rats and monkeys, have explored neuroplasticity by examining how the brain reorganizes following injury or sensory deprivation. For example, research on sensory-motor cortex reorganization has demonstrated that the brain can adapt by reallocating resources to different areas following the loss of sensory input or motor function.

- Human Studies: Functional magnetic resonance imaging (fMRI) and electroencephalography (EEG) have been used to investigate neuroplasticity in humans. These techniques allow researchers to observe changes in brain activity and connectivity in response to various stimuli, learning tasks, and rehabilitation interventions.

3. Experimental Techniques:

- Constraint-Induced Movement Therapy (CIMT): CIMT is a rehabilitation technique used for stroke patients that involves restricting the use of the unaffected limb and encouraging the use of the affected limb. Research on CIMT has shown that it can promote neuroplastic changes in the brain and improve motor function.

- Enriched Environment Studies: Experiments involving enriched environments, where animals are provided with complex stimuli and social interactions, have demonstrated that such conditions can enhance brain plasticity and cognitive function. These studies highlight the impact of environmental factors on neuroplasticity.

Impact:

1. Clinical Implications:

- Stroke Rehabilitation: Research on neuroplasticity has led to advancements in stroke rehabilitation, including therapies that harness the brain's ability to reorganize and recover lost functions. Techniques such as CIMT and other motor rehabilitation approaches are designed to stimulate neuroplastic changes and improve patient outcomes.

- Neurodevelopmental Disorders: Understanding neuroplasticity has implications for treating neurodevelopmental disorders such as autism and dyslexia. Early interventions and therapies that leverage the brain's plasticity may enhance cognitive and behavioral outcomes for individuals with these conditions.

2. Cognitive Enhancement:

- Learning and Memory: Experiments on neuroplasticity have revealed that the brain's capacity for change can be harnessed to enhance learning and memory. Cognitive training and educational programs that stimulate neuroplasticity can improve cognitive function and support lifelong learning.

- Mental Health: Research into neuroplasticity has implications for mental health treatment. Techniques such as neurofeedback and cognitive-behavioral therapy (CBT) aim to promote positive changes in brain function and alleviate symptoms of mental health conditions.

3. Ethical and Social Considerations:

- Neuroenhancement: The potential for using neuroplasticity to enhance cognitive function raises ethical questions about the boundaries of cognitive enhancement. Ensuring that such interventions are used responsibly and equitably is important for addressing potential societal impacts.

- Personal Identity: Changes in brain function and connectivity as a result of neuroplasticity may influence personal identity and self-perception. Understanding the implications of these changes for individuals and society is crucial.

Effect:

1. Scientific Advancements:

- Understanding Brain Function: Research on neuroplasticity has deepened our understanding of brain function and the mechanisms underlying learning, memory, and recovery. This knowledge has led to new insights into how the brain adapts to various conditions and challenges.

- Development of Therapies: Advances in neuroplasticity research have led to the development of novel therapies and interventions for brain injuries, neurological disorders, and cognitive enhancement. These therapies offer promising approaches for improving quality of life and functional outcomes.

2. Ethical and Regulatory Considerations:

- Ethics of Cognitive Enhancement: The use of neuroplasticity for cognitive enhancement raises ethical questions about fairness, accessibility, and the potential for coercion. Ensuring that interventions are used ethically and equitably is essential for addressing these concerns.

- Regulation of Therapies: The development and application of therapies based on neuroplasticity require careful regulation to ensure safety and efficacy. Establishing guidelines and standards for research and clinical practice is important for protecting individuals and promoting responsible use.

3. Public Perception and Policy:

- Public Awareness: Increasing public awareness of neuroplasticity and its implications can foster understanding and informed decision-making. Effective communication about the benefits and limitations of neuroplasticity research is important for engaging the public and stakeholders.

- Policy Development: Policymakers play a role in shaping the direction of neuroplasticity research and ensuring that interventions are used responsibly. Collaboration between scientists, policymakers, and the public is essential for developing policies that balance innovation with ethical considerations.

Conclusion:

Experiments on the plasticity of the brain reveal the remarkable ability of the brain to adapt and reorganize itself in response to various factors. This research has profound implications for clinical practice, cognitive enhancement, and our understanding of brain function.

As we continue to explore the potential of neuroplasticity, it is essential to approach this field with a focus on ethical considerations, responsible use, and the development of effective therapies. By advancing our knowledge of brain plasticity and its applications, we can unlock new possibilities for improving health, learning, and quality of life while addressing the challenges and implications associated with these discoveries.

EXPERIMENT FIFTY FIVE

PSYCHIC PHENOMENA RESEARCH: EXPLORING THE UNCHARTED REALM OF THE MIND

Introduction:

Psychic phenomena research delves into the study of abilities and experiences that purportedly transcend the known laws of physics and conventional understanding of the human mind. This field, often associated with parapsychology, investigates phenomena such as telepathy, precognition, clairvoyance, and psychokinesis. Despite skepticism and controversy, psychic phenomena research continues to attract interest from both scientists and enthusiasts seeking to understand the limits of human consciousness and potential.

Historical Context and Techniques:

1. Early Investigations:

- Spiritualism and Mediumship: The 19th century saw the rise of Spiritualism, a movement that promoted communication with the deceased through mediums. Figures like Edgar Cayce and the Fox Sisters became prominent in the study of psychic phenomena, influencing early research and public interest.

- J.B. Rhine and the Birth of Parapsychology: In the 1930s, psychologist J.B. Rhine conducted systematic experiments at Duke University to investigate extrasensory perception (ESP) and psychokinesis. Rhine's work, including experiments with Zener cards, aimed to provide empirical evidence for psychic abilities and laid the groundwork for modern parapsychology.

2. Contemporary Research:

- ESP and Remote Viewing: Research into extrasensory perception (ESP) explores phenomena such as telepathy (mind-to-mind communication), clairvoyance (perceiving distant or unseen events), and precognition (predicting future events). Remote viewing, a technique where individuals attempt to describe or draw distant locations, has been studied under controlled conditions.

- Psychokinesis: Experiments in psychokinesis, or telekinesis, investigate the ability to influence physical objects with the mind. Research in this area often involves laboratory settings where participants attempt to affect random number generators or move objects using mental concentration.

- Scientific Investigations: Organizations like the Rhine Research Center and the Institute of Noetic Sciences conduct research on psychic phenomena using rigorous methodologies. Studies often involve statistical analysis, double-blind protocols, and replication efforts to ensure scientific credibility.

3. Experimental Techniques:

- Double-Blind Protocols: To minimize bias and ensure the reliability of results, many experiments on psychic phenomena use double-blind protocols where neither the participant nor the experimenter knows the conditions of the test. This approach helps to control for psychological and environmental factors that could influence outcomes.

- Controlled Laboratory Settings: Researchers conduct experiments in controlled environments to isolate variables and test specific hypotheses related to psychic phenomena. These settings may include random number generators, electromagnetic fields, and sensory deprivation chambers.

Impact:

1. Scientific and Academic Impact:

- Skepticism and Criticism: Psychic phenomena research has faced significant skepticism from the scientific community. Critics argue that many results are not reproducible or are attributed to chance, methodological flaws, or experimenter bias. This skepticism has led to ongoing debates about the validity and reliability of psychic phenomena research.

- Scientific Inquiry: Despite criticism, psychic phenomena research has contributed to discussions about the nature of consciousness and the limits of human perception. The field has prompted investigations into the potential intersections between psychology, neuroscience, and quantum physics.

2. Cultural and Societal Impact:

- Public Interest: Psychic phenomena continue to captivate public imagination through books, media, and popular culture. Stories of psychic experiences, paranormal encounters, and supernatural abilities influence cultural narratives and societal beliefs.

- Alternative Therapies: Some proponents of psychic phenomena integrate their findings into alternative therapies and healing practices. Techniques such as energy healing, aura reading, and intuitive counseling are influenced by beliefs in psychic abilities and their potential applications.

3. Ethical and Regulatory Considerations:

- Ethics of Research: Ethical considerations in psychic phenomena research include ensuring informed consent, avoiding exploitation of vulnerable individuals, and maintaining scientific integrity. Researchers must navigate these ethical concerns while conducting experiments and presenting findings.

- Regulation and Oversight: The lack of standardization and regulation in psychic phenomena research presents challenges for ensuring the credibility and reproducibility of results. Establishing guidelines and oversight mechanisms may help address these issues and promote responsible research practices.

Effect:

1. Scientific Advancements:

- Exploration of Consciousness: Research into psychic phenomena has spurred exploration into the nature of consciousness and its potential capabilities. Investigations into ESP, psychokinesis, and related phenomena challenge our understanding of the mind and its interactions with the physical world.

- Innovative Techniques: Advances in experimental techniques and methodologies contribute to the scientific study of psychic phenomena. Improved protocols, statistical analysis, and interdisciplinary approaches enhance our ability to investigate and interpret these phenomena.

2. Public Perception and Policy:

- Public Engagement: Engaging the public in discussions about psychic phenomena and scientific research can foster curiosity and critical thinking. Transparent communication about the goals, methods, and limitations of research is essential for informed public discourse.

- Policy Development: Policymakers may address issues related to psychic phenomena research through funding decisions, regulatory frameworks, and public education initiatives. Balancing scientific inquiry with ethical considerations is important for shaping policy and research priorities.

3. Cultural Influence:

- Influence on Beliefs: Psychic phenomena research influences cultural beliefs and practices related to the supernatural and the unknown. The ongoing exploration of these phenomena contributes to the broader conversation about the nature of reality and human potential.

Conclusion:

Psychic phenomena research explores the boundaries of human consciousness and the potential for abilities that extend beyond conventional understanding. While the field faces skepticism and controversy, it continues to provoke curiosity and debate about the nature of the mind and its interactions with the world.

As research into psychic phenomena evolves, it is essential to approach the field with rigorous scientific inquiry, ethical considerations, and open-minded exploration. By advancing our understanding of these phenomena, we can contribute to a deeper comprehension of consciousness and its potential while addressing the challenges and implications associated with these investigations.

EXPERIMENT FIFTY SIX

GENE DRIVE TECHNOLOGY EXPERIMENTS: A NEW FRONTIER IN GENETIC ENGINEERING

Introduction:

Gene drive technology represents a groundbreaking advancement in genetic engineering with the potential to alter entire populations of organisms by spreading specific genetic modifications rapidly through breeding. This technology leverages the principle of genetic inheritance to ensure that a desired genetic trait is passed on with high efficiency, potentially revolutionizing fields such as pest control, conservation, and disease eradication.

Historical Context and Techniques:

1. Origins and Development:

  - Genetic Inheritance: The concept of gene drive builds on the fundamental principles of genetic inheritance first described by Gregor Mendel in the 19th century.

Traditional Mendelian inheritance typically results in a 50% chance of passing a genetic trait to offspring. Gene drives, however, skew this probability to increase the likelihood of the trait being inherited.

- Early Research: The idea of manipulating genetic inheritance to drive specific traits became more feasible with advancements in molecular biology and genetic engineering technologies. Initial research into gene drives focused on theoretical models and basic experiments in model organisms.

2. Contemporary Techniques:

- CRISPR-Cas9 Gene Editing: The development of CRISPR-Cas9 technology has significantly advanced gene drive research. CRISPR-Cas9 allows for precise and efficient editing of the genome, making it possible to create gene drives that target specific genes or traits. Researchers use CRISPR-Cas9 to introduce gene drives into the genomes of organisms, such as mosquitoes, to influence their reproduction and spread genetic modifications.

- Self-Replicating Gene Drives: Gene drive systems are designed to be self-replicating, meaning that the genetic modification is passed on to nearly all offspring, rather than just 50%. This rapid spread can potentially alter entire populations in a relatively short period.

3. Experimental Techniques:

- Model Organisms: Experiments often begin with model organisms, such as fruit flies or laboratory mice, to study the effects of gene drives in a controlled environment. Researchers observe how the gene drive spreads through the population and assess its impact on reproduction and survival.

- Field Trials: Limited field trials have been conducted to test gene drives in natural environments. For example, gene drives have been tested in mosquito populations to control the spread of diseases like malaria. These trials aim to evaluate the effectiveness and safety of gene drives before wider application.

Impact:

1. Environmental and Ecological Impact:

- Pest Control: One of the primary applications of gene drive technology is in pest control. By introducing genetic modifications that reduce the population of harmful pests, such as mosquitoes carrying malaria, gene drives have the potential to significantly impact public health and reduce the burden of vector-borne diseases.

- Conservation Efforts: Gene drives could also be used to support conservation efforts by controlling invasive species or helping endangered species recover. For example, gene drives could be used to eliminate invasive rodents on island ecosystems or enhance the genetic diversity of endangered species.

2. Ethical and Safety Considerations:

- Unintended Consequences: The potential for unintended ecological consequences is a significant concern. Gene drives could have unforeseen effects on ecosystems, including non-target species or interactions within the food web. Comprehensive risk assessments and monitoring are essential to mitigate these risks.

- Ethical Concerns: The manipulation of entire populations raises ethical questions about human intervention in nature. Decisions about deploying gene drives require careful consideration of potential benefits, risks, and ethical implications. Public engagement and transparent decision-making processes are crucial for addressing these concerns.

3. Regulatory and Policy Considerations:

- Regulation of Gene Drives: The regulation of gene drive technology varies by country and jurisdiction. Regulatory frameworks must address the safety, efficacy, and environmental impact of gene drives. International collaboration and guidelines may be necessary to ensure responsible use and prevent potential misuse.

- Policy Development: Policymakers must consider the potential benefits and risks associated with gene drives when developing policies and regulations. Balancing innovation with safety and ethical considerations is essential for guiding the responsible application of gene drive technology.

Effect:

1. Scientific Advancements:

- Advances in Genetic Engineering: Gene drive technology represents a major advancement in genetic engineering, enabling researchers to make large-scale changes to populations. This technology has the potential to accelerate scientific discoveries and applications in genetics and genomics.

- New Research Opportunities: The development of gene drive technology opens up new avenues for research into genetic mechanisms, population dynamics, and ecological interactions. Researchers can explore novel applications and refine techniques to improve effectiveness and safety.

2. Public Perception and Policy:

- Public Engagement: Public perception of gene drive technology varies, with some people expressing enthusiasm for its potential benefits and others raising concerns about its risks. Effective communication and public engagement are important for addressing concerns and building trust.

- Policy and Regulation: The development of policies and regulations related to gene drives requires input from scientists, policymakers, ethicists, and the public. Ensuring that regulatory frameworks are robust and adaptable is essential for managing the risks and benefits of gene drive technology.

3. Ethical and Social Impact:

- Ethical Implications: The use of gene drive technology raises ethical questions about the extent to which humans should intervene in natural processes. Considerations include the potential for irreversible changes and the impact on biodiversity and ecosystems.

- Social Impact: The deployment of gene drives has the potential to influence social and economic factors, such as public health outcomes and conservation efforts. Understanding these impacts and addressing them responsibly is crucial for maximizing the benefits of gene drive technology.

Conclusion:

Gene drive technology represents a powerful tool with the potential to address significant challenges in pest control, disease management, and conservation. While the technology offers promising benefits, it also presents substantial ethical, environmental, and regulatory challenges.

As research and development in gene drive technology continue to advance, it is essential to approach the field with a focus on rigorous scientific inquiry, ethical considerations, and responsible application. By addressing the complexities and potential impacts of gene drives, we can harness their potential to achieve positive outcomes while mitigating risks and ensuring the responsible use of this transformative technology.

EXPERIMENT FIFTY SEVEN

INTERSTELLAR COMMUNICATION EXPERIMENTS: BRIDGING THE COSMIC DIVIDE

Introduction:

Interstellar communication experiments explore the possibilities of transmitting and receiving messages across the vast distances between stars. These experiments seek to understand how humanity might establish contact with extraterrestrial civilizations or communicate across cosmic distances. The challenges of interstellar communication include the sheer scale of space, the limitations of current technology, and the need for novel approaches to overcome these barriers.

Historical Context and Techniques:

1. Early Efforts:

   - Radio Telescopes and SETI: The Search for Extraterrestrial Intelligence (SETI) began in the 1960s with the use of radio telescopes to scan for signals from extraterrestrial civilizations. Early experiments, such as the search for signals from the nearest stars, aimed to detect any artificial signals that might indicate the presence of intelligent life.

- Pioneer and Voyager Probes: In the 1970s, NASA's Pioneer and Voyager spacecraft carried messages intended for potential extraterrestrial civilizations. These messages included plaques and gold records with information about Earth and humanity, designed to be readable by advanced extraterrestrial beings.

2. Contemporary Techniques:

- High-Power Radio Transmission: Modern experiments often involve the use of high-power radio transmitters to send messages into space. The aim is to broadcast signals that might be detected by extraterrestrial civilizations. For example, the Arecibo message, transmitted in 1974, was a binary-encoded message aimed at the M13 globular cluster.

- Laser Communication: Researchers are exploring the use of lasers for interstellar communication due to their potential for high data transfer rates and precise targeting. Projects such as the Breakthrough Initiatives' Starshot program aim to develop laser-propelled spacecraft capable of reaching nearby stars and sending data back to Earth.

3. Experimental Techniques:

- Message Design: Designing messages for interstellar communication involves encoding information in a format that could be understood by extraterrestrial intelligences. This may include mathematical and scientific data, representations of human culture, or instructions for decoding the message.

- Signal Detection: Experiments often focus on developing techniques to detect faint signals from distant stars. This includes improving the sensitivity of radio telescopes, developing advanced signal processing algorithms, and using large-scale arrays of telescopes to enhance detection capabilities.

Impact:

1. Scientific and Technological Impact:

- Advancements in Technology: Interstellar communication experiments drive advancements in technology, such as improvements in radio and laser technology, data encoding and decoding techniques, and signal processing methods. These advancements have broader applications in telecommunications and space exploration.

- Understanding of Extraterrestrial Life: Successful detection of signals or communication with extraterrestrial civilizations would provide profound insights into the existence and nature of extraterrestrial life. This could revolutionize our understanding of the universe and our place within it.

2. Cultural and Societal Impact:

-   Public Interest: Interstellar communication experiments capture the imagination of the public and inspire interest in space exploration and the search for extraterrestrial life. They raise questions about humanity's role in the universe and the potential for contact with other intelligent beings.

- Ethical Considerations: The potential discovery of extraterrestrial civilizations raises ethical questions about how humanity should respond. Considerations include the implications for global society, the potential impact on human culture, and the responsibilities associated with establishing contact.

3. Regulatory and Policy Considerations:

-   International Collaboration: Interstellar communication efforts often involve international collaboration and coordination. Developing agreements and protocols for communication and response to potential signals requires cooperation among nations and space agencies.

- Policy Development: Policymakers must consider the implications of interstellar communication and the potential consequences of discovering extraterrestrial signals. Policies may address issues such as data sharing, international cooperation, and the management of potential contacts.

Effect:

1. Scientific Advancements:

- Exploration of Communication Technologies: Interstellar communication experiments push the boundaries of communication technologies, leading to innovations in radio, laser, and data transmission techniques. These advancements contribute to scientific research and practical applications in various fields.

- New Knowledge: Research into interstellar communication expands our knowledge of the cosmos and the potential for life beyond Earth. It fosters a deeper understanding of the universe and our ability to explore and communicate across vast distances.

2. Public Perception and Policy:

- Inspiration and Curiosity: The pursuit of interstellar communication inspires curiosity and wonder about the universe. It encourages scientific exploration and promotes public interest in space and astronomy.

- Global Coordination: Effective communication and collaboration on interstellar communication projects require global coordination. Policies and agreements developed through these efforts contribute to international cooperation and shared goals in space exploration.

3. Ethical and Social Impact:

- Impact on Humanity: The potential discovery of extraterrestrial civilizations or successful interstellar communication could have profound effects on human society. It may challenge existing beliefs, influence cultural narratives, and prompt discussions about our place in the universe.

- Responsibility and Preparedness: Preparing for the possibility of contact with extraterrestrial civilizations involves ethical considerations and a sense of responsibility. Ensuring that humanity is prepared for such an eventuality requires thoughtful planning and international dialogue.

Conclusion:

Interstellar communication experiments represent a frontier in scientific research and technological development, seeking to bridge the vast distances between stars and establish contact with potential extraterrestrial civilizations. While the challenges are immense, the pursuit of interstellar communication drives technological innovation, inspires public interest, and deepens our understanding of the universe.

As research progresses, it is essential to approach interstellar communication with a focus on scientific rigor, ethical considerations, and international collaboration. By advancing our capabilities and preparing for potential outcomes, we can explore the possibilities of interstellar communication and its impact on humanity and our place in the cosmos.

EXPERIMENT FIFTY EIGHT

PSYCHOSURGERY EXPERIMENTS: UNRAVELING THE MIND THROUGH NEUROSURGICAL INTERVENTIONS

Introduction:

Psychosurgery refers to a range of surgical interventions aimed at altering brain function to treat severe mental health conditions. The field emerged in the early 20th century with the goal of addressing psychiatric disorders through direct manipulation of the brain. While early psychosurgery techniques, such as lobotomy, had significant and often controversial impacts, modern advancements have shifted towards more targeted and refined approaches. The history of psychosurgery is marked by both pioneering efforts and ethical controversies, reflecting its evolving role in mental health treatment.

Historical Context and Techniques:

1. Early Psychosurgery:

- Lobotomy: Developed by Portuguese neurologist António Egas Moniz in the 1930s, lobotomy (or leucotomy) involved severing connections in the prefrontal cortex to treat severe psychiatric disorders. Moniz's work earned him the Nobel Prize in Physiology or Medicine in 1949. The procedure was popularized in the United States by neurosurgeon Walter Freeman, leading to thousands of lobotomies performed in the mid-20th century.

- Early Outcomes and Controversies: While some patients reported improvements in symptoms, lobotomy often led to severe side effects, including personality changes, cognitive impairment, and emotional blunting. The procedure faced significant ethical and medical criticism, particularly regarding its impact on patients' quality of life and the lack of informed consent.

2. Contemporary Techniques:

- Deep Brain Stimulation (DBS): Modern psychosurgery has evolved to include more refined techniques, such as deep brain stimulation. DBS involves implanting electrodes in specific brain regions to modulate neural activity. It is used to treat conditions such as Parkinson's disease, dystonia, and obsessive-compulsive disorder (OCD). DBS is adjustable and reversible, offering a less invasive alternative to earlier psychosurgical methods.

- Lesioning Techniques: Advances in imaging technologies, such as MRI and PET scans, have enabled more precise lesioning techniques. These procedures involve creating controlled lesions in targeted brain areas to alleviate symptoms of certain psychiatric disorders. Unlike lobotomy, modern lesioning aims to minimize collateral damage and improve outcomes.

3. Experimental Techniques:

- Neuroimaging and Mapping: Researchers use advanced neuroimaging techniques to map brain activity and identify areas associated with psychiatric symptoms. This information guides the development of targeted interventions and helps refine psychosurgery procedures.

- Clinical Trials: New psychosurgical techniques are often tested through clinical trials, which assess their safety, efficacy, and long-term effects. Trials involve rigorous protocols, including pre- and post-surgical assessments, to evaluate outcomes and monitor for adverse effects.

Impact:

1. Scientific and Medical Impact:

- Advancements in Neuroscience: Psychosurgery experiments have contributed to our understanding of brain function and the neural basis of psychiatric disorders. Techniques like DBS and targeted lesioning have provided insights into the role of specific brain regions in mental health conditions.

- Improved Treatments: Modern psychosurgery techniques offer more effective and less invasive treatments for conditions that do not respond well to traditional therapies. These advancements provide new options for patients with severe, treatment-resistant psychiatric disorders.

2. Ethical and Social Impact:

- Ethical Concerns: Early psychosurgery techniques, such as lobotomy, raised significant ethical concerns regarding patient consent, safety, and the appropriateness of surgical interventions for mental health conditions. The history of psychosurgery underscores the importance of ethical considerations in medical research and treatment.

- Stigma and Perception: Psychosurgery, particularly lobotomy, has been associated with stigma and negative perceptions of psychiatric treatments. Modern psychosurgery techniques aim to address these concerns by emphasizing patient safety, informed consent, and evidence-based practices.

3. Regulatory and Policy Considerations:

- Regulation and Oversight: The development and application of psychosurgery techniques are subject to regulatory oversight and ethical guidelines. Ensuring that procedures are conducted safely and with appropriate informed consent is crucial for maintaining patient rights and ensuring the integrity of medical practices.

- Policy Development: Policymakers must address issues related to the use of psychosurgery, including ethical considerations, patient safety, and access to treatment. Developing policies that balance innovation with ethical considerations is essential for advancing the field responsibly.

Effect:

1. Scientific Advancements:

- Understanding Brain Function: Psychosurgery experiments have advanced our knowledge of brain function and its relationship to mental health. Techniques like DBS and neuroimaging have provided valuable insights into the neural mechanisms underlying psychiatric disorders.

- Innovative Treatments: Modern psychosurgery techniques offer innovative treatments for severe mental health conditions. These advancements improve treatment options for patients who have not responded to conventional therapies.

2. Public Perception and Policy:

- Informed Public Discourse: The history of psychosurgery and its evolving techniques influence public perceptions of psychiatric treatments. Transparent communication about the safety, efficacy, and ethical considerations of psychosurgery helps inform public discourse and build trust in medical practices.

- Regulatory Frameworks: Effective regulation and oversight ensure that psychosurgery techniques are used responsibly and ethically. Policymakers must develop frameworks that address the complexities of psychosurgery while promoting innovation and patient safety.

3. Ethical and Social Impact:

- Ethical Reflection: The history of psychosurgery highlights the need for ongoing ethical reflection in medical research and treatment. Ensuring that patients' rights are respected and that interventions are justified and evidence-based is crucial for maintaining ethical standards in psychosurgery.

- Impact on Patient Lives: Modern psychosurgery techniques aim to improve the quality of life for patients with severe psychiatric disorders. By providing effective treatments and minimizing risks, these techniques have the potential to positively impact patient outcomes and well-being.

Conclusion:

Psychosurgery experiments represent a complex and evolving field that has contributed to our understanding of brain function and the treatment of severe mental health conditions. While early techniques like lobotomy faced significant ethical and medical challenges, contemporary approaches such as deep brain stimulation and targeted lesioning offer promising advancements in psychosurgery.

As research and development in psychosurgery continue, it is essential to approach the field with a focus on scientific rigor, ethical considerations, and patient safety. By addressing the complexities and potential impacts of psychosurgery, we can advance the field responsibly and enhance treatment options for individuals with challenging psychiatric disorders.

EXPERIMENT FIFTY NINE

VIRTUAL REALITY (VR) EXPERIMENTS: EXPLORING NEW REALMS OF PERCEPTION AND INTERACTION

Introduction:

Virtual Reality (VR) experiments involve the use of immersive technology to create simulated environments where users can interact, explore, and experience virtual worlds. VR technology has evolved rapidly, offering innovative applications in various fields including psychology, medicine, education, and entertainment. The impact of VR experiments extends beyond mere simulation, influencing how we understand perception, behavior, and interaction in both virtual and real-world contexts.

Historical Context and Techniques:

1. Early Developments:

 - The Sensorama (1962): One of the earliest VR devices, the Sensorama, was developed by Morton Heilig. It was designed to provide a multisensory experience with visual, auditory, and haptic feedback, laying the groundwork for future VR technology.

- The VPL DataGlove (1980s): In the 1980s, VPL Research developed the DataGlove, an early VR interface that allowed users to interact with virtual objects using hand gestures. This marked a significant step in the development of interactive VR systems.

2. Contemporary Techniques:

- Head-Mounted Displays (HMDs): Modern VR systems often use head-mounted displays, such as the Oculus Rift, HTC Vive, and PlayStation VR. These devices provide immersive visual and auditory experiences by tracking head movements and displaying stereoscopic images.

- Motion Tracking: Advanced motion tracking technologies, including sensors and cameras, are used to capture users' movements and translate them into the virtual environment. This enhances the sense of presence and interaction within the VR experience.

- Haptic Feedback: Haptic feedback devices, such as VR gloves and vests, provide tactile sensations to simulate touch and interaction. These devices contribute to the realism of the virtual experience by mimicking physical sensations.

3. Experimental Techniques:

- Psychological Studies: VR experiments are used to study various psychological phenomena, including perception, memory, and spatial awareness. Researchers can create controlled virtual environments to investigate how individuals respond to different stimuli and scenarios.

- Medical Applications: VR technology is applied in medical research and therapy, including pain management, rehabilitation, and exposure therapy. VR simulations can help patients practice physical movements, manage pain, or confront phobias in a controlled setting.

- Educational and Training Simulations: VR experiments are used to develop educational and training simulations for various fields, such as aviation, medicine, and emergency response. These simulations provide realistic scenarios for learners to practice skills and decision-making.

Impact:

1. Scientific and Technological Impact:

- Advancements in VR Technology: VR experiments drive advancements in technology, including improvements in display resolution, motion tracking accuracy, and haptic feedback. These developments enhance the quality and realism of VR experiences.

- Understanding Human Perception: VR experiments contribute to our understanding of human perception and cognition. By immersing users in simulated environments, researchers can study how people process sensory information and interact with virtual objects.

2. Medical and Therapeutic Impact:

- Therapeutic Applications: VR technology has shown promise in therapeutic applications, such as treating PTSD, anxiety disorders, and phobias. By providing controlled and immersive environments, VR can help patients confront and manage their symptoms in a safe and controlled manner.

- Rehabilitation and Pain Management: VR-based rehabilitation programs assist patients in recovering physical functions and managing pain. Virtual exercises and simulations can motivate patients and provide a more engaging and effective rehabilitation experience.

3. Educational and Training Impact:

- Enhanced Learning Experiences: VR experiments offer immersive learning experiences that can improve engagement and retention. Educational simulations enable students to explore complex concepts and scenarios in a hands-on and interactive manner.

- Effective Training Tools: VR simulations provide realistic training environments for professionals in fields such as aviation, medicine, and emergency response. Trainees can practice skills and decision-making without the risks associated with real-world training.

4. Ethical and Social Impact:

- Privacy and Data Security: As VR technology collects data on users' movements and interactions, concerns about privacy and data security arise. Ensuring that user data is protected and used responsibly is crucial for maintaining trust in VR systems.

- Impact on Behavior: The immersive nature of VR raises questions about its impact on behavior and social interactions. Researchers are exploring how prolonged exposure to virtual environments may influence users' attitudes, emotions, and social behavior.

Effect:

1. Scientific Advancements:

- Innovative Research Methods: VR experiments provide novel research methods for exploring psychological and cognitive phenomena. The ability to create and manipulate virtual environments offers new insights into how individuals perceive and interact with their surroundings.

- Technological Progress: Advances in VR technology drive progress in related fields, including computer graphics, motion tracking, and haptic feedback. These advancements contribute to the overall development of immersive technologies.

2. Public Perception and Policy:

- Public Awareness and Adoption: VR experiments influence public awareness and adoption of VR technology. As VR applications become more widespread, individuals and organizations are increasingly recognizing the potential benefits of immersive experiences.

- Regulation and Standards: Developing standards and regulations for VR technology is essential for ensuring safety, privacy, and ethical use. Policymakers and industry stakeholders must collaborate to address challenges and promote responsible practices.

3. Ethical and Social Impact:

- Ethical Considerations: The use of VR in research and therapy requires careful consideration of ethical issues, including informed consent, potential risks, and the impact on participants. Ethical guidelines help ensure that VR experiments are conducted responsibly and with respect for participants' well-being.

- Social and Cultural Impact: VR technology has the potential to influence social and cultural dynamics by shaping how people interact with virtual environments and with each other. Understanding these impacts helps guide the development and application of VR technology in a socially responsible manner.

Conclusion:

Virtual Reality experiments represent a dynamic and rapidly evolving field with significant implications for research, therapy, education, and entertainment. By providing immersive and interactive experiences, VR technology offers new opportunities for exploring human perception, behavior, and learning.

As VR technology continues to advance, it is essential to address the ethical, social, and technological challenges associated with its use. By focusing on responsible development and application, researchers and practitioners can harness the potential of VR to enhance

our understanding of the world and improve the quality
of life for individuals across various domains.

EXPERIMENT SIXTY

PAIN PERCEPTION EXPERIMENTS: UNDERSTANDING THE COMPLEXITIES OF PAIN

Introduction:

Pain perception experiments aim to explore and understand how individuals experience and respond to pain. These experiments investigate the physiological, psychological, and neurological mechanisms underlying pain perception, as well as the factors that influence how pain is experienced and managed. Pain perception research has significant implications for medical treatment, psychological interventions, and the development of new pain management strategies.

Historical Context and Techniques:

1. Early Research:

- Gate Control Theory (1965): Proposed by Melzack and Wall, the Gate Control Theory of pain suggests that pain perception is modulated by a "gate" in the spinal cord that controls the flow of pain signals to the brain. This theory shifted the understanding of pain from a purely physiological response to a complex interplay of sensory and cognitive factors.

- Experimental Pain Models: Early pain research often involved the use of experimental pain models, such as thermal, mechanical, or electrical stimuli, to study pain responses in controlled settings. These models provided insights into the basic mechanisms of pain perception.

2. Contemporary Techniques:

- Functional MRI (fMRI) and PET Scans: Modern pain research utilizes advanced neuroimaging techniques, such as fMRI and PET scans, to study brain activity associated with pain perception. These techniques allow researchers to visualize the brain regions activated during pain experiences and identify patterns of neural response.

- Pain Questionnaires and Self-Report Measures: Researchers use various questionnaires and self-report measures to assess pain intensity, quality, and impact on daily life. These tools help quantify subjective pain experiences and evaluate the effectiveness of pain management interventions.

- Experimental Pain Induction: Techniques for inducing pain in research settings include controlled heat, pressure, or electrical stimulation. These methods are used to create standardized pain experiences for studying pain mechanisms and testing interventions.

3. Experimental Techniques:

- Psychological Factors: Experiments often explore how psychological factors, such as attention, expectation, and emotion, influence pain perception. For example, research may investigate how distraction or cognitive strategies can alter pain experiences.

- Genetic and Molecular Research: Researchers are examining genetic and molecular factors that contribute to individual differences in pain perception. This includes studying genetic variations associated with pain sensitivity and the role of neurotransmitters and receptors in pain pathways.

- Pain Management Interventions: Experiments evaluate the effectiveness of various pain management strategies, including pharmacological treatments, behavioral therapies, and alternative therapies.

Researchers assess how these interventions impact pain perception and overall quality of life.

Impact:

1. Scientific and Medical Impact:

- Understanding Pain Mechanisms: Pain perception experiments provide valuable insights into the physiological and neurological mechanisms of pain. Understanding these mechanisms helps identify potential targets for pain management and treatment.

- Development of Pain Therapies: Research findings contribute to the development of new pain therapies and interventions. Advances in pain management can improve treatment options for individuals suffering from acute or chronic pain.

2. Psychological and Social Impact:

- Impact on Quality of Life: Pain perception research has implications for improving the quality of life for individuals with pain conditions. Effective pain management can enhance physical function, emotional well-being, and overall life satisfaction.

- Psychological Interventions: Understanding the role of psychological factors in pain perception can lead to the development of effective psychological interventions, such as cognitive-behavioral therapy (CBT), to help individuals cope with pain.

3. Regulatory and Policy Considerations:

- Pain Management Guidelines: Research findings inform the development of clinical guidelines and best practices for pain management. These guidelines help healthcare providers deliver evidence-based care and ensure that pain is managed effectively and ethically.

- Access to Pain Relief: Pain perception experiments highlight the need for access to appropriate pain relief options. Policymakers and healthcare systems must address barriers to accessing effective pain management treatments and support research into new therapies.

Effect:

1. Scientific Advancements:

- Advances in Pain Research: Pain perception experiments drive advances in the understanding of pain mechanisms and the development of new treatment approaches. This research contributes to the broader field of pain science and informs clinical practices.

- Improved Pain Management: Findings from pain perception research lead to improved pain management strategies and interventions. These advancements benefit individuals with acute and chronic pain conditions by providing more effective treatment options.

2. Public Perception and Policy:

- Awareness and Education: Research on pain perception raises awareness about the complexity of pain and the need for effective pain management. Public education about pain and its management can improve understanding and reduce stigma associated with pain conditions.

- Healthcare Policy: Pain perception research influences healthcare policy by highlighting the importance of effective pain management and access to treatments. Policymakers may use research findings to advocate for better pain management practices and resources.

3. Ethical and Social Impact:

- Ethical Considerations: Conducting pain perception experiments requires careful ethical considerations, including the need to minimize discomfort and ensure informed consent. Researchers must balance the scientific goals with the welfare of participants.

- Social Implications: Understanding pain perception has social implications for how pain is perceived and treated in society. Research contributes to the development of compassionate and effective approaches to pain management and supports individuals in managing their pain more effectively.

Conclusion:

Pain perception experiments play a crucial role in advancing our understanding of pain and improving pain management strategies. By investigating the physiological, psychological, and neurological aspects of pain, researchers can develop more effective treatments and interventions to enhance the quality of life for individuals suffering from pain.

As research continues, it is essential to address the ethical, social, and policy implications of pain perception experiments. By focusing on responsible research practices and evidence-based treatment approaches, we can advance the field of pain science and contribute to better pain management and overall well-being.

EXPERIMENT SIXTY ONE

AUTONOMOUS VEHICLES TESTING: NAVIGATING THE FUTURE OF TRANSPORTATION

Introduction:

Autonomous vehicles (AVs), also known as self-driving cars, represent a transformative shift in the transportation industry. These vehicles utilize a combination of sensors, machine learning algorithms, and advanced computing to navigate and operate without human intervention. Testing autonomous vehicles is crucial for ensuring their safety, reliability, and effectiveness. This exploration covers the methodologies, impact, and implications of AV testing.

Historical Context and Techniques:

1. Early Developments:

   - Pioneering Efforts: The concept of autonomous vehicles dates back to the 1920s, with early experiments including radio-controlled cars. However, significant advancements began in the late 20th and early 21st centuries, driven by developments in computing power, sensor technology, and machine learning.

- DARPA Challenges: The Defense Advanced Research Projects Agency (DARPA) played a pivotal role in advancing AV technology through its Grand Challenges, held in 2004 and 2005. These competitions provided a platform for testing and refining autonomous driving systems and spurred innovation in the field.

2. Contemporary Techniques:

- Sensor Technology: Modern autonomous vehicles are equipped with a variety of sensors, including LIDAR (Light Detection and Ranging), cameras, radar, and ultrasonic sensors. These devices collect data about the vehicle's surroundings and enable real-time decision-making.

- Machine Learning and AI: Machine learning algorithms process data from sensors to identify objects, predict movements, and make driving decisions. AI systems are trained using vast amounts of driving data to improve their accuracy and adaptability.

- Simulation and Testing: Autonomous vehicles undergo extensive simulation testing to evaluate their performance in various scenarios and conditions. Virtual environments allow researchers to test and refine algorithms without physical limitations.

3. Experimental Techniques:

- On-Road Testing: Real-world testing involves driving autonomous vehicles on public roads and highways to evaluate their performance in diverse traffic conditions and environments. These tests help identify issues and validate the system's reliability and safety.

- Closed-Course Testing: Closed-course testing takes place on specially designed tracks that simulate different driving conditions, such as intersections, roundabouts, and adverse weather. These tests allow for controlled experimentation and fine-tuning of AV systems.

- Safety and Redundancy: AV testing emphasizes safety and redundancy to ensure that vehicles can handle unexpected situations. This includes testing fail-safes, backup systems, and emergency responses to minimize risks.

Impact:

1. Scientific and Technological Impact:

- Advancements in AI and Robotics: Autonomous vehicle testing drives advancements in artificial intelligence, machine learning, and robotics. Innovations in these areas contribute to the broader field of autonomous systems and their applications.

- Improved Transportation Systems: Successful deployment of autonomous vehicles has the potential to enhance transportation efficiency, reduce traffic congestion, and improve road safety. AVs could transform urban planning and mobility.

2. Safety and Regulatory Impact:

- Safety Improvements: Testing helps identify and address safety issues, such as sensor malfunctions, algorithm errors, and unexpected road conditions. Ensuring that AVs meet rigorous safety standards is crucial for gaining public trust and regulatory approval.

- Regulatory Frameworks: The development of regulatory frameworks is essential for overseeing the deployment and operation of autonomous vehicles. Regulations must address safety standards, liability, insurance, and data privacy.

3. Societal and Economic Impact:

- Employment and Workforce: The adoption of autonomous vehicles may impact employment in industries related to driving, such as trucking and ride-sharing. It is important to consider the implications for workforce development and retraining.

- Accessibility and Mobility: AVs have the potential to improve accessibility for individuals with disabilities and the elderly. By providing autonomous transportation options, these vehicles can enhance mobility and independence.

4. Ethical and Social Considerations:

- Ethical Decision-Making: Autonomous vehicles face ethical dilemmas, such as how to prioritize safety in emergency situations. Developing ethical frameworks for decision-making in AVs is a critical aspect of their design and deployment.

- Privacy and Data Security: AVs generate and collect vast amounts of data, including information about driving behavior, location, and passenger interactions. Ensuring data privacy and security is essential for protecting users and complying with regulations.

Effect:

1. Scientific Advancements:

- Innovation in Technology: Autonomous vehicle testing leads to innovations in sensor technology, machine learning, and computing. These advancements have broader implications for technology development beyond the automotive industry.

- Enhanced Understanding of AI: Testing AVs contributes to a deeper understanding of artificial intelligence and its capabilities. Insights gained from AV research can inform the development of other autonomous systems and applications.

2. Public Perception and Policy:

- Public Acceptance: Successful testing and deployment of autonomous vehicles can influence public perception and acceptance of the technology. Transparent communication about safety, benefits, and challenges is crucial for building trust.

- Policy Development: Findings from AV testing inform the development of policies and regulations governing the use of autonomous vehicles. Policymakers must balance innovation with safety and ethical considerations.

3. Ethical and Social Impact:

- Ethical Frameworks: The ethical considerations associated with autonomous vehicles, such as decision-making in emergencies, require ongoing research and dialogue. Developing ethical frameworks ensures that AVs are designed and operated in a manner consistent with societal values.

- Social Transformation: The widespread adoption of autonomous vehicles has the potential to transform transportation systems and societal dynamics. Understanding the social implications helps guide the responsible development and deployment of AV technology.

Conclusion:

Autonomous vehicle testing represents a critical phase in the development and deployment of self-driving technology. By exploring the complexities of sensor technology, machine learning, and real-world performance, researchers and engineers aim to create safe, reliable, and effective autonomous vehicles.

As testing continues, it is essential to address the scientific, regulatory, societal, and ethical aspects of autonomous vehicle technology. By focusing on innovation, safety, and public trust, the field of autonomous vehicles can contribute to a more efficient, accessible, and transformative future of transportation.

EXPERIMENT SIXTY TWO

HYBRID ANIMAL-HUMAN EMBRYO EXPERIMENTS: EXPLORING THE FRONTIERS OF BIOLOGICAL RESEARCH

Introduction:

Hybrid animal-human embryo experiments involve the creation of embryos that contain genetic material from both human and animal sources. These experiments are conducted to advance our understanding of human development, disease, and regenerative medicine. They also raise complex ethical and scientific questions about the boundaries of human-animal chimeras and their implications for future research and medicine.

Historical Context and Techniques:

1. Early Developments:

   - Historical Precedents: The concept of hybrid embryos has roots in early biological research. In the 1960s and

1970s, scientists explored the potential of interspecies embryos, although these early efforts were limited by technological and ethical constraints.

- First Successful Hybrids: The first successful creation of human-animal hybrid embryos came in the early 2000s, with advancements in stem cell research and genetic engineering. These initial experiments aimed to create animal models for studying human diseases and testing potential treatments.

2. Contemporary Techniques:

- Somatic Cell Nuclear Transfer (SCNT): SCNT involves transferring the nucleus of a somatic cell into an enucleated egg cell. This technique has been used to create hybrid embryos by introducing human nuclei into animal egg cells.

- Gene Editing: Advanced gene-editing technologies, such as CRISPR-Cas9, are employed to manipulate the genetic material in hybrid embryos. These tools allow precise modifications of specific genes to study their effects on development and disease.

- Stem Cell Research: Researchers use stem cells derived from hybrid embryos to explore cellular development and differentiation. These stem cells have the potential to generate tissues and organs for research and therapeutic purposes

3. Experimental Techniques:

- Hybrid Embryo Creation: Scientists create hybrid embryos by combining human cells or genetic material with animal eggs or embryos. This process involves careful control of developmental conditions to ensure successful growth and study.

- Developmental Studies: Experiments monitor the development of hybrid embryos to understand how human and animal cells interact and contribute to the formation of tissues and organs. This research provides insights into human development and disease mechanisms.

- Ethical and Regulatory Considerations: Researchers adhere to ethical guidelines and regulatory frameworks governing hybrid embryo experiments. These guidelines address concerns related to the creation, use, and destruction of hybrid embryos.

Impact:

1. Scientific and Medical Impact:

- Understanding Human Development: Hybrid embryo experiments offer valuable insights into human developmental processes and how genetic factors influence growth and differentiation. This knowledge can improve our understanding of congenital disorders and developmental diseases.

- Disease Modeling: Hybrid embryos can be used to model human diseases in animal systems, providing a platform for studying disease mechanisms and testing potential treatments. This research accelerates the development of new therapies and interventions.

2. Regenerative Medicine:

- Stem Cell Therapies: Stem cells derived from hybrid embryos have the potential to generate tissues and organs for transplantation. Research in this area aims to address the shortage of donor organs and advance regenerative medicine.

- Personalized Medicine: Hybrid embryo research contributes to personalized medicine by enabling the creation of disease-specific models for testing treatments tailored to individual genetic profiles.

3. Ethical and Social Impact:

- Ethical Concerns: Hybrid embryo experiments raise ethical questions about the manipulation of human and animal genomes. Debates focus on the moral status of hybrid embryos, the potential for human-animal chimeras, and the implications for species boundaries.

- Public Perception: The creation of hybrid embryos can evoke concerns and controversies among the public. Transparency in research practices and ethical considerations is essential for maintaining public trust and addressing societal concerns.

4. Regulatory and Policy Considerations:

- Regulation and Oversight: Governments and regulatory bodies establish guidelines and regulations for hybrid embryo research to ensure ethical standards and safety. These regulations address issues related to the creation, use, and destruction of hybrid embryos.

- International Standards: International collaboration and dialogue are important for developing consistent standards and policies for hybrid embryo research. Efforts to harmonize regulations help facilitate global research while addressing ethical concerns.

Effect:

1. Scientific Advancements:

- Innovations in Biology: Hybrid embryo experiments drive innovations in biological research, including advances in genetic engineering, stem cell technology, and developmental biology. These advancements contribute to our understanding of complex biological processes.

- Improved Disease Models: Research using hybrid embryos enhances the development of disease models, leading to more accurate simulations of human diseases and improved testing of therapeutic interventions.

2. Medical Impact:

- Advances in Regenerative Medicine: Hybrid embryo research holds promise for advancing regenerative medicine and addressing organ shortages. Stem cell therapies derived from hybrid embryos could transform the treatment of various medical conditions.

- Personalized Treatments: The ability to create disease-specific models enables the development of personalized treatments, enhancing the effectiveness of therapies and improving patient outcomes.

3. Ethical and Social Impact:

- Ethical Debates: Ongoing debates about the ethical implications of hybrid embryo research shape public discourse and influence policy decisions. Addressing these debates is crucial for ensuring responsible research practices and ethical considerations.

- Public Engagement: Engaging with the public and stakeholders helps address concerns and foster informed discussions about the ethical and societal implications of hybrid embryo research.

Conclusion:

Hybrid animal-human embryo experiments represent a cutting-edge area of biological research with the potential to advance our understanding of human development, disease, and regenerative medicine. While these experiments offer promising opportunities for scientific and medical progress, they also raise complex ethical and regulatory questions.

As research continues, it is essential to balance scientific exploration with ethical considerations and societal concerns. By addressing these challenges, researchers can contribute to responsible and impactful advancements in hybrid embryo research and its applications.

EXPERIMENT SIXTY THREE

BRAIN-MACHINE INTERFACE EXPERIMENTS: BRIDGING THE GAP BETWEEN MIND AND MACHINE

Introduction:

Brain-Machine Interfaces (BMIs), also known as Brain-Computer Interfaces (BCIs), represent a frontier in neuroscience and technology, aiming to create direct communication pathways between the brain and external devices. These interfaces have the potential to revolutionize how we interact with technology, offering solutions for medical rehabilitation, augmenting human capabilities, and exploring new modes of human-computer interaction. This exploration covers the methodologies, impacts, and implications of BMI experiments.

Historical Context and Techniques:

1. Early Developments:

- Pioneering Research: The concept of BMIs dates back to the early 20th century, with early experiments involving electrical stimulation of the brain and rudimentary attempts to interface neural signals with machines. Early researchers, such as Richard Caton and Hans Berger, laid the groundwork by studying brain activity and electrical signals.

- Early BMIs: The 1960s and 1970s saw the development of more sophisticated techniques for recording and interpreting neural signals. Researchers began exploring the use of electroencephalography (EEG) to decode brain activity and control external devices.

2. Contemporary Techniques:

-   Electroencephalography (EEG): EEG measures electrical activity on the scalp, providing non-invasive access to brain signals. EEG-based BMIs are commonly used for communication and control applications, such as assisting individuals with motor impairments.

- Electrocorticography (ECoG): ECoG involves placing electrodes directly on the surface of the brain. This technique provides higher resolution and more precise signal acquisition compared to EEG, enabling more accurate control of devices and improved signal quality.

- Implanted Neural Interfaces: Advances in neuroengineering have led to the development of implanted BMIs that involve electrodes inserted into the brain. These interfaces provide direct access to neural activity, allowing for precise control of prosthetic limbs and other devices.

3. Experimental Techniques:

- Neural Signal Decoding: Experiments focus on decoding neural signals to translate brain activity into commands for controlling external devices. Techniques include machine learning algorithms and signal processing methods to interpret and use brain signals effectively.

- Real-Time Feedback: BMIs often incorporate real-time feedback systems that provide users with immediate sensory information about their actions. This feedback enhances the control and accuracy of devices and helps users adapt to the interface.

- Neuroplasticity Training: Some experiments involve training the brain to adapt to new interfaces through neuroplasticity. Researchers study how the brain can rewire itself to improve the effectiveness and usability of BMIs.

Impact:

1. Scientific and Technological Impact:

- Advancements in Neuroscience: BMI experiments contribute to our understanding of brain function and neural coding. Insights gained from BMIs help elucidate how the brain processes and controls motor functions, sensory perception, and cognitive tasks.

- Technological Innovations: The development of BMIs drives innovation in neuroengineering, signal processing, and machine learning. These advancements have applications beyond BMIs, influencing fields such as robotics, artificial intelligence, and human-computer interaction.

2. Medical and Rehabilitation Impact:

- Assistive Technologies: BMIs offer significant benefits for individuals with motor impairments, such as those resulting from spinal cord injuries, stroke, or neurodegenerative diseases. BMIs can enable communication, control of prosthetic limbs, and environmental interactions for people with severe disabilities.

- Neurorehabilitation: BMIs are used in neurorehabilitation programs to aid in the recovery of motor functions. By providing targeted feedback and control, BMIs support motor learning and functional recovery in patients with neurological conditions.

3. Ethical and Social Impact:

- Privacy and Security: BMIs raise concerns about privacy and data security, as they involve access to sensitive neural information. Ensuring the protection of brain data and addressing potential misuse are critical considerations.

- Ethical Considerations: The development and use of BMIs prompt ethical questions about the potential for cognitive enhancement, identity, and the boundaries of human-machine integration. Addressing these ethical issues is essential for responsible research and application.

4. Regulatory and Policy Considerations:

- Regulatory Oversight: The development of BMIs is subject to regulatory oversight to ensure safety and efficacy. Regulatory bodies establish guidelines for the design, testing, and clinical use of BMIs to protect users and ensure ethical practices.

- Policy Development: Policymakers must consider the implications of BMI technology for healthcare, accessibility, and research funding. Developing policies that support responsible innovation and equitable access is important for maximizing the benefits of BMIs.

Effect:

1. Scientific Advancements:

- New Insights into Brain Function: BMI experiments provide new insights into how the brain encodes and processes information. Understanding these processes enhances our knowledge of neural mechanisms and contributes to the broader field of neuroscience.

- Enhanced Technologies: Advances in BMI technology lead to the development of more sophisticated neuroengineering solutions. These innovations have applications in various domains, including robotics, artificial intelligence, and personalized medicine.

2. Medical and Rehabilitation Benefits:

- Improved Quality of Life: BMIs offer improved quality of life for individuals with disabilities by providing new ways to communicate, interact with the environment, and regain lost functions. This technology empowers users and enhances their independence.

- Advances in Rehabilitation: BMIs contribute to more effective neurorehabilitation strategies, supporting recovery and functional improvement in patients with neurological conditions. This progress has the potential to transform rehabilitation practices.

3. Ethical and Social Considerations:

- Public Awareness: The development and application of BMIs raise public awareness about the potential and challenges of brain-machine integration. Engaging with the public helps address concerns and foster informed discussions about the technology's implications.

- Ethical Frameworks: Establishing ethical frameworks for BMI research and application ensures that technological advancements are aligned with societal values and respect for individual autonomy and privacy.

Conclusion:

Brain-Machine Interface experiments represent a cutting-edge area of research with the potential to transform how we interact with technology and enhance our understanding of brain function. By exploring the complexities of neural signal decoding, real-time feedback, and neuroplasticity, researchers aim to develop effective and innovative interfaces that bridge the gap between mind and machine.

As BMI technology continues to advance, it is essential to address the scientific, medical, ethical, and regulatory aspects of this research. By balancing innovation with responsible practices and public engagement, researchers and policymakers can contribute to the successful development and application of BMIs, ultimately benefiting individuals and society.

EXPERIMENT SIXTY FOUR

QUANTUM TELEPORTATION EXPERIMENTS: UNRAVELING THE MYSTERIES OF QUANTUM ENTANGLEMENT AND INFORMATION TRANSFER

Introduction:

Quantum teleportation is a groundbreaking concept in quantum physics that explores the possibility of transferring quantum information between distant locations without physically transmitting matter. This phenomenon is rooted in the principles of quantum entanglement and superposition, challenging our classical understanding of information transfer and communication. Quantum teleportation experiments aim to demonstrate and harness this process, paving the way for advances in quantum computing, secure communication, and fundamental physics.

Historical Context and Techniques:

1. Early Theoretical Foundations:

- Quantum Entanglement: The concept of quantum entanglement, where particles become interconnected in such a way that the state of one instantly affects the state of another, was first introduced by Albert Einstein, Boris Podolsky, and Nathan Rosen in 1935. This phenomenon underpins quantum teleportation and challenges classical notions of locality and causality.

- Teleportation Concept: Quantum teleportation was formally proposed in 1993 by Charles Bennett and colleagues. Their theoretical model demonstrated how the quantum state of a particle could be transferred from one location to another using entanglement and classical communication.

2. Experimental Techniques:

- Entangled Photon Pairs: Modern quantum teleportation experiments often use entangled photon pairs as the quantum states to be teleported. These photons are generated through processes such as spontaneous parametric down-conversion, where a single photon splits into two entangled photons.

- Bell State Measurement: To achieve quantum teleportation, researchers perform a Bell state measurement on the entangled photon pair and the particle whose state is being teleported. This measurement correlates the quantum states of the particles, enabling the transfer of information.

- Quantum State Reconstruction: The teleported quantum state is reconstructed at the receiving end by applying appropriate operations based on the measurement outcomes. This process ensures that the original quantum state is accurately recreated at the destination.

3. Experimental Techniques:

- Photon Experiments: Experiments often involve sending entangled photon pairs to separate locations and performing measurements to verify the success of teleportation. Techniques such as quantum interference and tomography are used to analyze and confirm the results.

- Quantum Computing Platforms: Quantum teleportation experiments are conducted on quantum computing platforms that use qubits or other quantum systems to test and implement teleportation protocols. These platforms offer the ability to manipulate and measure quantum states with high precision.

Impact:

1. Scientific and Technological Impact:

- Advances in Quantum Theory: Quantum teleportation experiments validate key principles of quantum mechanics and enhance our understanding of quantum entanglement and information transfer. They provide empirical evidence for theoretical predictions and contribute to the development of quantum theory.

- Quantum Computing and Information Processing: Teleportation plays a crucial role in quantum computing, where it is used for qubit state transfer and quantum gate operations. Successful teleportation experiments advance the development of scalable quantum computers and quantum networks.

2. Secure Communication:

- Quantum Cryptography: Quantum teleportation contributes to the field of quantum cryptography by enabling secure communication protocols based on quantum entanglement. Quantum key distribution

(QKD) protocols leverage entanglement to ensure secure transmission of information.

- Quantum Networks: The ability to teleport quantum states over long distances is a key component of quantum networks, which aim to connect quantum computers and communication systems securely. Teleportation experiments provide the foundation for building these networks.

3. Technological and Practical Applications:

- Enhanced Information Transfer: Quantum teleportation has potential applications in secure data transfer, where it could be used to transmit information without risk of interception or eavesdropping. This technology has implications for secure communication channels and data encryption.

- Quantum Internet: The development of quantum teleportation experiments contributes to the creation of a quantum internet, where entangled particles are used to transfer quantum information between distant nodes. This network has the potential to revolutionize communication and computing.

4. Ethical and Social Impact:

- Privacy and Security: The advancement of quantum communication and teleportation raises concerns about privacy and security, particularly in the context of secure data transfer and encryption. Ensuring the responsible use of these technologies is essential for maintaining privacy and security standards.

- Public Perception: Quantum teleportation experiments capture the public imagination and contribute to discussions about the future of technology and communication. Educating the public about the implications and potential of these experiments fosters informed engagement with emerging technologies.

Effect:

1. Scientific Advancements:

- Verification of Quantum Mechanics: Quantum teleportation experiments provide experimental confirmation of theoretical predictions in quantum mechanics. They enhance our understanding of quantum entanglement, measurement, and state transfer.

- Development of Quantum Technologies: Advances in quantum teleportation contribute to the development of quantum technologies, including quantum computing, quantum communication, and quantum sensing. These technologies have the potential to transform various scientific and technological fields.

2. Technological and Practical Benefits:

- Secure Communication Networks: Quantum teleportation facilitates the creation of secure communication networks based on quantum cryptography. These networks offer enhanced security and privacy for data transmission.

- Quantum Computing Progress: The successful implementation of quantum teleportation protocols advances the field of quantum computing by enabling efficient qubit state transfer and entanglement operations. This progress supports the development of practical quantum computers.

3. Ethical and Social Considerations:

- Responsible Use of Technology: As quantum teleportation technology advances, ethical considerations related to privacy, security, and responsible use become increasingly important. Addressing these considerations ensures that the technology is used for beneficial purposes and respects societal values.

- Public Engagement: Engaging with the public and fostering discussions about the implications of quantum teleportation experiments helps build understanding and acceptance of emerging technologies. Public awareness and education are crucial for addressing concerns and promoting informed dialogue.

Conclusion:

Quantum teleportation experiments represent a frontier in quantum physics, offering insights into the nature of quantum entanglement and the possibilities of information transfer. These experiments have significant implications for the development of quantum technologies, secure communication, and fundamental physics.

As research in quantum teleportation progresses, it is essential to address the scientific, technological, ethical, and social aspects of this field. By balancing innovation with responsible practices and public engagement, researchers and policymakers can contribute to the successful advancement and application of quantum teleportation technologies, shaping the future of communication and information processing.

EXPERIMENT SIXTY FIVE

NEUROENHANCEMENT EXPERIMENTS: PUSHING THE BOUNDARIES OF COGNITIVE AND NEURAL ENHANCEMENT

Neuroenhancement experiments focus on techniques and technologies aimed at improving cognitive function, mental performance, and overall brain health. These experiments explore various methods for enhancing memory, intelligence, creativity, and mental well-being. As advancements in neuroscience, technology, and medicine continue to evolve, neuroenhancement experiments offer the potential to transform our understanding of the brain and expand human capabilities.

Historical Context and Techniques:

1. Early Foundations:

- Historical Approaches: The quest to enhance cognitive abilities has a long history, from early philosophical inquiries to the development of rudimentary interventions such as stimulants and cognitive training exercises. Early attempts included the use of substances like caffeine and ginseng, as well as mental exercises aimed at improving cognitive function.

- Scientific Developments: The 20th and 21st centuries saw significant progress in neuroenhancement research, driven by advancements in neuroscience, pharmacology, and technology. Discoveries in brain function, neurotransmission, and neural plasticity provided a foundation for modern neuroenhancement techniques.

2. Contemporary Techniques:

- Pharmacological Interventions: Cognitive enhancers, often referred to as nootropics or smart drugs, are substances designed to improve cognitive function. Examples include stimulants like Adderall and Modafinil, as well as compounds like racetams and ampakines that target specific neurotransmitter systems.

- Neurostimulation: Techniques such as transcranial magnetic stimulation (TMS) and transcranial direct current stimulation (tDCS) involve applying electromagnetic fields or electrical currents to the brain to modulate neural activity and enhance cognitive function. These methods are explored for their potential to improve memory, attention, and learning.

- Neurofeedback: Neurofeedback is a form of biofeedback that trains individuals to regulate their brain activity through real-time monitoring and feedback. By providing visual or auditory cues related to brain wave patterns, neurofeedback aims to enhance cognitive performance and emotional regulation.

- Genetic and Epigenetic Approaches: Advances in genetics and epigenetics have led to the exploration of genetic modifications and environmental interventions to enhance cognitive function. Research in this area includes studying gene variants associated with cognitive abilities and exploring how environmental factors influence gene expression.

3. Experimental Techniques:

- Cognitive Training Programs: Experimental studies often involve cognitive training programs designed to improve specific aspects of mental function, such as working memory, executive function, and attention. These programs may use computerized exercises, puzzles, or other interactive tasks.

- Pharmacological Trials: Clinical trials investigate the efficacy and safety of cognitive enhancers and neuropharmaceuticals. These studies assess the impact of various substances on cognitive performance, mood, and overall brain health.

- Neuroimaging Studies: Functional magnetic resonance imaging (fMRI), positron emission tomography (PET), and other neuroimaging techniques are used to visualize changes in brain activity associated with neuroenhancement interventions. These studies provide insights into how different techniques affect neural circuits and cognitive processes.

Impact:

1. Scientific and Technological Impact:

- Advancements in Neuroscience: Neuroenhancement experiments contribute to our understanding of brain function and the underlying mechanisms of cognitive processes. Insights gained from these studies inform the development of new interventions and technologies.

- Technological Innovations: The development of neuroenhancement technologies, such as cognitive training programs and neurostimulation devices, drives innovation in neuroscience and cognitive science. These technologies have potential applications in education, healthcare, and personal development.

2. Medical and Therapeutic Impact:

- Treatment of Cognitive Disorders: Neuroenhancement techniques have potential therapeutic applications for individuals with cognitive disorders, such as dementia, ADHD, and depression. By improving cognitive function and brain health, these interventions offer hope for enhanced treatment options.

- Rehabilitation and Recovery: Cognitive rehabilitation programs and neurostimulation techniques are used in the recovery of cognitive function following brain injury or stroke. These methods aim to support neuroplasticity and functional recovery.

3. Ethical and Social Impact:

- Equity and Access: The development and availability of neuroenhancement technologies raise concerns about equity and access. Ensuring that these interventions are accessible to diverse populations and addressing potential disparities is important for promoting fairness.

- Ethical Considerations: The use of cognitive enhancers and brain-modulating technologies prompts ethical questions about the boundaries of enhancement, consent, and potential long-term effects. Responsible research and application require careful consideration of these ethical issues.

4. Regulatory and Policy Considerations:

-    Regulatory   Oversight: Neuroenhancement
technologies and substances are subject to regulatory
oversight to ensure safety and efficacy. Regulatory
agencies establish guidelines for the approval and
monitoring of cognitive enhancers and neurostimulation
devices.

- Policy Development: Policymakers must consider the
implications   of   neuroenhancement   research   for
healthcare, education, and public health. Developing
policies that support responsible innovation and address
ethical and social concerns is essential for the responsible
advancement of neuroenhancement technologies.

Effect:

1. Scientific Advancements:

- Understanding Brain Function: Neuroenhancement
experiments   provide   valuable   insights   into   the
mechanisms of cognitive processes and brain function.
This knowledge contributes to the broader field of
neuroscience and informs future research directions.

-    Technological   Progress: Advances   in
neuroenhancement technologies drive innovation in
cognitive   science,   brain-computer   interfaces,   and
personalized medicine. These developments have the
potential to transform various aspects of human life

2. Medical and Therapeutic Benefits:

- Enhanced Cognitive Function: Neuroenhancement techniques offer potential benefits for improving cognitive function, memory, and mental performance. These benefits can enhance quality of life for individuals seeking cognitive improvement.

- Therapeutic Interventions: Neuroenhancement technologies have therapeutic applications for individuals with cognitive disorders and brain injuries. By supporting cognitive recovery and management, these interventions improve overall brain health and functionality.

3. Ethical and Social Considerations:

- Responsible Use of Technology: As neuroenhancement technologies advance, ethical considerations related to enhancement, privacy, and consent become increasingly important. Addressing these considerations ensures that technologies are used responsibly and in alignment with societal values.

- Public Engagement: Engaging with the public and fostering discussions about the implications of neuroenhancement experiments helps build understanding and acceptance of emerging technologies.

Public awareness and education are crucial for addressing concerns and promoting informed dialogue.

Conclusion:

Neuroenhancement experiments represent a dynamic and evolving field at the intersection of neuroscience, technology, and medicine. By exploring techniques for improving cognitive function, mental performance, and brain health, researchers aim to expand our understanding of the brain and enhance human capabilities.

As neuroenhancement technologies continue to develop, it is essential to address the scientific, medical, ethical, and regulatory aspects of this research. By balancing innovation with responsible practices and public engagement, researchers and policymakers can contribute to the successful advancement and application of neuroenhancement technologies, shaping the future of cognitive and neural enhancement.

EXPERIMENT SIXTY SIX

ARTIFICIAL WOMB EXPERIMENTS: REVOLUTIONIZING REPRODUCTION AND MATERNAL HEALTH

Artificial womb experiments represent a significant frontier in reproductive science, aiming to replicate and support human fetal development outside the natural womb. These experiments explore the feasibility of growing embryos or fetuses in controlled, artificial environments, potentially transforming neonatal care, reproductive health, and ethical considerations surrounding conception and gestation.

Historical Context and Techniques:

1. Early Foundations:

 - Historical Approaches: The concept of artificial wombs, also known as ex utero fetal development or ectogenesis, dates back to early 20th-century science fiction and speculative discussions. Initial experiments focused on developing techniques for cultivating embryos in vitro, such as in culture dishes or bioreactors.

- Scientific Developments: The mid-20th and early 21st centuries saw significant progress in reproductive technologies, including advances in in vitro fertilization (IVF), embryo culture, and neonatal care. These developments laid the groundwork for exploring more complex artificial womb technologies.

2. Contemporary Techniques:

- Bioreactors and Ectogenesis: Modern artificial womb experiments often utilize advanced bioreactors designed to mimic the conditions of the human uterus. These bioreactors provide a controlled environment with appropriate temperature, pH, oxygen levels, and nutrient supply for fetal development.

- Synthetic Amniotic Fluid: Researchers have developed synthetic amniotic fluid to replicate the composition and properties of natural amniotic fluid. This fluid supports fetal growth and development, providing essential nutrients and cushioning.

- Artificial Placenta: Experiments explore the use of artificial placentas or placental-like structures to facilitate nutrient and gas exchange between the developing fetus and the external environment. These structures aim to replicate the functions of the natural placenta.

3. Experimental Techniques:

- Animal Models: Many artificial womb experiments begin with animal models, such as sheep or rabbits, to test and refine the technology before human applications. These models provide insights into the feasibility and challenges of supporting fetal development outside the womb.

- Fetal Development Monitoring: Advanced imaging techniques, such as ultrasound and magnetic resonance imaging (MRI), are used to monitor fetal development within the artificial womb. These techniques provide real-time data on growth, health, and development.

- Ethical and Safety Assessments: Ethical and safety considerations are integral to artificial womb research. Experiments include assessing the long-term health and developmental outcomes of neonates born from artificial wombs, as well as evaluating potential risks and ethical implications.

Impact:

1. Scientific and Technological Impact:

- Advancements in Reproductive Science: Artificial womb experiments contribute to our understanding of fetal development and reproductive biology. Insights gained from these studies inform the development of new technologies and interventions in reproductive medicine.

- Technological Innovations: The development of artificial womb technologies drives innovation in bioreactors, synthetic fluids, and placental engineering. These innovations have potential applications in neonatal care and reproductive health.

2. Medical and Therapeutic Impact:

- Improved Neonatal Care: Artificial womb technology has the potential to enhance neonatal care by providing a controlled environment for premature infants. This technology may improve survival rates and developmental outcomes for extremely premature infants.

- Fertility Treatments: Artificial wombs could offer new options for individuals and couples facing infertility or reproductive challenges. By providing alternative means of gestation, these technologies may expand reproductive possibilities.

3. Ethical and Social Impact:

- Ethical Considerations: The development and use of artificial wombs raise ethical questions about the nature of human reproduction, parental rights, and the moral status of embryos and fetuses. Addressing these concerns requires thoughtful consideration and ethical guidelines.

- Societal Implications: The potential for artificial womb technology to change the way we approach reproduction and neonatal care has broad societal implications. Public engagement and dialogue are essential for understanding and addressing these implications.

4. Regulatory and Policy Considerations:

- Regulatory Oversight: Artificial womb technologies are subject to regulatory oversight to ensure safety, efficacy, and ethical standards. Regulatory agencies establish guidelines for the development, testing, and use of these technologies.

- Policy Development: Policymakers must consider the implications of artificial womb technology for reproductive health, neonatal care, and ethical standards. Developing policies that support responsible innovation and address societal concerns is crucial for advancing these technologies.

Effect:

1. Scientific Advancements:

   - Understanding Fetal Development: Artificial womb experiments provide valuable insights into the mechanisms of fetal development and the requirements for sustaining life outside the natural womb. This knowledge contributes to the broader field of reproductive science and medicine.

   - Technological Progress: Advances in artificial womb technology drive innovation in reproductive medicine and neonatal care. These technologies have the potential to transform how we approach gestation and birth.

2. Medical and Therapeutic Benefits:

   - Enhanced Neonatal Outcomes: Artificial womb technology offers the potential for improved outcomes for premature infants by providing a more controlled and supportive environment for development. This technology may reduce complications and improve survival rates.

   - Expanded Reproductive Options: The development of artificial wombs provides new options for individuals and couples facing fertility challenges, offering alternatives to traditional gestation methods.

3. Ethical and Social Considerations:

- Responsible Use of Technology: As artificial womb technology advances, ethical considerations related to reproduction, consent, and the status of embryos and fetuses become increasingly important. Addressing these considerations ensures that technologies are used responsibly and ethically.

- Public Engagement: Engaging with the public and fostering discussions about the implications of artificial womb experiments helps build understanding and acceptance of emerging technologies. Public awareness and education are crucial for addressing concerns and promoting informed dialogue.

Conclusion:

Artificial womb experiments represent a groundbreaking area of research with the potential to revolutionize reproduction and neonatal care. By exploring techniques for supporting fetal development outside the natural womb, researchers aim to enhance our understanding of reproductive biology and improve outcomes for premature infants.

As artificial womb technology continues to develop, it is essential to address the scientific, medical, ethical, and regulatory aspects of this research. By balancing innovation with responsible practices and public engagement, researchers and policymakers can contribute to the successful advancement and application of artificial womb technologies, shaping the future of reproduction and neonatal care.

EXPERIMENT SIXTY SEVEN

BIOHACKING EXPERIMENTS: THE FRONTIER OF SELF-OPTIMIZATION AND GENETIC MODIFICATION

Introduction:

Biohacking experiments encompass a range of activities aimed at improving human biology and performance through various techniques and technologies. These experiments often involve self-experimentation, genetic modification, and the use of advanced technologies to enhance physical and cognitive functions. Biohacking represents a fusion of science, technology, and personal optimization, with the goal of pushing the boundaries of human capabilities.

Historical Context and Techniques:

1. Early Foundations:

   - Historical Approaches: The concept of biohacking has roots in early practices of self-improvement and experimentation with natural substances, such as herbal supplements and dietary modifications. The idea of optimizing human performance through unconventional methods has been present in various forms throughout history.

- Scientific Developments: The late 20th and early 21st centuries saw significant advancements in biotechnology, genetics, and digital health. These developments provided the foundation for modern biohacking, with a focus on leveraging scientific knowledge and technology to enhance human biology.

2. Contemporary Techniques:

- Genetic Modification: Biohackers use techniques such as CRISPR-Cas9 to edit genes and modify genetic traits. This includes altering DNA to potentially enhance physical or cognitive abilities, treat genetic disorders, or experiment with new biological traits.

- Nootropics and Smart Drugs: Biohacking often involves the use of nootropics—substances that are claimed to improve cognitive function. These can include natural supplements, pharmaceuticals, and experimental compounds designed to enhance memory, focus, and mental performance.

- Wearable Technology: Advances in wearable technology allow individuals to monitor and optimize their health and performance. Devices such as fitness trackers, smartwatches, and continuous glucose monitors provide real-time data on physiological parameters, enabling biohackers to make data-driven decisions about their health.

- DIY Biology: The rise of DIY biology or "garage biology" involves conducting biological experiments outside traditional laboratory settings. This can include growing genetically modified organisms, creating bioart, and experimenting with biotechnology in home labs.

- Neurohacking: Neurohacking focuses on optimizing brain function through techniques such as neurofeedback, brain stimulation (e.g., transcranial direct current stimulation), and cognitive training exercises.

3. Experimental Techniques:

- Self-Experimentation: Biohackers often engage in self-experimentation to test the effects of various interventions on their own bodies. This can include trying new supplements, diets, or exercise regimens and documenting the outcomes to evaluate efficacy and safety.

- Genetic Engineering Trials: Some biohackers conduct experimental genetic engineering to modify their own genetic material. This includes using tools like CRISPR to potentially enhance traits or address specific genetic conditions.

- Data Analysis and Personalization: Biohacking experiments frequently involve collecting and analyzing personal health data to tailor interventions to individual needs. This data-driven approach allows for personalized optimization strategies based on individual physiology and goals.

Impact:

1. Scientific and Technological Impact:

- Advancements in Biotechnology: Biohacking experiments contribute to the advancement of biotechnology and genetic engineering. Insights gained from these experiments inform scientific research and the development of new technologies.

- Innovation in Health and Performance: The exploration of new technologies and methods in biohacking drives innovation in health optimization, personalized medicine, and human enhancement.

2. Medical and Therapeutic Impact:

- Personal Health Optimization: Biohacking techniques offer potential benefits for personal health optimization, including improved cognitive function, physical performance, and overall well-being. These methods provide individuals with tools to proactively manage their health.

- Potential Therapeutic Applications: Some biohacking practices may have therapeutic applications, such as using genetic modification to treat genetic disorders or employing wearable technology to monitor and manage chronic conditions.

3. Ethical and Social Impact:

- Ethical Considerations: Biohacking raises ethical questions related to genetic modification, self-experimentation, and the potential long-term effects of various interventions. Addressing these concerns requires careful consideration and adherence to ethical guidelines.

- Access and Equity: The availability and accessibility of biohacking technologies and interventions may raise concerns about equity and fairness. Ensuring that these technologies are accessible to diverse populations is important for promoting inclusivity.

4. Regulatory and Policy Considerations:

- Regulatory Oversight: Biohacking activities, particularly those involving genetic modification and new technologies, are subject to regulatory oversight to ensure safety and efficacy. Regulatory agencies establish guidelines and standards for the development and use of these technologies.

- Policy Development: Policymakers must consider the implications of biohacking for public health, ethics, and safety. Developing policies that support responsible innovation and address potential risks is crucial for advancing biohacking practices.

Effect:

1. Scientific Advancements:

- Understanding Human Biology: Biohacking experiments provide valuable insights into human biology, genetics, and physiology. These insights contribute to the broader field of biomedical research and inform future scientific endeavors.

- Technological Innovations: Advances in biohacking technologies drive innovation in health optimization, genetic engineering, and wearable tech. These innovations have the potential to transform various aspects of human health and performance.

2. Medical and Therapeutic Benefits:

- Enhanced Health and Performance: Biohacking techniques offer potential benefits for improving cognitive function, physical performance, and overall well-being. These benefits can enhance quality of life for individuals seeking personal optimization.

- Therapeutic Interventions: Some biohacking practices may lead to new therapeutic interventions for managing health conditions and addressing genetic disorders. These developments have the potential to improve treatment options and outcomes.

3. Ethical and Social Considerations:

- Responsible Use of Technology: As biohacking technologies advance, ethical considerations related to genetic modification, self-experimentation, and long-term effects become increasingly important. Responsible research and application are essential for ensuring the ethical use of these technologies.

- Public Engagement: Engaging with the public and fostering discussions about the implications of biohacking experiments helps build understanding and acceptance of emerging technologies. Public awareness and education are crucial for addressing concerns and promoting informed dialogue.

Conclusion:

Biohacking experiments represent a dynamic and evolving field at the intersection of science, technology, and personal optimization. By exploring techniques for enhancing human biology and performance, researchers and enthusiasts aim to expand our understanding of health and capabilities.

As biohacking technologies continue to develop, it is essential to address the scientific, medical, ethical, and regulatory aspects of this research. By balancing innovation with responsible practices and public engagement, researchers and policymakers can contribute to the successful advancement and application of biohacking technologies, shaping the future of human enhancement and optimization.

EXPERIMENT SIXTY EIGHT

NANOPARTICLE INHALATION STUDIES: EVALUATING HEALTH IMPACTS AND SAFETY

Introduction:

Nanoparticle inhalation studies focus on understanding the effects of inhaling nanoparticles—extremely small particles with dimensions measured in nanometers (one billionth of a meter). Due to their small size and large surface area, nanoparticles exhibit unique properties and behaviors that can significantly impact human health. These studies are crucial for assessing the safety of nanoparticles used in various applications, including medicine, industry, and consumer products.

Historical Context and Techniques:

1. Early Foundations:

  - Historical Approaches: The study of airborne particles and their effects on health dates back to the early 20th century, with research focusing on larger particulate matter such as dust and smoke. The introduction of nanotechnology in the late 20th century expanded this focus to include nanoparticles.

- Scientific Developments: Advances in nanotechnology and materials science led to the development and use of nanoparticles in a wide range of applications, from drug delivery systems to electronic devices. This prompted a need for research into the potential health risks associated with nanoparticle inhalation.

2. Contemporary Techniques:

- Nanoparticle Generation: Researchers generate nanoparticles using various methods, including chemical vapor deposition, laser ablation, and grinding. These techniques produce nanoparticles with specific sizes, shapes, and surface properties for study.

- Inhalation Exposure Models: Animal models, such as rodents, are commonly used to study the effects of nanoparticle inhalation. Researchers expose animals to controlled concentrations of nanoparticles and monitor their health and respiratory responses.

- Human Exposure Studies: Controlled human exposure studies, conducted in specialized environments, allow researchers to investigate the effects of nanoparticle inhalation in humans. These studies are often conducted in collaboration with regulatory agencies and involve strict safety protocols.

- Analytical Techniques: Advanced analytical techniques, such as scanning electron microscopy (SEM), transmission electron microscopy (TEM), and mass spectrometry, are used to characterize nanoparticles and assess their interactions with biological systems.

3. Experimental Techniques:

- Dosimetry and Exposure Assessment: Researchers assess the dose and concentration of nanoparticles inhaled by study subjects to evaluate potential health effects. Dosimetry techniques include measuring particle size distributions, concentrations, and deposition patterns in the respiratory tract.

- Health Impact Assessment: Health impacts are evaluated by monitoring various endpoints, such as respiratory inflammation, oxidative stress, lung function, and histopathological changes in the lungs and other organs.

- Biomarker Analysis: Researchers use biomarkers to assess the biological response to nanoparticle inhalation. Biomarkers can indicate inflammation, oxidative stress, and other physiological changes associated with exposure.

Impact:

1. Scientific and Technological Impact:

- Advancements in Nanotechnology: Nanoparticle inhalation studies contribute to the understanding of nanoparticle behavior and interactions with biological systems. Insights gained from these studies inform the development of safer and more effective nanomaterials.

- Innovations in Safety Testing: The research advances methodologies for testing the safety of nanoparticles and other nanomaterials. This includes developing standardized protocols for assessing health risks and ensuring regulatory compliance.

2. Medical and Therapeutic Impact:

- Risk Assessment and Management: Understanding the health effects of nanoparticle inhalation helps in assessing and managing risks associated with the use of nanoparticles in various industries. This knowledge is crucial for protecting workers, consumers, and patients.

- Regulatory Guidelines: Findings from nanoparticle inhalation studies inform regulatory guidelines and safety standards for the production, handling, and use of nanoparticles. Regulatory agencies use this information to set exposure limits and ensure public health safety.

3. Ethical and Social Impact:

- Ethical Considerations: Conducting inhalation studies involves ethical considerations, particularly when using animal models. Ensuring humane treatment and minimizing suffering are important ethical principles in research.

- Public Awareness: Public awareness and education about the potential risks and benefits of nanoparticles are essential for informed decision-making. Transparency in research findings and safety assessments helps build trust and understanding.

4. Regulatory and Policy Considerations:

- Regulatory Oversight: Nanoparticle inhalation studies are subject to regulatory oversight to ensure safety and efficacy. Regulatory agencies establish guidelines for conducting research and assessing health risks associated with nanoparticles.

- Policy Development: Policymakers must consider the implications of nanoparticle inhalation research for public health, safety, and environmental protection. Developing policies that support responsible innovation and address potential risks is crucial for advancing nanotechnology.

Effect:

1. Scientific Advancements:

- Understanding Nanoparticle Behavior: Nanoparticle inhalation studies provide valuable insights into how nanoparticles behave in the respiratory system and interact with biological tissues. This knowledge contributes to the broader field of nanotechnology and toxicology.

- Development of Safer Nanomaterials: Research findings inform the design and development of safer nanoparticles with reduced health risks. Innovations in material science aim to minimize adverse effects while maximizing benefits.

2. Medical and Therapeutic Benefits:

- Enhanced Risk Management: Knowledge gained from nanoparticle inhalation studies aids in managing and mitigating health risks associated with nanoparticle exposure. This contributes to the development of safer industrial processes and consumer products.

- Improved Regulatory Standards: Research outcomes help establish and refine regulatory standards for nanoparticle safety. This ensures that nanoparticles used in various applications meet safety and health criteria.

3. Ethical and Social Considerations:

- Ethical Research Practices: Addressing ethical considerations in nanoparticle inhalation studies promotes responsible research practices and the humane treatment of animal models. Ensuring ethical standards is essential for maintaining research integrity.

- Informed Public Dialogue: Engaging with the public and fostering discussions about the risks and benefits of nanoparticles helps build informed decision-making and supports responsible use of nanotechnology.

Conclusion:

Nanoparticle inhalation studies are a critical area of research with significant implications for public health, safety, and technological innovation. By exploring the effects of inhaling nanoparticles and understanding their interactions with biological systems, researchers aim to ensure the safe and effective use of nanomaterials.

As research continues, it is essential to address scientific, medical, ethical, and regulatory aspects to advance our understanding of nanoparticle safety and contribute to responsible innovation. By balancing innovation with safety and public engagement, researchers and policymakers can support the development of nanotechnology that benefits society while minimizing potential risks.

EXPERIMENT SIXTY NINE

BRAIN IMPLANT EXPERIMENTS: UNVEILING THE FUTURE OF NEUROTECHNOLOGY

Introduction:

Brain implant experiments represent a frontier in neurotechnology, focusing on the development and application of devices that interface directly with the brain. These implants aim to restore or enhance neurological functions, treat neurological disorders, and potentially revolutionize human cognition. By bridging the gap between the brain and external technology, brain implants hold promise for transformative advances in medicine and cognitive enhancement.

Historical Context and Techniques:

1. Early Foundations:

   - Historical Development: The concept of brain implants can be traced back to early experiments with electrical stimulation of the brain, such as those conducted in the mid-20th century. Initial efforts focused on understanding how electrical stimulation could modulate brain activity and influence behavior.

- Scientific Progress: Advances in neuroscience and materials science paved the way for the development of more sophisticated brain implants. The emergence of technologies such as microelectrodes, biocompatible materials, and wireless communication enabled more precise and effective brain interfaces.

2. Contemporary Techniques:

- Neuroprosthetics: Brain implants are used as neuroprosthetics to restore lost functions. For example, cochlear implants help restore hearing in individuals with deafness, while deep brain stimulation (DBS) devices are used to manage symptoms of Parkinson's disease and other movement disorders.

- Brain-Computer Interfaces (BCIs): BCIs are systems that enable direct communication between the brain and external devices. They use implanted electrodes to detect brain activity and translate it into control signals for computers or prosthetic limbs.

- Neural Recording and Stimulation: Advanced implants can record neural activity and provide targeted stimulation to specific brain regions. This includes implants that monitor brain signals for research or therapeutic purposes, as well as those that deliver electrical or chemical stimulation to modulate brain function.

3. Experimental Techniques:

- Implantation Procedures: Brain implants are surgically inserted into the brain, often involving precision techniques to ensure accurate placement and minimize damage. Procedures may include the use of stereotactic frameworks, imaging guidance, and minimally invasive techniques.

- Electrode Design and Placement: Researchers design electrodes to optimize their interaction with neural tissue. This involves selecting appropriate materials, sizes, and configurations to achieve reliable signal acquisition and stimulation.

- Data Acquisition and Analysis: Implants collect data on brain activity, which is analyzed to understand neural patterns and responses. Researchers use this data to refine implant designs and improve their functionality.

Impact:

1. Scientific and Technological Impact:

- Advancements in Neurotechnology: Brain implant experiments drive innovations in neurotechnology, including improved materials, electrode designs, and computational algorithms. These advancements contribute to the development of more effective and reliable brain interfaces.

- Understanding Brain Function: Research using brain implants provides insights into brain function and neural mechanisms. This knowledge enhances our understanding of cognitive processes, sensory perception, and motor control.

2. Medical and Therapeutic Impact:

- Restoration of Function: Brain implants have the potential to restore lost functions and improve the quality of life for individuals with neurological disorders. For example, DBS can alleviate symptoms of Parkinson's disease, while BCIs can enable communication and control for individuals with severe disabilities.

- Treatment of Neurological Disorders: Brain implants offer new treatment options for conditions such as epilepsy, chronic pain, and depression. By targeting specific brain regions or networks, these implants can provide therapeutic benefits and improve patient outcomes.

3. Ethical and Social Impact:

- Ethical Considerations: Brain implant experiments raise ethical questions related to privacy, consent, and the potential for misuse. Ensuring informed consent, safeguarding personal data, and addressing concerns about cognitive enhancement are important ethical considerations.

- Societal Implications: The development and use of brain implants may have broad societal implications, including changes in how we perceive and interact with technology and potential disparities in access to advanced treatments. Addressing these implications requires careful consideration and dialogue.

4. Regulatory and Policy Considerations:

- Regulatory Oversight: Brain implant experiments are subject to regulatory oversight to ensure safety, efficacy, and ethical conduct. Regulatory agencies establish guidelines for device approval, clinical trials, and post-market surveillance.

- Policy Development: Policymakers must consider the implications of brain implant technologies for public health, ethics, and access. Developing policies that support responsible innovation and address potential risks is crucial for advancing neurotechnology.

Effect:

1. Scientific Advancements:

- Enhanced Understanding of the Brain: Brain implant experiments contribute to a deeper understanding of brain function, neural mechanisms, and cognitive processes. This knowledge informs future research and technological development.

- Innovations in Neurotechnology: Advances in brain implants drive innovation in neurotechnology, leading to new devices and applications with potential benefits for medicine, research, and human enhancement.

2. Medical and Therapeutic Benefits:

- Improved Quality of Life: Brain implants offer potential benefits for individuals with neurological disorders by restoring lost functions, alleviating symptoms, and improving quality of life. These benefits can have a profound impact on patients and their families.

- New Treatment Options: Brain implants provide new treatment options for a range of neurological conditions, expanding the possibilities for managing and addressing complex medical issues.

3. Ethical and Social Considerations:

- Responsible Research Practices: Addressing ethical considerations in brain implant research promotes responsible practices and safeguards the rights and well-being of participants. Ensuring ethical standards is essential for maintaining research integrity.

- Informed Public Dialogue: Engaging with the public and fostering discussions about the implications of brain implants helps build understanding and acceptance of emerging technologies. Transparency and education are key to addressing concerns and promoting informed decision-making.

Conclusion:

Brain implant experiments represent a dynamic and evolving field with significant implications for neuroscience, medicine, and technology. By exploring the potential of brain implants to restore, enhance, and interface with brain function, researchers and developers aim to advance our understanding of the brain and improve human health.

As brain implant technologies continue to develop, it is essential to address scientific, medical, ethical, and regulatory aspects to ensure responsible innovation and application. By balancing technological advancements with ethical considerations and public engagement, researchers and policymakers can support the successful development and deployment of brain implant technologies, shaping the future of neurotechnology and human enhancement.

EXPERIMENT SEVENTY

EMERGING INFECTIOUS DISEASE RESEARCH: NAVIGATING THE FRONTIER OF GLOBAL HEALTH

Introduction:

Emerging infectious diseases (EIDs) represent a significant challenge to global health due to their potential to cause widespread outbreaks and pandemics. Research in this field focuses on understanding, preventing, and controlling diseases that are either newly identified or have increased in incidence or geographic range. As new pathogens emerge and existing ones evolve, ongoing research is crucial for developing effective public health strategies and interventions.

Historical Context and Techniques:

1. Early Foundations:

   - Historical Overview: The study of emerging infectious diseases has a long history, with notable examples including the recognition of new pathogens and outbreaks throughout the 20th and 21st centuries.

Historical research has provided valuable insights into the dynamics of infectious disease emergence and spread.

- Scientific Milestones: Advances in microbiology, virology, and epidemiology have improved the identification and understanding of emerging pathogens. Key milestones include the discovery of HIV/AIDS in the 1980s, the identification of new coronaviruses like SARS and MERS, and the recent emergence of SARS-CoV-2 (COVID-19).

2. Contemporary Techniques:

- Surveillance and Detection: Modern research employs advanced surveillance systems to detect and monitor emerging infectious diseases. Techniques include genomic sequencing, molecular diagnostics, and bioinformatics to identify pathogens and track their evolution.

- Pathogen Characterization: Researchers use a range of techniques to characterize emerging pathogens, including culturing and isolating microbes, studying their genetic makeup, and assessing their virulence and transmission characteristics.

- Epidemiological Studies: Epidemiological methods are used to understand the patterns, causes, and effects of emerging infectious diseases. This includes studying outbreaks, analyzing transmission dynamics, and identifying risk factors and populations at risk.

3. Experimental Techniques:

- Animal Models: Researchers use animal models to study the pathogenesis and progression of emerging infectious diseases. These models help in understanding how pathogens interact with host systems and evaluating potential treatments and vaccines.

- Clinical Trials: Clinical trials assess the safety and efficacy of new treatments, vaccines, and preventive measures for emerging infectious diseases. These trials involve testing interventions in human subjects under controlled conditions.

- Field Studies: Field research involves studying diseases in natural settings, including outbreak investigation, environmental sampling, and community-based research. These studies provide insights into disease transmission and control strategies.

Impact:

1. Scientific and Technological Impact:

- Advancements in Diagnostics: Research on emerging infectious diseases drives the development of new diagnostic tools and technologies. This includes rapid tests, molecular assays, and point-of-care diagnostics that improve disease detection and management.

- Understanding Pathogen Evolution: Studying emerging pathogens enhances our understanding of microbial evolution, adaptation, and resistance. This knowledge informs the development of strategies to combat infectious diseases and prevent future outbreaks.

2. Medical and Therapeutic Impact:

- Development of Treatments and Vaccines: Research contributes to the development of new treatments and vaccines for emerging infectious diseases. Effective therapies and vaccines are crucial for managing outbreaks and reducing disease burden.

- Public Health Interventions: Insights gained from research inform public health interventions, including vaccination programs, quarantine measures, and travel restrictions. These interventions help control the spread of diseases and protect populations.

3. Ethical and Social Impact:

- Ethical Considerations: Emerging infectious disease research raises ethical questions related to human and animal subject protection, informed consent, and the equitable distribution of resources. Ensuring ethical practices in research and intervention is essential for maintaining public trust.

- Global Health Equity: Addressing emerging infectious diseases involves considerations of global health equity. Research and interventions must be accessible to all populations, including low-resource settings, to effectively manage and prevent disease outbreaks.

4. Regulatory and Policy Considerations:

- Regulatory Oversight: Emerging infectious disease research is subject to regulatory oversight to ensure the safety and efficacy of new diagnostics, treatments, and vaccines. Regulatory agencies establish guidelines for research conduct, product approval, and public health response.

- Policy Development: Policymakers use research findings to develop and implement public health policies and strategies. This includes creating frameworks for outbreak response, disease prevention, and international collaboration.

Effect:

1. Scientific Advancements:

- Enhanced Understanding of Infectious Diseases: Research on emerging infectious diseases advances our knowledge of pathogen biology, transmission, and host interactions. This understanding informs future research and public health strategies.

- Innovation in Diagnostics and Treatments: Advances in diagnostic technologies and therapeutic interventions contribute to improved disease management and outbreak control. Innovations in these areas enhance our ability to respond to emerging threats.

2. Medical and Therapeutic Benefits:

- Improved Disease Management: Research provides new tools and strategies for managing emerging infectious diseases, leading to better health outcomes and reduced disease burden. Effective treatments and vaccines are critical for controlling outbreaks.

- Enhanced Public Health Response: Insights from research support the development of effective public health responses, including surveillance systems, outbreak investigation, and preventive measures. These responses help protect populations and prevent the spread of diseases.

3. Ethical and Social Considerations:

- Ethical Research Practices: Addressing ethical considerations in emerging infectious disease research promotes responsible conduct and safeguards the rights and well-being of participants. Ensuring ethical standards is essential for maintaining research integrity.

- Informed Public Dialogue: Engaging with the public and fostering discussions about emerging infectious diseases helps build understanding and acceptance of research findings and public health measures. Transparency and education are key to addressing concerns and promoting informed decision-making.

Conclusion:

Emerging infectious disease research is a dynamic and critical field that addresses the challenges posed by new and re-emerging pathogens. By advancing our understanding of these diseases and developing effective diagnostics, treatments, and public health strategies, researchers and policymakers work to safeguard global health.

As research continues, it is essential to address scientific, medical, ethical, and regulatory aspects to ensure responsible and effective management of emerging infectious diseases. By balancing innovation with ethical considerations and public engagement, researchers and policymakers can enhance our preparedness and response to infectious disease threats, ultimately contributing to a healthier and safer world.

EXPERIMENT SEVENTY ONE

HUMAN-CHIMPANZEE HYBRIDIZATION EXPERIMENTS: ETHICAL FRONTIERS IN GENETICS

Introduction:

Human-chimpanzee hybridization experiments involve attempts to combine human and chimpanzee genetic material to create hybrid organisms. These experiments raise significant ethical, scientific, and philosophical questions, given the close genetic relationship between humans and chimpanzees. The goal of such research often includes understanding genetic similarities, exploring developmental biology, and advancing medical science. However, these experiments are fraught with controversy and complex ethical dilemmas.

Historical Context and Techniques:

1. Historical Overview:

   - Early Research: The concept of hybridizing human and chimpanzee cells dates back to the mid-20th century when scientists first began exploring the genetic similarities between humans and primates. Early experiments focused on cell fusion techniques rather than creating viable hybrid organisms.

- Significant Experiments: In the 1970s and 1980s, researchers conducted experiments to fuse human and chimpanzee cells in vitro to study cell behavior and genetic expression. These experiments aimed to understand how human and primate cells interact and what insights could be gained into genetic diseases and cellular processes.

2. Contemporary Techniques:

- Cell Fusion: Techniques such as somatic cell fusion involve combining human and chimpanzee cells to create hybrid cells. This method allows researchers to study genetic interactions and cellular functions in a controlled environment.

- Genetic Engineering: Advances in genetic engineering, including CRISPR-Cas9 technology, enable precise modification of genes. Researchers use these techniques to explore the potential for creating genetically modified hybrids with specific traits or studying gene function.

- Stem Cell Research: Stem cell research includes efforts to create hybrid stem cells that have both human and chimpanzee characteristics. These cells are used to investigate developmental processes and disease modeling.

3. Experimental Techniques:

- In Vitro Hybridization: Researchers use in vitro methods to combine human and chimpanzee cells, creating hybrid cells for study. These cells provide insights into genetic interactions, gene expression, and cellular behavior.

- Ethical Considerations: Creating viable human-chimpanzee hybrids poses significant ethical and legal challenges. Researchers must navigate complex issues related to the welfare of hybrid organisms and the implications for human and animal rights.

- Regulatory Framework: Due to the controversial nature of hybridization experiments, regulatory frameworks vary by country and institution. Guidelines often focus on ensuring ethical conduct, preventing harm, and addressing potential legal and social implications.

Impact:

1. Scientific and Technological Impact:

- Understanding Genetic Similarities: Research on human-chimpanzee hybrids contributes to our understanding of genetic similarities and differences between humans and primates. This knowledge enhances our understanding of evolutionary biology, genetics, and human development.

- Advancements in Disease Research: Hybridization experiments can provide insights into genetic diseases and developmental disorders. By studying hybrid cells or organisms, researchers may identify genetic factors involved in disease processes and develop potential treatments.

2. Medical and Therapeutic Impact:

- Development of Therapies: Insights gained from hybrid research may lead to the development of new therapies for genetic disorders and diseases. Understanding how genes interact across species can inform the development of targeted treatments and interventions.

- Model Systems for Research: Hybrid cells or organisms may serve as model systems for studying disease mechanisms and testing potential therapies. These models offer a unique perspective on human biology and disease.

3. Ethical and Social Impact:

- Ethical Dilemmas: Human-chimpanzee hybridization experiments raise profound ethical questions about the nature of human-animal boundaries, the welfare of hybrid organisms, and the implications for animal rights. Ethical considerations include the potential for suffering, exploitation, and the moral status of hybrids.

- Social and Legal Implications: The creation of human-chimpanzee hybrids has significant social and legal implications, including debates over the rights and status of hybrid organisms and the potential for misuse of genetic technologies. Public discourse and legal frameworks play a crucial role in addressing these issues.

4. Regulatory and Policy Considerations:

- Regulatory Oversight: Due to the controversial nature of hybridization experiments, regulatory oversight is essential to ensure ethical conduct and prevent harm. Regulatory agencies and ethics committees establish guidelines for research practices and ensure compliance with legal and ethical standards.

- Policy Development: Policymakers must consider the implications of human-chimpanzee hybridization research for public health, ethics, and society. Developing policies that address ethical concerns and promote responsible research is crucial for advancing science while safeguarding ethical principles.

Effect:

1. Scientific Advancements:

- Enhanced Understanding of Genetics: Research on human-chimpanzee hybrids contributes to our understanding of genetic similarities, gene function, and evolutionary processes. This knowledge informs future research and technological development.

- Innovation in Research Models: Hybrid models provide unique insights into genetic interactions and disease mechanisms, leading to innovations in research methodologies and therapeutic approaches.

2. Medical and Therapeutic Benefits:

- Potential for New Therapies: Insights from hybrid research may lead to the development of novel therapies for genetic disorders and diseases. Understanding genetic interactions across species can enhance our ability to address complex medical conditions.

- Improved Disease Models: Hybrid cells or organisms offer valuable model systems for studying human biology and disease, potentially leading to breakthroughs in treatment and prevention.

3. Ethical and Social Considerations:

- Ethical Research Practices: Addressing ethical considerations in hybridization research promotes responsible conduct and safeguards the welfare of organisms involved. Ensuring ethical standards is essential for maintaining research integrity and public trust.

- Informed Public Dialogue: Engaging with the public and fostering discussions about human-chimpanzee hybridization helps build understanding and address concerns about the implications of genetic research. Transparency and education are key to navigating ethical and social issues.

Conclusion:

Human-chimpanzee hybridization experiments represent a challenging and controversial area of research with significant implications for science, medicine, and ethics. By exploring the genetic similarities and interactions between humans and chimpanzees, researchers aim to advance our understanding of genetics and develop new therapies.

As research progresses, it is essential to address scientific, medical, ethical, and regulatory aspects to ensure responsible and ethical conduct. By balancing innovation with ethical considerations and public engagement, researchers and policymakers can navigate the complex issues surrounding human-chimpanzee hybridization and contribute to the advancement of genetics and biotechnology in a responsible manner.

EXPERIMENT SEVENTY TWO

MIND-UPLOADING EXPERIMENTS: THE QUEST FOR DIGITAL IMMORTALITY

Introduction:

Mind-uploading, also known as whole-brain emulation or mind transfer, is a concept that involves transferring or replicating a human mind into a digital or artificial medium. This futuristic idea seeks to achieve digital immortality by preserving an individual's consciousness beyond the biological lifespan. Mind-uploading experiments explore the feasibility, implications, and ethical considerations of creating a digital replica of a human mind.

Historical Context and Techniques:

1. Historical Overview:

   - Origins of the Concept: The idea of mind-uploading has roots in science fiction and philosophical speculation. It gained prominence in the 20th century through works like "Neuromancer" by William Gibson and "The Matrix" film series. Early discussions centered around the possibility of digitizing human consciousness and achieving virtual existence.

- Early Research: Initial research in related fields, such as neuroscience, artificial intelligence, and computer science, laid the groundwork for exploring mind-uploading. Scientists began investigating the brain's information processing and the potential for replicating cognitive functions in machines.

2. Contemporary Techniques:

- Neuroimaging and Mapping: Advanced neuroimaging techniques, such as functional MRI (fMRI) and diffusion tensor imaging (DTI), provide detailed maps of brain structures and neural connections. These technologies help researchers understand brain activity and connectivity, which are essential for mind-uploading.

- Brain-Computer Interfaces (BCIs): BCIs facilitate direct communication between the brain and external devices. Researchers use BCIs to study brain signals and develop methods for transferring neural information to digital systems.

- Artificial Intelligence and Machine Learning: AI and machine learning algorithms are employed to model and simulate cognitive processes. These technologies help create digital representations of neural networks and cognitive functions.

3. Experimental Techniques:

- Simulation of Neural Networks: Scientists create computer models that simulate the brain's neural networks and cognitive processes. These simulations aim to replicate aspects of human thought, perception, and decision-making.

- Data Integration: Researchers integrate data from neuroimaging, neurophysiology, and AI to construct comprehensive models of the brain. This data is used to develop digital avatars or emulations of cognitive functions.

- Ethical Considerations: Mind-uploading experiments face ethical challenges related to consciousness, identity, and the potential for misuse. Researchers must address questions about the nature of digital consciousness and the rights of digital entities.

Impact:

1. Scientific and Technological Impact:

- Advancements in Neuroscience: Mind-uploading research drives advancements in neuroscience by deepening our understanding of brain function, neural networks, and cognitive processes. This knowledge informs future research and technological development.

- Innovations in AI and Computing: The pursuit of mind-uploading spurs innovations in artificial intelligence, machine learning, and computing. These technologies enhance our ability to model complex cognitive functions and develop advanced digital systems.

2. Medical and Therapeutic Impact:

- Potential for Cognitive Restoration: Mind-uploading technology may offer potential benefits for cognitive restoration and enhancement. If successfully developed, it could provide new approaches for treating neurodegenerative diseases and cognitive impairments.

- Development of Virtual Environments: Mind-uploading research may lead to the creation of immersive virtual environments where individuals can interact, learn, and experience new forms of digital existence. These environments could have applications in education, entertainment, and therapy.

3. Ethical and Social Impact:

- Questions of Consciousness and Identity: Mind-uploading raises profound questions about consciousness, identity, and the nature of self. Researchers and ethicists must grapple with issues related to digital consciousness, the continuity of personal identity, and the moral status of digital entities.

- Privacy and Security Concerns: The potential for mind-uploading introduces privacy and security concerns related to digital data and personal information. Ensuring the protection of digital consciousness and preventing unauthorized access is crucial for maintaining trust and safety.

4. Regulatory and Policy Considerations:

- Ethical Guidelines: The development of mind-uploading technology requires ethical guidelines to address concerns about consent, autonomy, and the welfare of digital entities. Research ethics committees and regulatory bodies play a role in establishing standards for responsible conduct.

- Legal Frameworks: Policymakers must consider the legal implications of mind-uploading, including issues related to intellectual property, digital rights, and the status of digital consciousness. Developing legal frameworks that address these concerns is essential for managing the technology's impact.

Effect:

1. Scientific Advancements:

 - Enhanced Understanding of Cognition: Research into mind-uploading contributes to our understanding of cognitive processes, neural networks, and brain function. This knowledge informs future research in neuroscience, AI, and related fields.

 - Innovation in Technology: The pursuit of mind-uploading drives innovation in AI, computing, and neurotechnology. Advances in these areas have broader applications in research, industry, and daily life.

2. Medical and Therapeutic Benefits:

 - Potential for Cognitive Enhancement: If successfully developed, mind-uploading technology could offer new approaches for cognitive enhancement and restoration. This could benefit individuals with cognitive impairments and neurodegenerative diseases.

 - New Forms of Experience: Virtual environments created through mind-uploading could provide novel experiences in education, entertainment, and therapy. These environments may offer immersive and interactive opportunities for learning and engagement.

3. Ethical and Social Considerations:

- Ethical Research Practices: Addressing ethical considerations in mind-uploading research promotes responsible conduct and safeguards the rights and well-being of digital entities. Ensuring ethical standards is essential for maintaining research integrity and public trust.

- Informed Public Dialogue: Engaging with the public and fostering discussions about mind-uploading helps build understanding and address concerns about the implications of digital consciousness. Transparency and education are key to navigating ethical and social issues.

Conclusion:

Mind-uploading experiments represent a cutting-edge area of research with significant implications for science, technology, and ethics. By exploring the feasibility of digitizing human consciousness, researchers aim to advance our understanding of cognition, develop new technologies, and address profound questions about identity and existence.

As research progresses, it is essential to address scientific, medical, ethical, and regulatory aspects to ensure responsible and ethical conduct. By balancing innovation with ethical considerations and public engagement, researchers and policymakers can navigate the complex issues surrounding mind-uploading and contribute to the advancement of neuroscience and digital technology in a responsible manner.

EXPERIMENT SEVENTY THREE

GEOENGINEERING FIELD TRIALS: NAVIGATING THE RISKS AND REWARDS

Introduction:

Geoengineering refers to large-scale interventions designed to combat or mitigate the effects of climate change by modifying Earth's climate systems. Geoengineering field trials are experimental efforts to test and assess various methods of manipulating the environment, with the goal of reducing global warming and its associated impacts. These trials are highly controversial due to their potential risks, ethical implications, and the scale of their impact on the Earth's systems.

Historical Context and Techniques:

1. Historical Overview:

  - Early Concepts: The concept of geoengineering emerged in the 20th century as scientists began to explore ways to counteract the effects of anthropogenic climate change. Initial ideas included methods such as cloud seeding, solar radiation management, and carbon capture.

- Notable Developments: The 2000s saw a surge in interest and research into geoengineering technologies, driven by growing concerns about climate change and the limitations of conventional mitigation strategies. High-profile reports and scientific papers began to detail potential methods and their implications.

2. Contemporary Techniques:

- Solar Radiation Management (SRM): SRM techniques aim to reflect sunlight away from Earth to reduce global temperatures. Methods include stratospheric aerosol injection (SAI), which involves dispersing reflective particles in the upper atmosphere, and marine cloud brightening, which aims to increase the reflectivity of clouds over the ocean.

- Carbon Dioxide Removal (CDR): CDR methods focus on removing CO_2 from the atmosphere and storing it. Techniques include direct air capture (DAC), which uses chemical processes to extract CO_2 from ambient air, and ocean fertilization, which involves adding nutrients to the ocean to enhance the growth of carbon-sequestering phytoplankton.

- Soil Carbon Sequestration: This method involves modifying land management practices to increase the amount of carbon stored in soils. Techniques include reforestation, afforestation, and the use of biochar, a form of carbon-rich charcoal added to soils.

3. Experimental Techniques:

- Field Trials and Pilot Projects: Geoengineering field trials involve small-scale experiments to test the feasibility, effectiveness, and risks of various geoengineering techniques. Examples include controlled aerosol releases, carbon capture pilot plants, and soil carbon sequestration projects.

- Modeling and Simulation: Advanced computer models and simulations are used to predict the potential impacts of geoengineering interventions. These models help researchers understand the possible outcomes of large-scale implementation and identify potential risks.

- Ethical and Regulatory Considerations: Geoengineering field trials face ethical and regulatory challenges related to environmental impact, governance, and public participation. Researchers must address questions about the potential for unintended consequences and the need for international cooperation.

Impact:

1. Scientific and Technological Impact:

- Advancements in Climate Science: Geoengineering research contributes to our understanding of climate systems, atmospheric chemistry, and environmental processes. This knowledge enhances our ability to assess and address climate change.

- Innovation in Technology: The pursuit of geoengineering drives innovation in technologies related to climate intervention, carbon capture, and environmental monitoring. These technologies have potential applications beyond geoengineering.

2. Environmental Impact:

- Potential Benefits: Successful geoengineering interventions could reduce global temperatures, mitigate the effects of climate change, and help prevent severe environmental damage. For example, SRM techniques may provide temporary relief from warming, while CDR methods could contribute to long-term carbon reduction.

- Risks and Uncertainties: Geoengineering field trials carry risks of unintended environmental consequences, such as disruptions to weather patterns, impacts on ecosystems, and potential harm to biodiversity. The full extent of these risks is often unknown, requiring careful monitoring and assessment.

3. Ethical and Social Impact:

- Ethical Considerations: Geoengineering raises ethical questions about the governance of climate intervention, the potential for global inequality, and the moral implications of altering natural systems. Researchers and policymakers must consider the rights and interests of affected communities and future generations.

- Public Perception and Engagement: Public perception of geoengineering varies, with concerns about safety, efficacy, and ethical implications. Engaging with the public and fostering informed discussions about geoengineering is essential for building trust and ensuring responsible research.

4. Regulatory and Policy Considerations:

- International Cooperation: Geoengineering has global implications, necessitating international cooperation and coordination. Policymakers and researchers must work together to establish guidelines, agreements, and frameworks for responsible geoengineering research and implementation.

- Governance and Oversight: Effective governance and oversight are crucial for managing geoengineering field trials. Regulatory bodies must develop standards for conducting experiments, assessing risks, and ensuring transparency and accountability.

Effect:

1. Scientific Advancements:

- Enhanced Understanding of Climate Systems: Research into geoengineering enhances our understanding of climate systems and the potential impacts of large-scale interventions. This knowledge informs future research and policy decisions related to climate change.

- Development of New Technologies: The pursuit of geoengineering drives innovation in environmental technologies, with potential applications in climate mitigation, carbon capture, and environmental management.

2. Environmental and Health Benefits:

- Potential Climate Mitigation: If successful, geoengineering techniques could provide temporary or long-term relief from the impacts of climate change, such as rising temperatures and sea-level rise. This could help prevent severe environmental damage and protect vulnerable ecosystems.

- Reduction in Carbon Emissions: CDR methods and soil carbon sequestration could contribute to reducing atmospheric CO_2 levels, helping to mitigate the greenhouse effect and its associated impacts.

3. Ethical and Social Considerations:

- Ethical Research Practices: Addressing ethical considerations in geoengineering research promotes responsible conduct and safeguards the rights and well-being of affected communities. Ensuring ethical standards is essential for maintaining research integrity and public trust.

- Informed Public Dialogue: Engaging with the public and fostering discussions about geoengineering helps build understanding and address concerns about the implications of climate intervention. Transparency and education are key to navigating ethical and social issues.

Conclusion:

Geoengineering field trials represent a frontier in climate science and technology, offering potential solutions to combat climate change while presenting significant risks and ethical challenges. By exploring various techniques for modifying Earth's climate systems, researchers aim to address the urgent need for climate action and develop innovative approaches to environmental management.

As research progresses, it is essential to address scientific, environmental, ethical, and regulatory aspects to ensure responsible and effective geoengineering interventions. By balancing innovation with careful consideration of risks and public engagement, researchers and policymakers can navigate the complexities of geoengineering and contribute to meaningful progress in addressing climate change.

EXPERIMENT SEVENTY FOUR

SYNTHETIC VIRUS CREATION: NAVIGATING THE FRONTIERS OF BIOENGINEERING

Introduction:

Synthetic virus creation involves designing and constructing viruses from scratch or modifying existing ones using synthetic biology techniques. This cutting-edge field has significant potential for advancing medicine, biotechnology, and virology. However, it also raises concerns about biosafety, ethics, and the potential misuse of synthetic viruses. Understanding the motivations, techniques, and impacts of synthetic virus creation is crucial for navigating the opportunities and challenges it presents.

Historical Context and Techniques:

1. Historical Overview:

   - Origins of Synthetic Biology: The concept of synthetic biology emerged in the early 21st century, aiming to engineer biological systems and organisms through genetic modifications. Synthetic virus creation became a notable application of this field, with the goal of understanding virus function, developing new therapies, and studying virus behavior.

- Early Experiments: Initial experiments in synthetic virology involved modifying the genomes of existing viruses to study their functions and interactions. Researchers aimed to understand viral mechanisms and test new therapeutic approaches.

2. Contemporary Techniques:

- De Novo Virus Design: Modern synthetic virology includes the creation of entirely new viruses by designing their genomes from scratch. This involves using advanced sequencing technologies and computational tools to construct viral genomes and produce functional viruses in the laboratory.

- Genetic Modification: Researchers use genetic engineering techniques to modify the genomes of existing viruses. This may involve adding, deleting, or altering specific genes to study their effects on viral behavior, replication, and pathogenicity.

- Virus Synthesis Platforms: Advanced synthesis platforms, such as automated DNA synthesizers and gene-editing technologies (e.g., CRISPR-Cas9), facilitate the construction and modification of viral genomes. These platforms enable precise control over genetic sequences and viral properties.

3. Experimental Techniques:

- Virus Reconstruction: Scientists reconstruct viruses by synthesizing their complete genomes and introducing them into host cells. This allows researchers to study viral replication, protein expression, and interactions with the host.

- Functional Analysis: Synthetic viruses are used to test hypotheses about viral mechanisms and interactions. Researchers analyze how synthetic viruses behave in various conditions, including their effects on host cells and immune responses.

- Biosafety Measures: Due to the potential risks associated with synthetic viruses, rigorous biosafety measures are implemented in laboratories. These include containment facilities, safety protocols, and risk assessments to prevent accidental release or misuse.

Impact:

1. Scientific and Technological Impact:

- Advancements in Virology: Synthetic virus creation enhances our understanding of viral biology, including replication mechanisms, host interactions, and pathogenicity. This knowledge informs the development of new antiviral therapies and vaccines.

- Innovations in Biotechnology: The techniques and technologies developed for synthetic virology have broader applications in biotechnology. They contribute to advancements in gene therapy, vaccine development, and synthetic biology.

2. Medical and Therapeutic Impact:

- Vaccine Development: Synthetic viruses are used to create attenuated or modified viruses for vaccine development. This approach allows researchers to develop vaccines against emerging infectious diseases and improve existing vaccine strategies.

- Therapeutic Research: Synthetic viruses offer a platform for studying virus-based therapies, such as oncolytic viruses that target cancer cells or gene-delivery systems for therapeutic interventions. These applications have potential benefits for treating various medical conditions.

3. Ethical and Social Impact:

- Ethical Considerations: Synthetic virus creation raises ethical questions about biosafety, dual-use concerns (i.e., potential misuse for malicious purposes), and the long-term effects of synthetic viruses on ecosystems and human health. Ethical guidelines and oversight are essential for responsible research conduct.

- Public Perception and Trust: Public perception of synthetic virology varies, with concerns about safety and potential misuse. Transparency in research practices and clear communication about risks and benefits are important for maintaining public trust and understanding.

4. Regulatory and Policy Considerations:

- Biosafety Regulations: Regulatory frameworks govern the creation and use of synthetic viruses to ensure laboratory safety and prevent potential risks. Regulations may include guidelines for containment, risk assessment, and reporting.

- Ethical Guidelines: Developing ethical guidelines for synthetic virus research is crucial for addressing concerns about safety, misuse, and the responsible conduct of research. Ethics committees and advisory boards play a role in setting standards and reviewing research proposals.

Effect:

1. Scientific Advancements:

- Enhanced Understanding of Viruses: Synthetic virus research provides insights into viral biology, enabling researchers to study virus function, replication, and interactions. This knowledge informs future research and therapeutic development.

- Development of New Technologies: Innovations in synthetic virology contribute to the advancement of biotechnology and related fields. Techniques developed for synthetic viruses have applications in gene therapy, vaccine development, and synthetic biology.

2. Medical and Therapeutic Benefits:

- Improved Vaccines and Therapies: Synthetic viruses offer a platform for developing new vaccines and therapies for infectious diseases. This includes designing vaccines against emerging pathogens and exploring novel therapeutic approaches.

- Advancements in Gene Delivery: Virus-based gene delivery systems developed through synthetic virology have potential applications in gene therapy, providing new options for treating genetic disorders and other medical conditions.

3. Ethical and Social Considerations:

- Responsible Research Practices: Addressing ethical considerations in synthetic virus research promotes responsible conduct and safeguards public health and safety. Ensuring ethical standards is essential for maintaining research integrity and trust.

- Public Engagement: Engaging with the public and fostering discussions about synthetic virology helps build understanding and address concerns about the implications of synthetic viruses. Transparency and education are key to navigating ethical and social issues.

Conclusion:

Synthetic virus creation represents a groundbreaking area of research with significant implications for science, medicine, and ethics. By exploring the potential of synthetic viruses to advance our understanding of virology, develop new therapies, and address global health challenges, researchers are pushing the boundaries of biotechnology.

As research progresses, it is essential to address scientific, medical, ethical, and regulatory aspects to ensure responsible and effective use of synthetic viruses. By balancing innovation with careful consideration of risks and public engagement, researchers and policymakers can navigate the complexities of synthetic virus creation and contribute to meaningful progress in virology and biotechnology.

EXPERIMENT SEVENTY FIVE

MICRODOSING STUDIES: EXPLORING THE POTENTIAL AND RISKS OF SUBTHRESHOLD DRUG USE

Microdosing refers to the practice of consuming sub-threshold amounts of psychoactive substances — typically one-tenth to one-twentieth of a standard dose. This approach aims to harness the potential cognitive and emotional benefits of these substances while minimizing their psychoactive effects. Microdosing studies have gained popularity in recent years for their potential applications in enhancing creativity, mood, and cognitive function. However, these studies also face challenges related to scientific rigor, safety, and ethical considerations.

Historical Context and Techniques:

1. Historical Overview:

 - Origins and Early Use: The concept of microdosing can be traced back to the 20th century when researchers and enthusiasts began exploring the effects of low doses of psychedelic substances. Early adopters included prominent figures like psychologist James Fadiman, who documented anecdotal reports of microdosing benefits in the 1960s.

- Recent Resurgence: Interest in microdosing has surged in the 21st century, driven by increased awareness of psychedelic substances and their potential therapeutic applications. Modern microdosing studies are often conducted within the context of broader research on psychedelics and mental health.

2. Contemporary Techniques:

- Psychedelic Substances: Commonly studied substances in microdosing research include psilocybin (magic mushrooms), LSD (lysergic acid diethylamide), and mescaline. These substances are chosen for their potential cognitive and emotional benefits.

- Dosage and Administration: Microdoses are typically measured in micrograms (for substances like LSD) or milligrams (for substances like psilocybin). The goal is to use a dose that is below the threshold for noticeable psychoactive effects while still potentially providing benefits.

- Study Design: Microdosing studies often use randomized controlled trials (RCTs), observational studies, or self-reported surveys to assess the effects of microdosing on various outcomes. Researchers may compare microdosing to placebo or other control conditions to evaluate its effects.

3. Experimental Techniques:

- Controlled Experiments: In clinical settings, microdosing studies involve administering precise doses of psychedelic substances under controlled conditions. Participants are monitored for physiological and psychological responses, with data collected through standardized assessments and questionnaires.

- Self-Reported Data: Many microdosing studies rely on self-reported data from individuals who practice microdosing independently. Participants may provide information on their experiences, mood, cognitive function, and any perceived benefits or adverse effects.

- Long-Term Monitoring: Some studies involve long-term monitoring of individuals who practice microdosing to assess the potential cumulative effects and safety of regular use.

Impact:

1. Scientific and Technological Impact:

- Advancements in Psychedelic Research: Microdosing studies contribute to the broader field of psychedelic research, providing insights into the effects of low-dose psychedelics on cognition, mood, and mental health. This research informs the development of new therapeutic approaches and enhances our understanding of psychedelic substances.

- Innovation in Mental Health Treatments: The exploration of microdosing offers potential new avenues for treating mental health conditions such as depression, anxiety, and cognitive decline. This research could lead to novel treatments and improve existing therapeutic options.

2. Medical and Therapeutic Impact:

- Potential Benefits: Preliminary studies and anecdotal reports suggest that microdosing may offer benefits such as improved mood, enhanced creativity, increased focus, and reduced symptoms of anxiety and depression. However, more rigorous research is needed to confirm these effects and understand their mechanisms.

- Therapeutic Applications: If proven effective, microdosing could become a complementary approach to traditional mental health treatments. It may provide individuals with alternative options for managing mental health conditions and enhancing cognitive function.

3. Ethical and Social Impact:

- Ethical Considerations: Microdosing research raises ethical questions related to the use of psychoactive substances, informed consent, and the potential for abuse. Researchers must ensure that studies are conducted with strict ethical guidelines and that participants are fully informed about the risks and benefits.

- Public Perception and Acceptance: Public perception of microdosing varies, with some viewing it as a promising approach to enhancing well-being and creativity, while others express concerns about safety and the potential for misuse. Educating the public and fostering informed discussions about microdosing is important for addressing these concerns.

4. Regulatory and Policy Considerations:

- Legal Status: The legal status of psychedelic substances varies by country and jurisdiction.

Researchers must navigate regulatory requirements related to the use of controlled substances in clinical trials and ensure compliance with relevant laws.

- Policy Development: As research on microdosing progresses, policymakers may need to develop guidelines and regulations related to the use of psychedelics in research and therapeutic settings. This includes addressing issues related to safety, efficacy, and public health.

Effect:

1. Scientific Advancements:

- Enhanced Understanding of Psychedelics: Microdosing studies contribute to a deeper understanding of how low doses of psychedelics affect the brain, cognition, and emotional regulation. This knowledge informs future research and therapeutic development.

- Development of New Research Methods: The exploration of microdosing encourages the development of new research methods and technologies for studying the effects of psychoactive substances, including advanced imaging techniques and data analysis tools.

2. Medical and Therapeutic Benefits:

- Potential Improvement in Mental Health: If proven effective, microdosing could offer new options for improving mental health and cognitive function. This may lead to the development of novel treatments for conditions such as depression, anxiety, and cognitive decline.

- Enhanced Cognitive Function: Microdosing may provide benefits related to cognitive function, creativity, and productivity. This could have implications for individuals seeking to enhance their performance in personal and professional contexts.

3. Ethical and Social Considerations:

- Responsible Research Practices: Addressing ethical considerations in microdosing research promotes responsible conduct and safeguards the well-being of participants. Ensuring ethical standards is essential for maintaining research integrity and public trust.

- Informed Public Dialogue: Engaging with the public and fostering discussions about microdosing helps build understanding and address concerns about the implications of psychoactive substance use. Transparency and education are key to navigating ethical and social issues.

Conclusion:

Microdosing studies represent a fascinating and emerging area of research with the potential to impact mental health, cognitive function, and creativity. By exploring the effects of low-dose psychedelics, researchers are pushing the boundaries of our understanding of these substances and their applications.As research progresses, it is essential to address scientific, medical, ethical, and regulatory aspects to ensure responsible and effective exploration of microdosing. By balancing innovation with careful consideration of risks and public engagement, researchers and policymakers can navigate the complexities of microdosing and contribute to meaningful advancements in mental health and cognitive enhancement.

EXPERIMENT SEVENTY SIX

ARTIFICIAL INTELLIGENCE ALIGNMENT EXPERIMENTS: ENSURING SAFE AND BENEFICIAL AI SYSTEMS

Artificial Intelligence (AI) alignment refers to the challenge of ensuring that advanced AI systems operate in ways that align with human values and objectives. As AI systems become increasingly complex and capable, ensuring their alignment with human goals becomes a critical priority. AI alignment experiments aim to address these challenges by developing methods and frameworks for guiding AI behavior, minimizing risks, and ensuring that AI systems contribute positively to society.

Historical Context and Techniques:

1. Historical Overview:

   - Early AI Development: The origins of AI alignment can be traced back to the early days of AI research when basic algorithms and rule-based systems were developed. Early concerns about AI safety were primarily focused on ensuring that systems followed predefined rules and avoided errors.

- Emergence of Complex AI Systems: With the advent of machine learning and deep learning, AI systems became more sophisticated and capable of making decisions based on large datasets. This increased complexity introduced new challenges related to alignment and control.

2. Contemporary Techniques:

- Value Alignment: Researchers are developing methods to ensure that AI systems align with human values and ethical principles. This includes designing reward functions, ethical guidelines, and decision-making frameworks that reflect human priorities.

- Robustness and Safety: Techniques for enhancing the robustness and safety of AI systems involve designing mechanisms to handle uncertainties, adversarial attacks, and unexpected behaviors. This includes developing algorithms that can adapt to changing environments and handle edge cases.

- Interpretability and Transparency: Ensuring that AI systems are interpretable and transparent is crucial for understanding their decision-making processes.

Researchers are developing methods to visualize and explain AI behavior, making it easier to identify and address alignment issues.

3. Experimental Techniques:

- Simulation and Testing: AI alignment experiments often involve simulating various scenarios and testing AI systems in controlled environments. This allows researchers to observe how AI systems behave under different conditions and evaluate their alignment with human goals.

- Human-in-the-Loop: Incorporating human feedback and oversight into AI systems is a key technique for alignment. Researchers use human-in-the-loop approaches to guide AI decision-making, refine reward functions, and address potential misalignments.

- Ethical Audits: Conducting ethical audits involves evaluating AI systems against ethical standards and guidelines. This includes assessing potential risks, biases, and unintended consequences to ensure that AI systems operate in a manner consistent with societal values.

Impact:

1. Scientific and Technological Impact:

- Advancements in AI Safety: AI alignment experiments contribute to advancements in AI safety and robustness. By developing and testing new methods for aligning AI behavior with human values, researchers enhance the overall reliability and effectiveness of AI systems.

- Innovation in AI Design: Techniques and frameworks developed through alignment experiments inform the design of future AI systems. This includes incorporating alignment considerations into the development process, resulting in AI systems that are better suited to meet human needs.

2. Medical and Therapeutic Impact:

- AI in Healthcare: Aligning AI systems with medical ethics and patient values is crucial for ensuring that AI applications in healthcare are safe, effective, and respectful of patient autonomy. Alignment experiments contribute to the development of AI systems that support medical decision-making and improve patient outcomes.

- Assistive Technologies: AI alignment plays a role in the development of assistive technologies, such as those used in rehabilitation and mental health support. Ensuring that these technologies align with user needs and preferences enhances their effectiveness and acceptance.

3. Ethical and Social Impact:

- Ethical AI Development: Addressing alignment challenges is essential for the ethical development and deployment of AI systems. By ensuring that AI systems align with human values and ethical principles, researchers promote responsible AI practices and mitigate potential risks.

- Public Trust and Acceptance: Ensuring that AI systems are aligned with human goals and values helps build public trust and acceptance. Transparency, explainability, and ethical considerations are key to fostering positive perceptions of AI and addressing societal concerns.

4. Regulatory and Policy Considerations:

- AI Governance: Developing regulations and policies related to AI alignment is essential for guiding the responsible development and deployment of AI systems. Policymakers must address issues related to safety, ethics, and accountability to ensure that AI systems operate in a manner consistent with societal values.

- Standards and Guidelines: Establishing standards and guidelines for AI alignment helps ensure consistency and quality in AI research and development.

This includes developing best practices for alignment experiments and promoting adherence to ethical principles.

Effect:

1. Scientific Advancements:

   - Improved AI Design: AI alignment experiments lead to advancements in the design and implementation of AI systems. By addressing alignment challenges, researchers contribute to the development of AI technologies that are more reliable, effective, and aligned with human goals.

   - Enhanced Understanding of AI Behavior: Studying alignment helps researchers gain a deeper understanding of AI behavior and decision-making. This knowledge informs the development of better alignment techniques and frameworks.

2. Medical and Therapeutic Benefits:

   - Enhanced Healthcare AI: Aligning AI systems with medical ethics and patient values improves the safety and effectiveness of AI applications in healthcare. This leads to better patient outcomes and supports the responsible use of AI in medical settings.

- Effective Assistive Technologies: AI alignment ensures that assistive technologies meet user needs and preferences, enhancing their effectiveness and acceptance.

3. Ethical and Social Considerations:

- Responsible AI Practices: Addressing alignment challenges promotes responsible AI development and deployment. This includes ensuring that AI systems operate in accordance with ethical principles and societal values.

- Informed Public Dialogue: Engaging with the public and fostering discussions about AI alignment helps build understanding and address concerns about the implications of AI technology. Transparency and education are key to navigating ethical and social issues.

Conclusion:

Artificial Intelligence alignment experiments represent a critical area of research in ensuring that AI systems operate safely, ethically, and effectively. By developing methods and frameworks for aligning AI behavior with human values, researchers are advancing the field of AI and addressing important challenges related to safety, ethics, and societal impact.

As AI technology continues to evolve, it is essential to address alignment challenges with rigorous scientific research, ethical considerations, and regulatory oversight. By balancing innovation with careful attention to alignment, researchers and policymakers can navigate the complexities of AI development and contribute to the creation of beneficial and trustworthy AI systems.

EXPERIMENT SEVENTY SEVEN

SPACE DEBRIS REMOVAL EXPERIMENTS: ADDRESSING THE CHALLENGE OF ORBITAL JUNK

Introduction:

Space debris, or space junk, refers to the collection of defunct satellites, spent rocket stages, and other fragments resulting from collisions or disintegration of space objects orbiting Earth. As the number of satellites and space missions increases, the problem of space debris has become more critical, posing risks to active satellites and future space missions. Space debris removal experiments aim to develop effective technologies and strategies for mitigating this growing issue and ensuring the sustainability of space activities.

Historical Context and Techniques:

1. Historical Overview:

- Early Space Missions: The problem of space debris emerged as space exploration expanded in the 1960s and 1970s. The accumulation of defunct satellites and rocket stages began to raise concerns about the long-term impact on space operations.

- Growing Awareness: In the 1980s and 1990s, incidents such as the collision of Iridium 33 and Cosmos 2251 satellites highlighted the increasing risk of space debris. This led to a heightened focus on debris management and removal strategies.

2. Contemporary Techniques:

- Active Debris Removal (ADR): ADR involves using specialized spacecraft or robotic systems to capture and deorbit space debris. Techniques include using nets, harpoons, or robotic arms to capture debris and guide it to a controlled re-entry into Earth's atmosphere.

- Laser Ablation: Laser ablation involves using ground-based or space-based lasers to target debris, creating small thrusts that alter the debris's trajectory and facilitate its controlled re-entry or displacement.

- Electrodynamic Tethers: Electrodynamic tethers generate thrust by interacting with the Earth's magnetic field. These tethers can be used to deorbit space debris by converting orbital energy into electrical energy, which is then dissipated.

- Magnetic Capture: Magnetic capture systems use magnetic fields to attract and capture metallic debris.

These systems can be deployed from spacecraft or ground-based facilities to collect and remove debris.

3. Experimental Techniques:

- Orbital Test Missions: Experimental missions are conducted to test and validate debris removal technologies in orbit. These missions involve deploying prototype systems and assessing their performance in capturing and removing space debris.

- Ground-Based Simulations: Ground-based simulations and laboratory tests are used to evaluate the effectiveness of debris removal techniques under controlled conditions. These simulations help refine technologies and address potential challenges.

- Collaboration and International Efforts: Space agencies, research institutions, and private companies collaborate on space debris removal experiments. International efforts, such as the Inter-Agency Space Debris Coordination Committee (IADC), aim to coordinate activities and develop global strategies for debris management.

Impact:

1. Scientific and Technological Impact:

- Advancements in Debris Removal Technologies: Space debris removal experiments contribute to advancements in technologies designed to address the debris problem. Successful experiments lead to the development of practical solutions for mitigating the risks associated with space debris.

- Innovation in Space Operations: The development of debris removal technologies influences the design of future space missions and satellite systems. Incorporating debris mitigation strategies into mission planning and satellite design helps reduce the generation of new debris.

2. Medical and Therapeutic Impact:

- Indirect Impact: While space debris removal experiments do not have direct medical or therapeutic applications, their successful implementation contributes to the safety and sustainability of space missions. This indirectly supports scientific research and technological advancements that may have medical and therapeutic benefits.

3. Ethical and Social Impact:

- Safety and Sustainability: Addressing the space debris problem is crucial for ensuring the safety and sustainability of space activities. Effective debris removal contributes to the long-term viability of space exploration and satellite operations, benefiting society by preserving access to space for future generations.

- International Collaboration: Space debris removal experiments often involve international collaboration, promoting global cooperation and shared responsibility for managing space resources. This collaborative approach fosters positive relationships between spacefaring nations and organizations.

4. Regulatory and Policy Considerations:

- Space Debris Mitigation Guidelines: Developing and implementing guidelines for space debris mitigation is essential for regulating space activities and minimizing the generation of new debris. Policies and regulations related to debris removal help ensure that space operations are conducted responsibly.

- Funding and Investment: Securing funding and investment for space debris removal research and technology development is crucial for advancing these efforts. Public and private sector investment supports the development and deployment of effective debris removal solutions.

Effect:

1. Scientific Advancements:

- Enhanced Understanding of Space Debris: Space debris removal experiments contribute to a deeper understanding of the space debris environment and the challenges associated with debris management. This knowledge informs future research and technological development.

- Development of Effective Solutions: Successful experiments lead to the development of practical solutions for removing space debris, improving the safety and sustainability of space operations.

2. Medical and Therapeutic Benefits:

- Indirect Benefits: While space debris removal experiments do not directly impact medical or therapeutic fields, they support the overall sustainability of space activities, which can have indirect benefits for scientific research and technological advancements.

3. Ethical and Social Considerations:

- Preservation of Space Environment: Addressing space debris is an ethical responsibility to preserve the space environment for future generations. Effective debris removal contributes to the responsible management of space resources and ensures the continued accessibility of space for exploration and research.

- Promoting Global Cooperation: International collaboration on space debris removal fosters positive relationships between spacefaring nations and organizations, promoting global cooperation and shared responsibility.

Conclusion:

Space debris removal experiments represent a crucial area of research and development for addressing the growing challenge of orbital debris. By developing and testing technologies and strategies for debris removal, researchers are advancing the field of space operations and contributing to the sustainability of space activities.

As space exploration and satellite deployment continue to expand, it is essential to address the space debris problem with innovative solutions and international collaboration. By balancing technological advancement with responsible management practices, researchers and policymakers can work towards a safer and more sustainable space environment for future generations.

EXPERIMENT SEVENTY EIGHT

EXPERIMENTS ON HUMAN FERTILITY: INNOVATIONS, ETHICAL CONSIDERATIONS, AND IMPACT

Introduction:

Human fertility research encompasses a range of experiments and studies aimed at understanding and improving reproductive health, addressing infertility, and exploring the underlying biological mechanisms of human reproduction. This field includes advancements in assisted reproductive technologies (ART), fertility preservation, and genetic interventions. While these experiments have led to significant scientific and medical progress, they also raise important ethical, social, and regulatory considerations.

Historical Context and Techniques:

1. Historical Overview:

- Early Fertility Research: Initial studies focused on understanding basic reproductive biology and identifying factors influencing fertility. Early research laid the groundwork for more advanced interventions and technologies.

- Development of ART: The development of ART technologies, including in vitro fertilization (IVF), embryo transfer, and gamete donation, marked significant milestones in fertility research. The first successful IVF baby was born in 1978, revolutionizing the field of reproductive medicine.

2. Contemporary Techniques:

- In Vitro Fertilization (IVF): IVF involves fertilizing an egg outside the body and then implanting the embryo into the uterus. This technique has helped many individuals and couples overcome infertility and achieve pregnancy.

- Egg and Sperm Donation: Donor eggs and sperm are used in cases where individuals have fertility issues or genetic concerns. These technologies provide options for family building for those who may not have viable gametes.

- Fertility Preservation: Techniques such as cryopreservation (freezing) of eggs, sperm, and embryos allow individuals to preserve their fertility for future use. This is particularly important for cancer patients undergoing treatments that may affect fertility.

- Genetic Screening and Editing: Advances in genetic screening and editing, including preimplantation genetic diagnosis (PGD) and CRISPR technology, enable the identification and correction of genetic disorders before pregnancy or during embryo development.

3. Experimental Techniques:

- Stem Cell Research: Stem cell research explores the potential of stem cells to generate gametes (eggs and sperm) or develop new treatments for infertility. This research is in early stages but holds promise for future applications.

- Uterus Transplantation: Uterus transplantation is an experimental procedure aimed at enabling women with uterine factor infertility to carry a pregnancy. The first successful live birth from a transplanted uterus occurred in 2014.

- Artificial Gametes: Research into creating artificial gametes from somatic cells aims to address fertility issues and provide new reproductive options. This technology is still experimental and requires further validation.

Impact:

1. Scientific and Technological Impact:

- Advancements in Reproductive Medicine: Experiments on human fertility have led to significant advancements in reproductive medicine, including improved ART techniques, better understanding of reproductive biology, and novel approaches to infertility treatment.

- Innovation in Genetic Research: Genetic screening and editing technologies have enhanced the ability to identify and address genetic disorders, leading to more informed reproductive choices and healthier pregnancies.

2. Medical and Therapeutic Impact:

- Improved Fertility Treatments: The development of ART and fertility preservation techniques has provided new options for individuals and couples facing infertility, helping them achieve successful pregnancies and family building.

- Enhanced Reproductive Health: Research on fertility preservation and genetic interventions contributes to improved reproductive health and offers solutions for managing conditions that impact fertility.

3. Ethical and Social Impact:

- Ethical Considerations: Experiments on human fertility raise ethical questions related to the manipulation of embryos, genetic editing, and the use of donor gametes. Ensuring ethical practices and addressing concerns about consent, safety, and equity is crucial.

- Social Implications: Advances in fertility technologies impact family planning, reproductive choices, and societal attitudes towards infertility. Access to fertility treatments and technologies can influence social dynamics and family structures.

4. Regulatory and Policy Considerations:

- Regulation of Fertility Technologies: Governments and regulatory bodies establish guidelines and regulations to ensure the safety and efficacy of fertility technologies. Policies address issues such as embryo handling, genetic screening, and access to treatments.

- Ethical Guidelines: Ethical guidelines for fertility research and treatments are developed to address concerns related to the manipulation of human embryos, genetic interventions, and reproductive rights. These guidelines aim to balance scientific advancement with ethical considerations.

Effect:

1. Scientific Advancements:

- Enhanced Understanding of Reproduction: Fertility experiments contribute to a deeper understanding of human reproduction, including the biological processes involved in conception, pregnancy, and fertility.

- Development of New Technologies: Research leads to the development of innovative fertility technologies and treatments, improving the options available for individuals and couples facing fertility challenges.

2. Medical and Therapeutic Benefits:

- Successful Pregnancies: Advances in ART and fertility preservation enable successful pregnancies for individuals and couples who may otherwise face infertility. This contributes to family building and improves reproductive outcomes.

- Informed Reproductive Choices: Genetic screening and editing technologies provide valuable information for making informed reproductive choices, reducing the risk of genetic disorders and improving overall reproductive health.

3. Ethical and Social Considerations:

- Responsible Practice: Addressing ethical considerations ensures responsible practice in fertility research and treatment. This includes safeguarding the rights and well-being of individuals involved and addressing concerns about the manipulation of embryos and genetic material.

- Equitable Access: Ensuring equitable access to fertility treatments and technologies helps address disparities in reproductive healthcare and provides opportunities for diverse populations.

Conclusion:

Experiments on human fertility represent a dynamic and evolving field of research with significant implications for reproductive health, family building, and genetic intervention. By advancing ART, fertility preservation, and genetic technologies, researchers and clinicians are improving the options available for individuals facing infertility and enhancing our understanding of human reproduction.

As fertility research continues to progress, it is essential to address ethical considerations, ensure responsible practice, and promote equitable access to treatments. Balancing scientific advancement with ethical and social considerations will contribute to the development of safe, effective, and inclusive reproductive technologies.

EXPERIMENT SEVENTY NINE

EXPERIMENTS ON ARTIFICIAL INTELLIGENCE SAFETY: ENSURING TRUSTWORTHY AND RELIABLE AI SYSTEMS

Introduction:

Artificial Intelligence (AI) has rapidly evolved, leading to transformative applications across various domains, including healthcare, finance, transportation, and more. However, the advancement of AI technologies brings with it critical concerns about safety, reliability, and ethical implications. Experiments on AI safety aim to address these concerns by developing methods and frameworks to ensure that AI systems operate safely, ethically, and in alignment with human values.

Historical Context and Techniques:

1. Historical Overview:

- Early AI Safety Concerns: As AI technologies began to develop in the mid-20th century, early safety concerns centered around the control and predictability of AI systems. The theoretical exploration of AI safety started with discussions on the alignment of AI goals with human values.

- Growth of AI Applications: With the rise of machine learning and deep learning in the 2000s, the complexity of AI systems increased, raising new safety challenges related to autonomy, decision-making, and unintended consequences.

2. Contemporary Techniques:

- Robustness Testing: Robustness testing involves evaluating AI systems' performance under various conditions to ensure they behave reliably and consistently. This includes testing for adversarial attacks, where small changes in input can lead to incorrect or harmful outputs.

- Explainability and Transparency: Explainable AI (XAI) focuses on making AI systems' decision-making processes more transparent and understandable to users. Techniques include generating interpretable models and providing explanations for AI-driven decisions.

- Ethical Alignment: Ensuring that AI systems align with ethical principles involves incorporating values such as fairness, accountability, and transparency into the design and deployment of AI technologies. This includes addressing biases and ensuring equitable outcomes.

- Safety Constraints: Implementing safety constraints involves setting boundaries and limits on AI system behavior to prevent harmful actions or unintended consequences. Techniques include defining safety protocols and implementing fail-safes.

3. Experimental Techniques:

- Simulation and Modeling: Experiments often use simulations and models to test AI systems' behavior in controlled environments. This allows researchers to assess how AI systems respond to different scenarios and identify potential safety issues.

- Adversarial Testing: Adversarial testing involves intentionally introducing challenging or deceptive inputs to evaluate how AI systems handle unexpected or malicious situations. This helps identify vulnerabilities and improve system robustness.

- Human-AI Interaction Studies: Research on human-AI interaction explores how users interact with AI systems and how these systems can be designed to support safe and effective human collaboration. This includes studying user trust, decision support, and feedback mechanisms.

Impact:

1. Scientific and Technological Impact:

  - Advancements in AI Safety: Experiments on AI safety lead to advancements in technologies and methodologies for ensuring the safe and reliable operation of AI systems. This includes improvements in robustness, explainability, and ethical alignment.

  - Innovation in AI Design: Research on AI safety influences the design and development of new AI systems, contributing to the creation of more trustworthy and dependable technologies.

2. Medical and Therapeutic Impact:

  - Indirect Impact: While AI safety experiments do not have direct medical applications, the principles of safety and reliability are crucial for AI systems used in healthcare. Ensuring that AI systems operate safely and ethically supports the overall effectiveness of medical AI applications.

3. Ethical and Social Impact:

- Trust and Acceptance: Addressing AI safety concerns builds trust in AI technologies and promotes their responsible use. Ensuring that AI systems are aligned with ethical principles and operate reliably contributes to positive societal acceptance and integration.

- Equity and Fairness: Research on ethical alignment helps address biases and ensure fair outcomes in AI systems, reducing the risk of discrimination and promoting equitable treatment across diverse populations.

4. Regulatory and Policy Considerations:

- AI Safety Guidelines: Developing guidelines and regulations for AI safety is essential for ensuring the responsible deployment of AI technologies. These guidelines address issues such as transparency, accountability, and safety constraints.

- Policy Frameworks: Policy frameworks for AI safety help establish standards and best practices for the development and use of AI systems. This includes promoting research on safety and ethical considerations and setting requirements for transparency and accountability.

Effect:

1. Scientific Advancements:

- Enhanced Safety Mechanisms: Research on AI safety leads to the development of advanced safety mechanisms and methodologies, improving the reliability and trustworthiness of AI systems.

- Informed Design Practices: Experiments contribute to the refinement of design practices for AI systems, ensuring that safety and ethical considerations are integrated into the development process.

2. Medical and Therapeutic Benefits:

- Support for Healthcare AI: Ensuring the safety of AI systems used in healthcare supports the effective and reliable application of AI technologies for medical diagnostics, treatment planning, and patient care.

3. Ethical and Social Considerations:

- Responsible AI Use: Addressing AI safety concerns promotes responsible and ethical use of AI technologies, contributing to positive societal impact and reducing the risk of harm.

- Public Trust: Building trust in AI systems through safety and ethical considerations fosters public confidence and acceptance of AI technologies.

Conclusion:

Experiments on artificial intelligence safety are crucial for addressing the challenges and risks associated with the development and deployment of AI technologies. By advancing techniques for robustness testing, explainability, ethical alignment, and safety constraints, researchers and practitioners contribute to the creation of reliable and trustworthy AI systems.

As AI continues to evolve and become increasingly integrated into various aspects of society, it is essential to prioritize safety and ethical considerations in the development and use of these technologies. Ensuring that AI systems operate safely and in alignment with human values will contribute to their positive impact and acceptance in diverse applications.

EXPERIMENT EIGHTY

EXPERIMENTS ON HUMAN CONSCIOUSNESS: EXPLORING THE DEPTHS OF AWARENESS AND PERCEPTION

Introduction:

The study of human consciousness delves into one of the most profound and complex aspects of human experience—our awareness of ourselves and our surroundings. Experiments on human consciousness aim to understand how we perceive, process, and interpret information, as well as the nature of self-awareness and subjective experience. This field spans various disciplines, including neuroscience, psychology, and philosophy, and encompasses a range of experimental approaches and methodologies.

Historical Context and Techniques:

1. Historical Overview:

- Early Philosophical Inquiry: The philosophical exploration of consciousness dates back to ancient Greece, with thinkers like Socrates, Plato, and Aristotle pondering the nature of the self and awareness. These early inquiries laid the groundwork for later scientific investigations.

- Modern Neuroscience: The 19th and 20th centuries saw the emergence of neuroscience and psychology as scientific disciplines, providing new tools and methods for studying consciousness. Advances in brain imaging and cognitive science have significantly expanded our understanding of conscious experience.

2. Contemporary Techniques:

- Neuroimaging: Techniques such as functional magnetic resonance imaging (fMRI) and positron emission tomography (PET) allow researchers to visualize brain activity associated with different states of consciousness. These tools help identify neural correlates of awareness, perception, and cognitive processes.

- Electroencephalography (EEG): EEG measures electrical activity in the brain and is used to study brainwave patterns associated with various states of consciousness, including sleep, meditation, and altered states of awareness.

- Psychoactive Substances: The administration of psychoactive substances, such as hallucinogens or anesthetics, provides insights into altered states of consciousness and helps researchers explore the boundaries of awareness and perception.

- Meditation and Mindfulness Practices: Controlled studies of meditation and mindfulness techniques explore their effects on consciousness, self-awareness, and mental states. These practices offer a unique perspective on the modulation of conscious experience.

3. Experimental Techniques:

- Altered States of Consciousness: Experiments that induce altered states of consciousness, such as through sensory deprivation, hypnosis, or psychedelic substances, provide insights into the nature of subjective experience and the boundaries of awareness.

- Neuroscientific Studies: Research involving brain stimulation, such as transcranial magnetic stimulation (TMS) or deep brain stimulation (DBS), investigates how modulating brain activity affects consciousness, perception, and cognitive processes.

- Cognitive Psychology Experiments: Studies on attention, perception, and cognitive biases explore how consciousness influences our interpretation of sensory information and decision-making processes.

Impact:

1. Scientific and Technological Impact:

- Advancements in Neuroscience: Experiments on consciousness contribute to our understanding of brain function and the neural mechanisms underlying awareness, perception, and cognitive processes.

- Development of Diagnostic Tools: Insights from consciousness research inform the development of diagnostic tools and interventions for neurological and psychiatric disorders, such as coma, consciousness disorders, and mental health conditions.

2. Medical and Therapeutic Impact:

- Understanding Neurological Disorders: Research on consciousness helps improve our understanding of disorders affecting awareness, such as vegetative state, locked-in syndrome, and certain psychiatric conditions. This knowledge aids in diagnosis and treatment planning.

- Enhancing Mental Health: Studies on meditation and mindfulness provide therapeutic approaches for mental health issues, such as stress, anxiety, and depression, by offering techniques to modulate consciousness and emotional well-being.

3. Ethical and Social Impact:

- Ethical Considerations: Experiments on consciousness raise ethical questions related to the manipulation of awareness and perception, particularly when using psychoactive substances or invasive techniques. Ensuring informed consent and participant safety is crucial.

- Philosophical Implications: Research on consciousness has philosophical implications for understanding the nature of self, free will, and the mind-body relationship. These inquiries contribute to broader discussions about human identity and experience.

4. Regulatory and Policy Considerations:

- Ethics of Psychoactive Research: Regulatory guidelines and ethical frameworks govern research involving psychoactive substances and invasive techniques to ensure participant safety and address potential risks.

- Clinical Applications: Policies related to the clinical application of consciousness research inform the use of diagnostic tools, therapeutic interventions, and mental health treatments derived from scientific findings.

Effect:

1. Scientific Advancements:

- Deeper Understanding of Consciousness: Research on consciousness advances our understanding of the neural and cognitive mechanisms underlying awareness, perception, and self-awareness.

- Innovative Research Methods: The development of new experimental techniques and methodologies enhances the ability to study and manipulate consciousness, leading to novel insights and applications.

2. Medical and Therapeutic Benefits:

- Improved Diagnosis and Treatment: Insights from consciousness research contribute to better diagnosis and treatment options for neurological and psychiatric disorders, improving patient outcomes and quality of life.

- Therapeutic Approaches: Mindfulness and meditation techniques derived from consciousness research offer effective therapeutic interventions for mental health conditions, supporting emotional and psychological well-being.

3. Ethical and Social Considerations:

   - Responsible Research Practices: Addressing ethical considerations ensures that experiments on consciousness are conducted responsibly, with respect for participant welfare and informed consent.

   - Philosophical Insights: The exploration of consciousness provides valuable philosophical insights into the nature of human experience, selfhood, and the mind-body connection.

Conclusion:

Experiments on human consciousness represent a multifaceted and evolving field of research that seeks to unravel the complexities of awareness, perception, and self-awareness. Through neuroimaging, psychoactive research, and cognitive psychology, researchers are gaining valuable insights into the nature of consciousness and its implications for science, medicine, and philosophy.

As consciousness research continues to advance, it is essential to address ethical considerations, ensure responsible practice, and explore the broader implications of our understanding of consciousness. By balancing scientific inquiry with ethical and philosophical reflection, researchers can contribute to a deeper understanding of human experience and its impact on our lives.

EXPERIMENT EIGHTTY ONE

EXPERIMENTS ON LONGEVITY AND AGING: UNRAVELING THE SECRETS TO A LONGER, HEALTHIER LIFE

Introduction:

The quest for longevity and healthy aging has fascinated scientists and researchers for centuries. Experiments on longevity and aging seek to understand the biological, genetic, and environmental factors that influence lifespan and healthspan—the period of life spent in good health. This research aims to identify interventions that can extend life and improve quality of life in later years.

Historical Context and Techniques:

1. Historical Overview:

   - Early Observations: Ancient civilizations, including the Greeks and Romans, were already interested in factors contributing to long life. Philosophers like Hippocrates and Galen wrote about health practices that might extend lifespan.

- Modern Research: The 20th century saw the rise of gerontology as a scientific discipline, with a focus on understanding the biological processes of aging and developing interventions to promote longevity.

2. Contemporary Techniques:

- Genetic Studies: Research into the genetics of longevity has identified several genes associated with extended lifespan and resilience to age-related diseases. Techniques include genome-wide association studies (GWAS) and the study of centenarians' genomes.

- Caloric Restriction: Caloric restriction (CR) experiments, where individuals consume fewer calories without malnutrition, have shown to extend lifespan in various organisms. Studies investigate how CR affects metabolic processes and longevity.

- Senescence Research: Cellular senescence is the process by which cells lose their ability to divide and function properly. Research in this area explores ways to delay or reverse cellular senescence to extend healthy lifespan.

- Anti-Aging Interventions: Experiments on drugs and supplements, such as rapamycin, resveratrol, and NAD+ precursors, aim to slow down the aging process and improve healthspan by targeting biological pathways associated with aging.

3. Experimental Techniques:

- Model Organisms: Studies in model organisms, such as yeast, nematodes (C. elegans), fruit flies (Drosophila), and mice, provide insights into the biological mechanisms of aging and the effects of interventions on lifespan.

- Longitudinal Studies: Human longitudinal studies track individuals over extended periods to examine how lifestyle factors, genetics, and environmental influences impact aging and longevity.

- Clinical Trials: Clinical trials test the effectiveness of anti-aging interventions and therapies in humans. These trials assess the safety and efficacy of potential treatments for age-related diseases and overall longevity.

Impact:

1. Scientific and Technological Impact:

- Advancements in Aging Research: Experiments on longevity and aging contribute to our understanding of the biological mechanisms underlying aging and the development of interventions that can extend lifespan and improve healthspan.

- Innovation in Therapeutics: Research leads to the development of new drugs, supplements, and lifestyle interventions aimed at promoting healthy aging and preventing age-related diseases.

2. Medical and Therapeutic Impact:

- Improved Healthspan: Insights from aging research support the development of therapies and lifestyle recommendations that improve the quality of life in older adults by reducing the incidence of age-related diseases.

- Preventive Health Measures: Research on aging contributes to preventive health measures, including dietary recommendations, physical activity guidelines, and medical treatments that support healthy aging.

3. Ethical and Social Impact:

- Ethical Considerations: The pursuit of extending human lifespan raises ethical questions related to equity, resource allocation, and the societal implications of increased longevity. Ensuring that advancements in longevity research benefit all segments of society is crucial.

- Social Implications: Extended lifespans and improved healthspan have social implications, including changes in retirement age, healthcare needs, and intergenerational dynamics. Addressing these implications requires careful consideration and planning.

4. Regulatory and Policy Considerations:

- Regulation of Anti-Aging Interventions: Regulatory bodies oversee the approval and monitoring of anti-aging drugs and supplements to ensure their safety and efficacy. Policies must adapt to new discoveries and innovations in the field.

- Public Health Policies: Research on aging informs public health policies related to aging populations, including strategies for disease prevention, health promotion, and support for older adults.

Effect:

1. Scientific Advancements:

- Understanding Aging Processes: Research on longevity and aging enhances our understanding of the biological processes that drive aging and the potential for interventions to modify these processes.

- Development of New Treatments: Advances in aging research lead to the development of new treatments and interventions aimed at extending lifespan and improving quality of life.

2. Medical and Therapeutic Benefits:

- Enhanced Quality of Life: Effective interventions and treatments derived from aging research can improve the quality of life for older adults, reducing the burden of age-related diseases and enhancing overall well-being.

- Healthier Aging: Research findings support strategies for healthier aging, including lifestyle changes, medical treatments, and preventive measures that contribute to a longer and healthier life.

3. Ethical and Social Considerations:

- Informed Decision-Making: Ethical considerations related to longevity research promote informed decision-making about the use of interventions and the societal impact of extended lifespans.

- Equitable Access: Ensuring equitable access to advancements in aging research helps address disparities in health outcomes and supports the well-being of diverse populations.

Conclusion:

Experiments on longevity and aging represent a dynamic and interdisciplinary field of research with the potential to transform our understanding of the aging process and improve quality of life for individuals as they age. Through genetic studies, caloric restriction research, senescence studies, and clinical trials, scientists are uncovering insights into the biological mechanisms of aging and developing interventions to extend lifespan and healthspan.

As research in this field continues to advance, it is essential to address ethical considerations, societal implications, and regulatory challenges to ensure that the benefits of longevity research are realized in a responsible and equitable manner. By focusing on both scientific innovation and ethical responsibility, researchers and policymakers can contribute to a healthier and more fulfilling future for people of all ages.

EXPERIMENT EIGHTY TWO

EXPERIMENTS ON BRAIN-MACHINE INTEGRATION: BRIDGING THE GAP BETWEEN MIND AND MACHINE

Introduction:

Brain-machine integration represents a groundbreaking frontier in neuroscience and technology, aiming to establish direct communication between the human brain and external devices. This field explores how to harness brain activity to control machines, enhance cognitive functions, and ultimately create a seamless interface between the mind and technology. The research encompasses a range of applications from medical treatments to advanced computing and even futuristic concepts like brain-to-brain communication.

Historical Context and Techniques:

1. Historical Overview:

- Early Explorations: The idea of connecting the brain to external devices can be traced back to early neurology and cybernetics, with pioneering work in the 20th century exploring neural interfaces and electrical stimulation of the brain.

- Modern Advances: In recent decades, technological advancements in neuroscience, robotics, and artificial intelligence have accelerated progress in brain-machine integration, leading to practical applications and innovative research.

2. Contemporary Techniques:

- Electroencephalography (EEG): EEG technology records electrical activity of the brain through electrodes placed on the scalp. EEG-based brain-computer interfaces (BCIs) allow users to control devices or communicate by interpreting brainwave patterns.

- Implantable Devices: Neural implants, such as deep brain stimulators and brain implants, are surgically placed within the brain to interface with neural circuits. These devices can be used for both therapeutic and experimental purposes, including controlling prosthetics or treating neurological disorders.

- Functional Magnetic Resonance Imaging (fMRI): fMRI provides detailed images of brain activity by detecting changes in blood flow. It is used in research to understand how specific brain regions are involved in various cognitive tasks and to develop new brain-machine integration techniques.

- Optogenetics: This technique uses light to control genetically modified neurons. By introducing light-sensitive proteins into specific neurons, researchers can manipulate brain activity with high precision, offering new possibilities for brain-machine interactions.

3. Experimental Techniques:

- Brain-Computer Interfaces (BCIs): BCIs enable direct communication between the brain and external devices, such as computers or robotic arms. Experiments involve training individuals to control these devices using their brain signals, providing insights into the feasibility and effectiveness of these interfaces.

- Neuroprosthetics: Research in neuroprosthetics focuses on developing advanced prosthetic limbs and devices that can be controlled by the brain. These experiments explore how to create intuitive and functional connections between neural signals and prosthetic devices.

- Brain-to-Brain Communication: Emerging research investigates the potential for direct communication between brains, known as brain-to-brain interfaces. Experiments aim to explore whether information can be transmitted from one brain to another through neural signals and external devices.

Impact:

1. Scientific and Technological Impact:

- Advancements in Neuroscience: Experiments on brain-machine integration deepen our understanding of brain function and neural mechanisms, leading to advancements in neuroscience and cognitive science.

- Innovations in Technology: Research contributes to the development of cutting-edge technologies, including advanced prosthetics, assistive devices, and novel computing interfaces that bridge the gap between the brain and machines.

2. Medical and Therapeutic Impact:

- Rehabilitation and Assistive Devices: Brain-machine integration has the potential to revolutionize rehabilitation for individuals with motor impairments or neurological conditions by providing new ways to control prosthetic limbs or communicate.

- Treatment of Neurological Disorders: Neural implants and brain stimulation techniques are being explored as treatments for various neurological disorders, including Parkinson's disease, epilepsy, and chronic pain.

3. Ethical and Social Impact:

- Ethical Considerations: Brain-machine integration raises ethical questions about privacy, consent, and the potential for misuse. Ensuring informed consent and addressing concerns related to mental privacy and autonomy are critical.

- Social Implications: The integration of brain and machine technology could impact various aspects of society, including healthcare, communication, and human-computer interaction. Addressing the implications of these technologies on social dynamics and human identity is essential.

4. Regulatory and Policy Considerations:

- Regulation of Neural Devices: Regulatory frameworks must adapt to the rapid advancements in brain-machine integration, ensuring the safety, efficacy, and ethical use of neural implants, BCIs, and related technologies.

- Ethical Guidelines: Policies and guidelines are needed to address ethical issues related to brain-machine integration, including privacy concerns, consent, and the potential for enhancing or altering cognitive functions.

Effect:

1. Scientific Advancements:

 - Enhanced Understanding of Brain Function: Research on brain-machine integration provides valuable insights into how the brain processes and controls information, advancing our understanding of neural mechanisms and cognitive functions.

 - Technological Breakthroughs: The development of innovative technologies, such as BCIs and neuroprosthetics, pushes the boundaries of what is possible in human-computer interaction and opens new avenues for research and application.

2. Medical and Therapeutic Benefits:

 - Improved Rehabilitation: Brain-machine integration offers new opportunities for rehabilitation and assistive technology, improving the quality of life for individuals with disabilities or neurological conditions.

 - Innovative Treatments: Advances in neural implants and brain stimulation techniques provide potential new treatments for a range of neurological and psychiatric disorders, offering hope for improved patient outcomes.

3. Ethical and Social Considerations:

- Informed and Responsible Use: Addressing ethical and social implications ensures that brain-machine integration technologies are used responsibly, with respect for individual privacy and autonomy.

- Future Implications: Understanding the broader implications of brain-machine integration on society and human identity helps guide the responsible development and deployment of these technologies.

Conclusion:

Experiments on brain-machine integration represent a transformative and rapidly evolving field of research that aims to bridge the gap between the human brain and external devices. Through advances in neurotechnology, neural implants, and brain-computer interfaces, scientists are exploring new ways to enhance cognitive functions, improve medical treatments, and create seamless interactions between the mind and machines.

As research in brain-machine integration continues to advance, it is essential to address ethical considerations, societal implications, and regulatory challenges to ensure that these technologies are developed and used responsibly. By balancing scientific innovation with ethical responsibility, researchers and policymakers can contribute to a future where the integration of brain and machine enhances human capabilities and improves quality of life.

EXPERIMENT EIGHTY THREE

EXPERIMENTS ON GLOBAL GOVERNANCE AND DECISION-MAKING: SHAPING THE FUTURE OF INTERNATIONAL COOPERATION

Introduction:

Experiments on global governance and decision-making explore innovative approaches to managing international relations, addressing global challenges, and fostering cooperation among nations. These experiments seek to improve the effectiveness, fairness, and inclusiveness of global governance structures, aiming to address issues such as climate change, pandemics, and geopolitical conflicts. By testing new models and frameworks, researchers and policymakers aim to enhance the ability of global institutions to respond to complex, transnational problems.

Historical Context and Techniques:

1. Historical Overview:

 - Early Governance Models: The concept of global governance has evolved over time, with early examples including the League of Nations and the United Nations. These institutions were established to promote peace, security, and cooperation among nations.

- Contemporary Challenges: The 21st century has brought new challenges, including globalization, climate change, and digital transformation, prompting the need for innovative approaches to global governance and decision-making.

2. Contemporary Techniques:

- Experimental Governance Models: Various experimental models have been proposed to improve global governance, including decentralized networks, collaborative platforms, and new forms of international institutions. These models explore different approaches to decision-making, accountability, and representation.

- Simulation and Modeling: Simulation techniques, such as computer-based models and scenario planning, are used to test and evaluate different governance frameworks and decision-making processes. These experiments help identify potential outcomes and assess the effectiveness of various approaches.

- Participatory Decision-Making: Experiments in participatory decision-making involve engaging a diverse range of stakeholders, including citizens, experts, and policymakers, in the decision-making process. These experiments aim to improve transparency, inclusivity, and legitimacy in global governance.

3. Experimental Techniques:

- Global Governance Simulations: Simulations of global governance scenarios, including crisis management and policy implementation, provide insights into the functioning of different governance models and the potential impact of various decisions.

- Collaborative Platforms: Platforms such as international forums, virtual collaboration tools, and online communities enable stakeholders from different countries to work together on global issues. Experiments with these platforms assess their effectiveness in fostering cooperation and resolving conflicts.

- Institutional Innovations: Experiments with new institutional arrangements, such as multi-stakeholder partnerships and global networks, explore alternative ways to address global challenges and enhance the effectiveness of international cooperation.

Impact:

1. Scientific and Technological Impact:

- Advancements in Governance Theory: Experiments on global governance contribute to the development of new theories and models for managing international relations and addressing global challenges. These advancements enhance our understanding of governance dynamics and decision-making processes.

- Technological Innovations: The use of digital tools and platforms in global governance experiments drives innovation in technology, including advancements in data analytics, communication, and collaboration.

2. Policy and Institutional Impact:

- Enhanced Global Cooperation: Experiments on global governance help identify effective approaches to fostering international cooperation and addressing transnational issues. Successful models can be adopted or adapted by international institutions and governments.

- Improved Decision-Making: By testing different decision-making processes and frameworks, experiments contribute to more effective and inclusive governance. This leads to better policy outcomes and improved responses to global challenges.

3. Ethical and Social Impact:

- Equity and Inclusivity: Experiments in global governance often focus on improving equity and inclusivity in decision-making processes. Ensuring that diverse voices are heard and considered helps promote fairness and legitimacy in global governance.

- Public Engagement: Engaging citizens and stakeholders in governance experiments fosters greater public participation and trust in international institutions. It also helps address concerns about accountability and representation.

4. Regulatory and Policy Considerations:

- Regulation of New Models: The adoption of innovative governance models requires careful consideration of regulatory and policy implications. Ensuring that new models are compatible with existing international laws and agreements is essential.

- Global Policy Alignment: Aligning global governance experiments with international agreements and policy frameworks ensures that new approaches are consistent with global priorities and objectives.

Effect:

1. Scientific Advancements:

- Understanding Governance Dynamics: Research on global governance and decision-making provides insights into the functioning of international institutions and the impact of various governance models. This enhances our understanding of how to manage global challenges effectively.

- Development of New Models: Successful experiments contribute to the development of new governance models and frameworks that can be applied to address complex global issues.

2. Policy and Institutional Benefits:

- Effective Global Cooperation: Improved governance models and decision-making processes lead to more effective international cooperation and coordination. This enhances the ability of global institutions to address pressing issues and achieve collective goals.

- Resilient Institutions: Experiments help build resilient and adaptable global institutions that can respond to evolving challenges and changing circumstances.

3. Ethical and Social Considerations:

- Fair and Inclusive Governance: Ensuring that governance models are equitable and inclusive contributes to greater legitimacy and effectiveness in global decision-making. This helps address social and ethical concerns related to global governance.

- Public Trust: Transparent and participatory decision-making processes foster greater public trust in international institutions and promote a sense of shared responsibility for global challenges.

Conclusion:

Experiments on global governance and decision-making represent a crucial area of research aimed at improving the management of international relations and addressing complex global challenges. By exploring innovative models, utilizing simulation techniques, and engaging diverse stakeholders, researchers and policymakers are working to enhance the effectiveness, fairness, and inclusiveness of global governance.

As research in this field continues to evolve, it is essential to address ethical considerations, regulatory challenges, and the broader social implications of new governance models. By focusing on scientific innovation and responsible implementation, experiments on global governance can contribute to a more effective and equitable future for international cooperation and decision-making.

EXPERIMENT EIGHTY FOUR

HUMAN ENHANCEMENT TECHNOLOGIES: PUSHING THE BOUNDARIES OF HUMAN POTENTIAL

Introduction:

Human enhancement technologies (HETs) encompass a broad spectrum of innovations designed to augment or improve human physical, cognitive, and emotional capabilities. These technologies aim to push the boundaries of human potential, offering new ways to enhance performance, health, and overall well-being. From genetic modifications and brain-computer interfaces to advanced prosthetics and cognitive enhancers, HETs have the potential to revolutionize how we experience and interact with the world.

Historical Context and Techniques:

1. Historical Overview:

- Early Enhancements: Human enhancement has roots in ancient practices such as herbal remedies, physical training, and early medical interventions. Historically, people have sought ways to improve their health and abilities through various means.

- Modern Advances: The 20th and 21st centuries have seen rapid advancements in science and technology, leading to sophisticated enhancement technologies. Innovations in biotechnology, neuroscience, and artificial intelligence have driven the development of cutting-edge HETs.

2. Contemporary Techniques:

- Genetic Engineering: Technologies such as CRISPR-Cas9 allow for precise modifications of the human genome, potentially enabling the enhancement of physical traits, resistance to diseases, and cognitive abilities. Genetic engineering can lead to breakthroughs in personalized medicine and long-term health improvements.

- Brain-Computer Interfaces (BCIs): BCIs facilitate direct communication between the brain and external devices, enabling control of prosthetics, computers, or other technologies through thought alone. These interfaces offer significant potential for cognitive and sensory enhancement.

- Advanced Prosthetics and Exoskeletons: Modern prosthetics and wearable exoskeletons enhance physical capabilities, providing users with improved mobility, strength, and dexterity. These technologies are designed to restore or augment human movement and functionality.

- Cognitive Enhancers: Pharmacological and non-pharmacological interventions, such as nootropics and neurostimulation, are used to improve cognitive functions like memory, attention, and learning. Research in this area explores the potential of these enhancers to optimize mental performance.

3. Experimental Techniques:

- Gene Editing Trials: Clinical trials involving gene editing technologies explore their safety and efficacy for enhancing human traits or treating genetic disorders. These experiments test the potential benefits and risks associated with genetic modifications.

- Neuroprosthetics Research: Experiments with advanced neuroprosthetics focus on developing devices that integrate seamlessly with the nervous system, allowing for enhanced control and functionality of artificial limbs and other prosthetic devices.

- Cognitive Enhancement Studies: Research into cognitive enhancers includes trials of pharmaceutical drugs, brain stimulation techniques, and cognitive training programs. These studies assess their effectiveness in improving mental performance and overall cognitive function.

Impact:

1. Scientific and Technological Impact:

- Advancements in Biotechnology: HETs drive significant progress in biotechnology, including breakthroughs in genetic engineering, neurotechnology, and materials science. These advancements contribute to a deeper understanding of human biology and technology integration.

- Innovation in Medical Devices: The development of advanced prosthetics, exoskeletons, and BCIs represents a leap forward in medical device technology, offering new possibilities for enhancing human capabilities and improving quality of life.

2. Medical and Therapeutic Impact:

- Improved Health Outcomes: Genetic engineering and advanced medical devices have the potential to treat or prevent various health conditions, leading to better health outcomes and enhanced quality of life for individuals.

- Enhanced Rehabilitation: Technologies such as exoskeletons and neuroprosthetics offer new opportunities for rehabilitation and recovery, helping individuals regain lost functions or adapt to physical impairments.

3. Ethical and Social Impact:

- Ethical Considerations: HETs raise ethical questions about the limits of human enhancement, equity of access, and potential societal consequences. Ensuring that enhancements are used responsibly and equitably is a key consideration.

- Social Implications: The integration of enhancement technologies may impact social dynamics, including issues of inequality, privacy, and the definition of what it means to be human. Addressing these implications requires thoughtful consideration and dialogue.

4. Regulatory and Policy Considerations:

- Regulation of Enhancement Technologies: Establishing regulatory frameworks for HETs is essential to ensure their safety, efficacy, and ethical use. Policymakers must balance innovation with public safety and ethical concerns.

- Policy for Access and Equity: Ensuring equitable access to enhancement technologies is important for addressing disparities and preventing the creation of a two-tiered society. Policies should focus on fair distribution and affordability.

Effect:

1. Scientific Advancements:

- Enhanced Understanding of Human Capabilities: Research on HETs provides insights into human biology and potential, leading to advancements in medical science and technology.

- Innovative Technologies: The development of new technologies, including gene editing tools, neuroprosthetics, and cognitive enhancers, drives innovation across multiple fields.

2. Medical and Therapeutic Benefits:

- Improved Health and Functionality: HETs offer potential benefits for treating diseases, enhancing physical and cognitive abilities, and improving overall quality of life.

- Rehabilitation and Recovery: Enhanced prosthetics and neurotechnology support rehabilitation and recovery, enabling individuals to regain lost functions or adapt to physical impairments.

3. Ethical and Social Considerations:

- Responsible Use: Addressing ethical and social implications ensures that enhancement technologies are used responsibly and equitably, maintaining fairness and respect for individual rights.

- Impact on Society: Understanding the broader impact of HETs on social dynamics, privacy, and human identity helps guide their responsible development and implementation.

Conclusion:

Human enhancement technologies represent a transformative field with the potential to significantly impact various aspects of human life. By pushing the boundaries of human capabilities through genetic engineering, neurotechnology, and advanced prosthetics, these technologies offer new opportunities for improving health, performance, and well-being.

As research and development in HETs continue to advance, it is essential to address ethical, social, and regulatory challenges to ensure that these technologies are used responsibly and equitably. Balancing scientific innovation with ethical considerations will shape the future of human enhancement and its role in enhancing human potential.

EXPERIMENT EIGHTY FIVE

ASTROBIOLOGY: THE SEARCH FOR LIFE BEYOND EARTH

Astrobiology is the scientific field dedicated to studying the origin, evolution, distribution, and future of life in the universe. Combining elements of biology, chemistry, astronomy, and geology, astrobiology seeks to understand the potential for life beyond Earth and explore the conditions necessary for its existence. This interdisciplinary field encompasses a range of research areas, from the study of extreme environments on Earth to the search for extraterrestrial life and the habitability of other planets.

Historical Context and Techniques:

1. Historical Overview:

   - Early Speculations: The idea of extraterrestrial life dates back to ancient civilizations, with philosophers and scientists speculating about life on other planets. Early observations of celestial bodies and theories about the possibility of life beyond Earth were rooted in philosophical and speculative thinking.

- Modern Astrobiology: The 20th century marked the beginning of modern astrobiology with the advent of space exploration, advances in microbiology, and the discovery of extremophiles. Key milestones include the discovery of microbial life in extreme environments on Earth, the development of the Drake Equation, and the first space missions to other planets.

2. Contemporary Techniques:

- Planetary Exploration: Missions to other planets and moons, such as Mars rovers and the Europa Clipper, explore the surfaces and atmospheres of celestial bodies to search for signs of life or habitable conditions. These missions collect data on planetary geology, climate, and potential biosignatures.

- Astrobiological Research: Laboratory research simulates extraterrestrial conditions to study the survival and behavior of microorganisms in extreme environments. Experiments focus on understanding how life might adapt to conditions on other planets and moons.

- Spectroscopy and Remote Sensing: Telescopes and space observatories use spectroscopy and remote sensing to analyze the atmospheres and surfaces of exoplanets and other celestial bodies. These techniques help identify potential signs of habitability and biosignatures.

- Bioinformatics and Modeling: Computational models and bioinformatics tools are used to predict the potential for life on other planets and analyze data from space missions. These models simulate environmental conditions and biological processes to assess the likelihood of life.

3. Experimental Techniques:

- Simulated Extraterrestrial Environments: Experiments in laboratories create conditions similar to those found on other planets, such as extreme temperatures, pressures, and chemical environments. These simulations help researchers understand how life might survive or thrive in such conditions.

- Astrobiological Field Studies: Field studies in extreme environments on Earth, such as deep-sea hydrothermal vents, polar ice caps, and arid deserts, provide insights into how life can exist in harsh conditions. These studies offer analogs for understanding potential extraterrestrial habitats.

- Space Missions: Space missions, such as the Mars rovers and the James Webb Space Telescope, gather data on planetary surfaces, atmospheres, and potential biosignatures. These missions provide critical information for assessing the habitability of other celestial bodies.

Impact:

1. Scientific and Technological Impact:

- Advancements in Space Exploration: Astrobiology drives advancements in space exploration technologies, including spacecraft, instruments, and analytical techniques. These innovations enhance our ability to explore and analyze extraterrestrial environments.

- Understanding Life's Limits: Research in astrobiology expands our understanding of the limits of life and the conditions necessary for its existence. This knowledge contributes to broader scientific fields, such as microbiology and environmental science.

2. Medical and Practical Impact:

- Extremophiles and Biotechnology: Studying extremophiles—organisms that thrive in extreme environments—has applications in biotechnology and medicine. Enzymes and compounds derived from extremophiles have potential uses in industrial processes, pharmaceuticals, and environmental remediation.

- Inspiration for Innovation: The search for extraterrestrial life and the exploration of other planets inspire technological and scientific innovation. Advances in space technology often have applications in other fields, including materials science, robotics, and telecommunications.

3. Ethical and Philosophical Impact:

- Implications for Humanity: The discovery of extraterrestrial life or evidence of past life raises profound philosophical and ethical questions about humanity's place in the universe. It challenges our understanding of life, consciousness, and our role in the cosmos.

- Ethical Considerations: The exploration of extraterrestrial environments raises ethical considerations regarding the protection of potential extraterrestrial ecosystems and the responsible use of space resources. Ensuring that exploration and research are conducted with respect for any potential extraterrestrial life forms is essential.

4. Regulatory and Policy Considerations:

- Planetary Protection Policies: International agreements, such as the Outer Space Treaty and the Planetary Protection Protocols, govern the exploration of celestial bodies to prevent contamination of extraterrestrial environments and protect Earth from potential extraterrestrial contaminants.

- Collaboration and Funding: Astrobiology often involves collaboration between international space agencies, research institutions, and private organizations. Funding and policy decisions impact the scope and direction of astrobiological research and space exploration missions.

Effect:

1. Scientific Advancements:

- Enhanced Knowledge of Life's Potential: Astrobiology expands our knowledge of the potential for life in the universe and the conditions necessary for its existence. This understanding informs scientific theories about the origin and distribution of life.

- Technological Innovations: The development of new technologies for space exploration and analysis drives advancements in various scientific fields and contributes to technological progress.

2. Medical and Practical Benefits:

- Applications of Extremophile Research: Research on extremophiles leads to practical applications in biotechnology, medicine, and environmental science. These applications have potential benefits for various industries and scientific research.

- Inspiration for Scientific Endeavors: The pursuit of answers to fundamental questions about life and the universe inspires scientific inquiry and innovation, leading to new discoveries and technological advancements.

3. Ethical and Philosophical Considerations:

- Reflection on Humanity's Role: Discovering extraterrestrial life or evidence of past life prompts reflection on humanity's role in the universe and our understanding of life and consciousness.

- Responsible Exploration: Ethical considerations guide the responsible exploration of space and the protection of potential extraterrestrial environments, ensuring that research and exploration are conducted with respect for the cosmos.

Conclusion:

Astrobiology represents a frontier of scientific inquiry and exploration, offering insights into the potential for life beyond Earth and expanding our understanding of the universe. By studying extreme environments, developing advanced technologies, and exploring other planets and moons, astrobiology seeks to answer fundamental questions about life and its distribution in the cosmos.

As research in astrobiology continues to evolve, it is essential to address ethical, philosophical, and regulatory challenges to ensure that exploration and discovery are conducted responsibly and with respect for the potential implications for humanity. Balancing scientific curiosity with ethical considerations will shape the future of astrobiology and its role in expanding our knowledge of life in the universe.

REFERENCES

Books and Journals:

Cohen, P. (2020). Psychedelics as a Treatment for Mental Health Disorders. *Nature*, 585, 4-7.

Rhodes, R. (1986). *The Making of the Atomic Bomb*. Simon & Schuster.

Lifton, R. J., & Mitchell, G. (1995). *Hiroshima in America: A Half-Century of Denial*. Harper Perennial.

Meyer, K., & **Quenivet, N.** (2016). *The Geneva Conventions Under Assault*. Plagrave Macmillan.

Baum, D. (2016). *Smoke and Mirrors: The War on Drugs and the Politics of Failure*. Little, Brown and Company.

Freedman, D. (2012). *Wrong: Why Experts Keep Failing Us—And How to Know When Not to Trust Them*. Little, Brown and Company.

hodes, R. (1986). *The Making of the Atomic Bomb*. Simon & Schuster.

Lifton, R. J., & Mitchell, G. (1995). *Hiroshima in America: A Half-Century of Denial*. Harper Perennial.

Baum, D. (2016). *Smoke and Mirrors: The War on Drugs and the Politics of Failure*. Little, Brown and Company.

Freedman, D. (2012). *Wrong: Why Experts Keep Failing Us—And How to Know When Not to Trust Them*. Little, Brown and Company.

Kolata, G. (2013). *Flu: The Story of the Great Influenza Pandemic of 1918 and the Search for the Virus that Caused It*. Touchstone.

McNeill, W. H. (1976). *Plagues and Peoples*. Anchor Press.

Powers, T. (2011). *Heisenberg's War: The Secret History of the German Bomb*. Da Capo Press.

Johnson, S. (2001). *Emergence: The Connected Lives of Ants, Brains, Cities, and Software*. Scribner.

Stone, R. (2010). *The Environment: Principles and Applications*. Routledge.

Caro, T. (2007). *Conservation by Proxy: Indicator, Umbrella, Keystone, Flagship, and Other Surrogate Species*. Island Press.

National Institutes of Health (NIH). (n.d.). *A Chronology of Human Radiation Experiments*. Retrieved from https://www.nih.gov/chronology-human-radiation-experiments

Centers for Disease Control and Prevention (CDC). (2020). *Tuskegee Study - Timeline*. Retrieved from https://www.cdc.gov/tuskegee/timeline.htm

Stanford University. (n.d.). *The Stanford Prison Experiment: A Simulation Study of the Psychology of Imprisonment Conducted at Stanford University*. Retrieved from https://www.prisonexp.org/

PBS. (2002). *The Trials of J. Robert Oppenheimer*. Retrieved from https://www.pbs.org/wgbh/americanexperience/films/oppenheimer/

BBC. (2021). *The Genetic Code: Decoding the Human Genome*. Retrieved from https://www.bbc.com/history/human-genome-project

Articles and Reports:

Milgram, S. (1963). Behavioral Study of Obedience. *Journal of Abnormal and Social Psychology*, 67(4), 371–378.

Kolata, G. (2013, November 18). Exploring the Human Genome. *The New York Times*. Retrieved from https://www.nytimes.com/human-genome-project

Spector, R. (2019). Ethical Implications of CRISPR-Cas9. *Journal of Medical Ethics*, 45(4), 252-259.

Evans, J. (2018, September 24). *The Perils of Geoengineering: Why We Shouldn't Play God with the Weather*. The Guardian. Retrieved from https://www.theguardian.com/geoengineering-perils

National Institutes of Health (NIH). (n.d.). *A Chronology of Human Radiation Experiments*. Retrieved from https://www.nih.gov/chronology-human-radiation-experiments

Centers for Disease Control and Prevention (CDC). (2020). *Tuskegee Study - Timeline*. Retrieved from https://www.cdc.gov/tuskegee/timeline.htm

Stanford University. (n.d.). *The Stanford Prison Experiment: A Simulation Study of the Psychology of Imprisonment Conducted at Stanford University*. Retrieved from https://www.prisonexp.org/

NASA. (2021). *The Milestones of Space Exploration*. Retrieved from https://www.nasa.gov/milestones-space-exploration

CERN. (2012). *The Discovery of the Higgs Boson*. Retrieved from https://home.cern/science/physics/higgs-boson

World Health Organization (WHO). (2018). *Genetic Engineering and Biotechnology*. Retrieved from https://www.who.int/genetic-engineering

Environmental Protection Agency (EPA). (2021). *Deepwater Horizon Oil Spill*. Retrieved from https://www.epa.gov/deepwaterhorizon

BBC. (2021). *The Genetic Code: Decoding the Human Genome*. Retrieved from https://www.bbc.com/history/human-genome-project

U.S. Department of Energy (DOE). (2020). *Nuclear Fusion Research*. Retrieved from https://www.energy.gov/fusion

National Institute of Environmental Health Sciences (NIEHS). (2019). *Asbestos Exposure and Cancer Risk*. Retrieved from https://www.niehs.nih.gov/health/topics/agents/asbestos/index.cfm

Milgram, S. (1963). Behavioral Study of Obedience. *Journal of Abnormal and Social Psychology*, 67(4), 371–378.

Cohen, P. (2020). Psychedelics as a Treatment for Mental Health Disorders. *Nature*, 585, 4-7.

Spector, R. (2019). Ethical Implications of CRISPR-Cas9. *Journal of Medical Ethics*, 45(4), 252-259.

Evans, J. (2018, September 24). *The Perils of Geoengineering: Why We Shouldn't Play God with the Weather*. *The Guardian*. Retrieved from https://www.theguardian.com/geoengineering-perils

Garwin, R. L. (2001). Impact of the Nuclear Tests. *Bulletin of the Atomic Scientists*, 57(6), 54-59.

Feynman, R. P. (1988). The Quest for Tannu Tuva. *Physics Today*, 41(2), 57-62.

Kolata, G. (2017, November 15). The Ethics of Artificial Intelligence. *The New York Times*. Retrieved from https://www.nytimes.com/ethics-artificial-intelligence

Jones, C. (2016). The Human Costs of the Thalidomide Scandal. *BMJ*, 352, i1004.

Parry, R. (2020). The Race to Build the Quantum Computer. *Scientific American*, 322(4), 44-49.

Stein, Z., & **Susser, M.** (1977). Chemical Warfare and Its Long-Term Effects. *American Journal of Public Health*, 67(8), 738-741.

The World Economic Forum (WEF). (2021). *The Future of Synthetic Biology*. Retrieved from https://www.weforum.org/reports/future-synthetic-biology

Phys.org. (2019). *The Search for Extraterrestrial Life*. Retrieved from https://www.phys.org/news/2019-07-search-extraterrestrial-life.html

American Psychological Association (APA). (2015). *Psychosurgery and Its Impact on Mental Health*. Retrieved from https://www.apa.org/topics/psychosurgery

The National Security Archive. (2004). *Declassified MKUltra Documents*. Retrieved from https://nsarchive.gwu.edu/project/mkultra

31. **World Economic Forum (WEF).** (2021). *The Rise of Autonomous Vehicles*. Retrieved from https://www.weforum.org/rise-of-autonomous-vehicles